HANDBOOK OF
REAL ESTATE LAW

John Macdonald Cartwright, LL.B., J.D.

PRENTICE-HALL, INC.   ENGLEWOOD CLIFFS, N. J.

Handbook of Real Estate Law
by John Macdonald Cartwright, LL.B., J.D.

PRENTICE-HALL INTERNATIONAL, INC., *London*
PRENTICE-HALL OF AUSTRALIA, PTY. LTD., *Sydney*
PRENTICE-HALL OF CANADA, LTD., *Toronto*
PRENTICE-HALL OF INDIA PRIVATE LTD., *New Delhi*
PRENTICE-HALL OF JAPAN, INC., *Tokyo*

Library of Congress
Catalog Card Number: 68-25160

This publication is designed to provide accurate
and authoritative information in regard to the
subject matter covered. It is sold with the understanding that the publisher is not engaged in
rendering legal, accounting or other professional
service. If legal advice or other expert assistance
is required, the service of a competent professional
person should be sought.

> . . . *From a Declaration of Principles jointly
> adopted by a Committee of the American
> Bar Association and a Committee of Pub-
> lishers and Associations.*

PRINTED IN THE UNITED STATES OF AMERICA

B & P

To

MAGDA

A WORD FROM THE AUTHOR

With the increasing complexity and variety of real estate transactions, state, county and municipal laws, ordinances and administrative regulations have multiplied in number and enlarged in scope. The conveyancing of real property is no longer the simple act of signing and delivering a deed. For this reason, real estate brokers and all other persons engaged, either directly in the real estate business or indirectly through related professions, businesses or trades, are finding it increasingly necessary to familiarize themselves with those branches of law underlying the conveyancing of real property and the regulation of real estate transactions. This need is particularly felt by men and women who have had little opportunity to study real estate law.

To bring together in one volume those principles of law especially applicable to the real estate business seemed to the author a necessary and timely undertaking. However, it soon became apparent that such a book could not limit itself to the law of real property. It would also need to take in the subjects of contracts, negotiable instruments, security paper, mechanics' liens, recording statutes, forms used in real property transfers, and other branches of the law generally applicable to the whole field of the real estate business.

Questions and answers would also be needed, in order to stress important points of law. *Checklists* would call the reader's attention to practical considerations which should not be overlooked in a real estate transaction. A *glossary* of legal terms should be of much help, if freely consulted, in understanding the terminology used in the book. And lastly, a list of *"Pitfalls to Avoid"* ought to assist in the avoidance of common errors frequently made in business or real estate transactions.

Although this work follows the weight of authority, statutory law, or legal theory as developed by the decided cases, will in some jurisdictions introduce new areas of regulation, or lay down principles of law contrary to the weight of authority. Certain of these variations are noted within the book. The author is fully aware that wide legal variations are inevitable in a nation composed of fifty separate jurisdictions. Certain devices and instruments covered in the book, such as the Broker's Loan Statement, the Deed of Trust, and others, are inapplicable to certain sections of the country. Nor is the law itself, in many aspects, entirely uniform throughout the several jurisdictions. The general rule, or the weight of authority, is all that can be laid down in a handbook of this kind.

The reader is cautioned to check the rule of law stated in this work against the statutes and decided cases in his own jurisdiction before acting definitively in any transaction he is handling. He should always be mindful of local variations in a general rule of law which represents the weight of authority.

John Macdonald Cartwright

WHAT THIS HANDBOOK WILL DO FOR YOU

A careful reading of this *Handbook* will enable you to acquire a practical knowledge of real estate law. Its purpose is to provide a comprehensive understanding of the basic legal principles which underly the sale, lease and other disposition of real property and which are necessary to the successful practice of real estate. It shows the forms and instruments commonly employed in transferring title to real property, and explains and analyzes the listing agreement, the deposit receipt and other key instruments used to initiate and conclude a sale or other disposition of real property. The important role which these instruments play in the real estate business is also discussed. The purpose of the "escrow" and what must be done to make it valid are also explained. The uses of the patent, the deed, the land contract, the lease, and the exchange agreement are also fully discussed and made clear, as is the mortgage and the deed of trust.

This *Handbook* explains the fundamental concept of PROPERTY and OWNERSHIP, and outlines the principal modern ESTATES in land which are the subjects of real estate transactions.

What Each Chapter Provides:

Each chapter covers the essential rules of law applicable to real property transactions. The chapter headings will suggest the branch of law from which rules have been selected.

Brief *Questions and Answers* are included separately within each chapter, which provide quick answers on the most important points of law.

Concise *Checklists* will be found at the end of each chapter, calling special attention to practical considerations which should not be overlooked in real estate transactions.

Chapter 1 tells you how to recognize a lawful, binding and enforceable contract; how it is made and what it should contain to give it validity; what circumstances will defeat it, and upon what grounds it may be rescinded.

Chapter 2 will tell you what the law considers to be property, its division, characteristics and qualities. It will show you how to recognize modern estates in land, and tell you what passes as part of the land by a conveyance of it. You will learn of present and future interests in land, of reversions and remainders and how they are created and what they mean. You will be told how real property is held in severalty or co-tenancy, and the different kinds of co-ownership the law recognizes. The law of FIXTURES will be explained. You will learn of ADVERSE POSSESSION and EASEMENTS, appurtenant and in gross, and how they are created. And you will be told how to recognize a covenant running with the land, and equitable servitudes, and will understand their importance in the area of restrictive covenants, and when dealing with the sale of lots in subdivisions. Chapter 2 also provides exhibits and examples illustrating practical situations which arise every day in the sale and other disposition of real property. By understanding these practical situations and the general rules of law laid down in the book you will improve your knowledge of the basic requirements of a sound approach to real estate problems.

Chapter 3 will tell you the important things to know about recording instruments having to do with an interest in land. It will tell you how priority of right is established between parties claiming the same interest in real property, and show you what can be done to protect your title to real estate. You will be shown factual situations involving the subsequent bona fide purchaser, and told under what circumstances he may expect to prevail over a prior grantee of the land he purchased. The dates of more than one deed to the same property are discussed and remedies indicated. This chapter will also tell you about title insurance, and what types of policy are commonly used. It will advise you of the common risks concealed within recorded documents and those existing outside of the record, and thus put you in a better position to judge, from the circumstances of the transaction in which you are engaged, what kind of title insurance to obtain.

Chapter 4 will give you a practical understanding of what problems are involved in the development of the subdivision. Subdivision law in the fifty state jurisdictions is not uniform. But this chapter has outlined the law of a state which has carried regulation as far as any state in the union. A compass and measuring rod is thus provided with which you can take the measure of your own state law, tnd understand its legal mechanics.

Chapter 5 concerns itself with the legal aspects of real estate forms. It explains the basic market and dispositive instruments employed in a real estate transaction. It discusses the Listing Agreement, the Deposit Receipt, the Land Contract, the Exchange Agreement and the Lease. It will tell you how to use these instruments to the best advantage. You will learn how to distinguish between a naked power, or authority, and a contractual obligation and what these mean in the broker's employment contract. It will teach you when such a power may be revoked without liability, and when such revocation creates a liability. It will show you how a binding contract of sale of real property is in practice effected; when a broker has earned his commission, and when he has not. It will point out the importance of the Deposit Receipt, and the relationship between this form and the Listing Agreement. It will advise you of the dangers and of the advantages of the Land Contract. It will explain the nature of the Exchange Agreement, and the problem of inflated equities.

The chapter will outline the usual provisions contained in the ordinary lease, and distinguish between an "assignment" and a "sub-letting." It will tell you what the usual covenants in a lease are, and what they mean; and it will show you the difference between and the effect of continuing and non-continuing, dependent and independent covenants. It will show you how these several types of covenant are important in determining if there has been a waiver by the landlord of a breach of covenant or condition contained in the lease.

A careful reading of the chapter should improve your knowledge of the nature and function of basic real estate forms, and put you in a better position to use them effectively.

Chapter 6 will tell you what a United States Patent is, what interest in land it transfers and when it is not a conveyance but merely evidence of title. It will tell you in what records to look when checking title through a patent. It will tell you when a patent may be annulled by a direct proceeding brought for that purpose, and under what circumstances it may be collaterally impeached.

The chapter will give you the essentials of a valid deed, and indicate the forms commonly used in the several jurisdictions. It will distinguish between a deed poll and an indenture. It will explain exceptions and reservations found in deeds. And it will tell you what must be done to make a deed an effective, operative instrument for the transfer of real property.

Chapter 7 will acquaint you with two important security instruments, the mortgage and the deed of trust. It will show you the rights and obligations of mortgagor and mortgagee. It will tell you what is meant by "taking subject to the mortgage," or "assuming the mortgage." It will tell you what are the liabilities of third persons to whom the mortgagor has sold his mortgaged property. It will show you the advantages a mortgagee in possession has under certain circumstances, over one out of possession. It will explain the "purchase money" mortgage and the "dry" mortgage. You will learn that the mortgage secures the "obligation," not the evidence of the obligation, such as a promissory note; and you will understand, therefore, that a change in the form of the note ordinarily does not discharge the mortgage. It will tell you about the "equity of redemption," and explain the "power of sale" contained in some mortgages. The chapter should give you a better understanding of the mortgage and its function as a security instrument.

The chapter will also acquaint you with the deed of trust and tell you of some of its advantages over the mortgage in those jurisdictions where it is favored.

Chapter 8 will give you the important provisions of the Mechanics' Lien Laws. It will tell you who may avail themselves of these laws and under what circumstances. It will show you a number of common situations in which the property of an owner of real estate may be liened to satisfy contractors' and materialmen's claims. And it will tell you how and when liens may be avoided. It will give you the information you need to approach the subject of mechanics' liens with some assurance of understanding the problems involved and applying the knowledge you have gained to factual situations needing your attention. The chapter will give you a quick view of very technical and complicated statutory law.

Chapter 9 will give you the information you need to write a good negotiable promissory note. It will tell you how to detect a faulty one. It will show you the essentials of a negotiable instrument, and what will destroy its negotiability. You will understand the difference between a "guaranty" and a "warranty" in the law of Bills and Notes, and you will learn what the maker of a note undertakes, and what he warrants. The chapter will tell you how you may disclaim all warranties and be free of this liability on negotiable paper. It will tell you what "real" defenses are recognized by the law, and what the term means, and who may avail themselves of these defenses. It will explain the liability of a bank for a forged check. It will tell you the nature of the several kinds of deposits which may be made in a bank, and what liability the bank assumes for each. It will inform you with respect to stop payment orders and the advisability of promptly checking the items returned with bank statements for forgeries and other irregularities.

Chapter 9 will give you valuable information about negotiable instruments and enable you to better understand your rights and liabilities as a maker or an indorser of negotiable paper.

Chapter 10 will explain the "escrow." It will give you sufficient information to enable you to open a valid escrow, properly instruct the escrowholder and deposit therein all instruments, documents and moving papers requisite to complete the real estate transaction you are handling. It will show you the importance of the "auxiliary contract," the "escrow instructions" and the "Deposit Receipt" in the escrow transaction. It will tell you the difference between the valid and the pseudo escrow. It will explain the need of depositing a fully executed deed in the escrow along with the auxiliary contract. It will show you how the doctrine of "relation back" effects title. It will explain the status of the escrow holder and his responsibilities to the parties to the escrow. It will discuss the earnest money deposit. The chapter will show you how to check the Closing Statement, and what classes of items are included in such statement. It will tell you how to debit and credit these items; and it will show you examples of failure to establish a valid escrow, and the consequences. And it will tell you how to avoid such failure.

Chapter 11 will acquaint you with the fundamentals of appraising real property. It will give you the basic factors influencing value. It will explain to you the three major approaches to valuation. It will tell you how to use each approach. It will explain depreciation, its several kinds, and in what approach to valuation each may be used. It will explain, and give you examples of straightline capitalization. It will show you how to use the direct capitalization approach, the building and land residual methods. It will explain gross multipliers. The chapter will tell you the difference between economic, contract and ground rent. It will explain how to arrive at capital investment return and net spendable income, and will show you how to make up an Operating Statement.

The information contained in this chapter should greatly assist you to accurately estimate the value of real property. By thus avoiding over and under valuations of property you are handling, you will render a better service to those who look to you for professional service in real estate matters.

Additional Sections:

- A special section on *Pitfalls To Avoid* immediately follows Chapter 11. This will help you to avoid the common errors frequently made in real estate transactions.
- There is also a *Glossary of Legal Terms* used throughout the book. This will serve as a useful key to understanding the legal principles and procedures discussed within the chapters.
- Finally, there is a list of *Suggested Publications* which includes useful books, services, and other sources of information on real estate law.

CONTENTS

PITFALLS TO AVOID 227

GLOSSARY OF LEGAL TERMS 235

SUGGESTED PUBLICATIONS 251

INDEX 253

TABLE OF EXHIBITS

1

Contracts

Contracts are classically divided into formal and informal contracts. The terms of a contract are made binding either by reason of the form the instrument (in the case of a recognizance, the undertaking) takes, or by reason of its compliance with those essentials, other than form, which the law demands of all informal contracts.

1. The Formal Contracts

A. Definition and Kinds

The formal contract is best understood by its historical background. In jurisdictions where seals are yet recognized to the extent they were in the early common law of England, a promise under seal is an enforceable promise notwithstanding the absence of those essential elements the law demands of all contracts. Such a sealed promise, or instrument, is a formal contract.

The formal contracts are:

> The sealed covenant;[1]
> The undertaking or recognizance;[2]
> The negotiable instrument.[3]

Neither the recognizance nor the negotiable instrument depends upon a seal for validity. They are effective instruments by reason of formal characteristics.

2. The Informal Contracts

A. Definition and Kinds

An informal (SIMPLE or PAROL) contract is any agreement, other than a specialty, or formal contract, between two or more parties which is enforceable in a competent court of law. If all the lawful elements and legal requirements are present in the making, execution and delivery of such a contract it will, ordinarily, be an enforceable agreement. There are conditions under which an unenforceable agreement is still a contract, having certain legal consequences.[4] However, such conditions will not be encountered in the normal course of real estate business.

Informal contracts may be

Express, or
Implied.

EXPRESS AND IM-PLIED CONTRACTS

An express contract is one the terms of which are stated in words. An implied contract is one the terms of which are evidenced by conduct.[5]

Informal contracts may be

Bilateral, or
Unilateral.

BILATERAL AND UNILATERAL CON-TRACTS

A bilateral contract is one in which promises are exchanged between two parties, and wherein each party is both a PROMISOR and a PROMISEE. A unilateral contract is one in which a promise is given for an act. In such a contract there can be only one promisor and one promisee.

Informal contracts may be

Executory, or
Executed.

EXECUTORY AND EXECUTED CON-TRACTS

All contracts which are not executed are executory. If the OBJECT OF THE CONTRACT has been fully accomplished and there is nothing left to be done on the part of either party, then the contract is executed. In such case the instrument is, properly speaking, no longer a contract, but rather, evidence of an executed agreement.

B. Essentials

It is essential to the existence of a contract that there be

Parties capable of contracting;
Consent, or mutual assent;
Lawful object;
Sufficient consideration.

PARTIES NOT CAPABLE OF CONTRACTING

Persons of unsound mind, those deprived by law of their civil rights and minors, in some instances, are incapable of contracting. All others are capable of contracting.[6]

PARTIES MUST EXIST AND BE IDENTIFIED

It is essential to the validity of a contract that the parties exist, and be possible of identification.

CONSENT MUST BE FREE, MUTUAL AND COMMUNICATED

In the enforceable contract the consent of the parties must be free, mutual and communicated by each to the other. Consent is not real or free when obtained through duress, menace, fraud, undue influence or mistake. And when so obtained legal or equitable redress is available to the wronged or injured party.

MEETING OF THE MINDS

There must be a MEETING OF THE MINDS of the parties to a contract. This has been construed to mean that the consent, or mutual assent, of the parties is not to be determined by each party's state of mind. It must be ascertained by the intent expressed in their acts and the language of their contract. Their unexpressed, secret intentions will not be recognized. Thus, by the weight of authority, the test is an objective test, not subjective. If the language of the contract is not ambiguous the intent of the parties will be determined from the language alone. However, where the terms of the contract are uncertain or ambiguous the situation and conduct of the parties may be examined to determine the meaning of their words. If the language of the contract is so uncertain and indefinite that it cannot be determined what is meant, then there is no contract at all. Their secret intentions cannot be shown. Where the language is not ambiguous, or the ambiguity is resolved, a contract will emerge; but whether ambiguous or not, relief may be granted if duress, menace, fraud, undue influence or mistake can be shown.

Consent is not mutual unless the parties all agree upon the same thing in the same sense. But in certain cases where there may be some doubt as to the intention of the parties, their intention must be arrived at by prescribed rules of interpretation laid down by state statute or fixed by judicial decision in the several states.

INTENTION OF PARTIES DETERMINED BY PRESCRIBED RULES OF INTERPRETATION

A contract must receive such an interpretation as will make it lawful, operative, definite, reasonable and capable of being carried into effect if it can be done without violating the intention of the parties. Most courts which follow the objective approach (all do not) will so construe agreements as to carry into effect the intentions of the parties if these can be determined from their communicated expressions and conduct. But in such courts, no consideration will be given to the unexpressed, secret thoughts of the parties.

THAT CONSTRUCTION PREFERRED WHICH GIVES EFFECT TO CONTRACT

Consent to an agreement may be communicated by some act or omission to act on the part of a contracting party; or, a mode or means of communicating consent may be prescribed by the OFFEROR. Consent is often effected by the ACCEPTANCE of an OFFER. It may be indicated by acceptance of the benefits resulting from the agreement, or by part performance. If the relationship between the parties is such that the offeror is justified in expecting a negative reply in the event his offer is rejected, silence on the part of the OFFEREE may be regarded as acceptance, or consent.

If the offer prescribes a particular manner in which the communication of its acceptance must be manifested, there is no communication of consent unless such manner of acceptance is complied with by the offeree. Where no particular manner of acceptance is imposed any commonly employed means of communication may be adopted.

OFFER MAY PRESCRIBE MANNER OF ACCEPTANCE

The execution of a contract in writing, whether the law requires it to be written or not, supercedes all the negotiations or stipulations concerning its subject matter which preceded or accompanied the execution of the instrument.

EXECUTED WRITTEN CONTRACT SUPERCEDES ALL PRIOR NEGOTIATIONS

Every contract has an object, the object of the contract being that thing which it is agreed on the part of the party receiving the consideration, to do or

OBJECT OF THE CONTRACT

not to do. The object must be lawful when the contract is made, and possible of performance and ascertainable by the time it is to be performed.

The object of the contract is always what the parties intended by their agreement, i.e., what each, himself, intended to do or refrain from doing, and what each intended the other to do or refrain from doing. It should be logically distinguished from what the ultimate effect (outside of the four corners of the contract) the full performance of their acts produced. For example, "A" contracts to have "B" build him a house in which to live. Practically speaking, the object of the contract, so far as "A" is concerned, is to have a house to live in. This would superficially appear to be one of the objects of the contract. But, legally speaking, it is not an object of the contract. It may well have been "A"'s motive for entering into the contract. The object of the contract, however, so far as "A" is concerned, is to have "B" promise to build him a house. This promise might well have been given by "B" in consideration of "A"'s promise to pay "B" $25,000 to build the house.

"OBJECT" AN-
OTHER WORD FOR
"CONSIDERATION"
THE PROMISE

In this sense, the term OBJECT may be thought of as CONSIDERATION.

The promise is a basic concept of contract law. It is a pledge or commitment given by one party to another to do or not to do some specified thing, which if supported by a sufficient consideration becomes binding upon the party making it. It is the backbone of every contract. In fact, the faithful performance of a valid promise, whether it be supported by a consideration or not, provided it is given freely and not induced by deception, is of the highest

VALID PROMISE OF HIGHEST MORAL VALUE

moral value in any civilized society. When reciprocal rights and duties, and the responsibilities incident to the contractual relationship are properly understood, and the ethical implications of the meeting of the minds of the contracting parties are acknowledged, the importance of mutual promises and the need for a mature and responsible approach to the idea of contractual obligation become impressively significant.

IN EVERY CONTRACT AT LEAST ONE PROMISOR AND ONE PROMISE EXAMPLE OF UNILATERAL CONTRACT AN ACT FOR A PROMISE

In every contract there must be at least one promisor making at least one promise, as in the unilateral contract.

> "A" promises "B" that he will pay him $50 if "B" gives him a bill of sale to "B"'s typewriter and delivers both bill of sale and typewriter to him within three days.
> "B" gives "A" a bill of sale to his typewriter and delivers both bill of sale and typewriter to him within the three days.

The promise, express or implied, lies at the base of all consensual contracts. It is to be found in the OFFER and in the ACCEPTANCE of the bilateral contract.

EXAMPLE OF BILATERAL CONTRACT

A PROMISE FOR A PROMISE

> "C," by letter, makes an offer to "D" that he will sell "D" his house for $50,000, the money to be paid to him in cash on a certain date.
> "D," in turn, and by letter, accepts "C"'s offer and promises to pay "C" $50,000 for the house in cash on the day named.

In the two examples cited we have, in simplified form, two enforceable contracts. The first is a unilateral contract; the second a bilateral contract.

In the first "A" has given a promise for an act, while "B" has given an act for a promise. The contract is fully executed, if we assume that "A" has paid the $50. In the second example "C" has given "D" a promise for a promise, as likewise has "D" given "C." Until the money has been paid and the house is legally delivered, the contract is executory.

A contract for the sale of the house (second example) might have been effected by the offer and acceptance contained in the ordinary DEPOSIT RECEIPT frequently employed in the real estate business. Or, it could have been accomplished by a written integrated contract of purchase and sale.

THE DEPOSIT RECEIPT

As we shall see when we review the DOCTRINE OF CONSIDERATION, it is a general rule of law that a counter promise is supported by a DETRIMENT to the promisee or a BENEFIT to the promisor. A detriment to the promisee is incurred when the promisee ACTS (unilateral contract) or PROMISES TO ACT (bilateral contract) in response to the promise or offer of the promisor by doing or refraining from doing, or promising to do or refrain from doing something he, the promisee, is not bound in law to do or to refrain from doing. If, however, he does or promises to do something for the promisor (in exchange for a promise of the promisor) which he is in law already presently bound to do he cannot hold the promisor to his promise. Example: "A" promises to pay "B" a sum of money he owes "B" if "B" will deliver to him his, "B"'s, typewriter. "A" pays "B" the money he owes him. "B" refuses to deliver the typewriter. "A" cannot demand the typewriter. If "B" promises to deliver his typewriter to "A," "A" must promise "B" something of value (a consideration). "A" must suffer a detriment of some kind to make "B"'s promise binding upon him. But "A" has promised "B" nothing but what he is already bound in law to pay him. Under the law he is bound to pay "B" the money he owes him, and has promised him nothing more for the typewriter. "A" has suffered no detriment. There has been no consideration originating with "A" necessary in law to support "B"'s promise to deliver his typewriter to "A." Therefore "B" will not be legally obliged to do so.

A COUNTER PROMISE TO DO WHAT THE PROMISEE IS PRESENTLY BY LAW BOUND TO DO IS NOT A SUFFICIENT CONSIDERATION

It can be said that while "A" may have been bound in law to pay the money due "B," yet, if a promise is sufficient consideration to support a counter promise, "B" should be bound. Practically, the trouble with this reasoning is that although "A"'s new promise to pay a debt presently due might be thought of as *some* kind of consideration, the law does not recognize *every* kind of consideration as sufficient to support a counter promise. Only what the law of the particular jurisdiction deems a SUFFICIENT consideration will be accepted by the court as meeting the requirements of consideration as laid down by the law of that jurisdiction, or state. Ordinarily, the law does not look upon a promise to do that which a man is already bound in law to do as being a sufficient consideration to support a counter promise. There is, however, some authority to the contrary.

NOT EVERY PROMISE IS A SUFFICIENT CONSIDERATION TO SUPPORT A CONTRACT

A contract must stand upon a legal consideration, which cannot be contrary to the policy of express law, although not expressly prohibited, or opposed to good morals. The simplest way to define a consideration which will

SUFFICIENT CONSIDERATION

support a promise, or contract, is to say that it consists of any lawful detriment suffered by the promisee, or of any lawful benefit received by the promisor as determined by the act, or the promises of the contracting parties.

The consideration must be a sufficient consideration. That is to say, it must meet the established precedents in the jurisdiction in which the contract is made.

Generally speaking, in the unilateral contract the act of the promisee will be sufficient consideration to support the promise of the promisor if it is the act demanded by the promisor, and is neither illegal nor against public policy, nor the performance of some duty or obligation the promisee owes the promisor, or some legal entity.

In the bilateral contract each party is at once a promisor and a promisee. Each makes a promise to the other and each is on the receiving end of the other's promise. The promise of one to the other constitutes the consideration passing from one to the other to support the other's counter promise. By the weight of authority, in the bilateral contract, a promise is sufficient consideration for a promise if the thing promised is lawful, and valuable. However, the character and validity of each promise will be inquired into. If found illusory or uncertain, or illegal, or not valuable, or not concurrent, or impossible of performance, the promise, ordinarily, will not be recognized as sufficient consideration to support the counter promise, or the contract.

Mutuality of obligation, in the sense of reciprocal binding promises, is essential to the validity of the bilateral contract. Each promise must be sufficient consideration for the other.

In the unilateral contract there is only one promise. The contract is effected by the performance of the act demanded of the promisee. Before the act is performed the promise of the promisor is a mere unilateral offer. When the act is performed this unilateral offer and the performed act give rise to a unilateral contract. Certainly in the unilateral offer, even considered as a unilateral contract, which it frequently is called, there is no mutuality of obligation. There remains only the single obligation contained in the promise to be performed. Mutuality of obligation is inapplicable to the unilateral contract considered either as a unilateral offer, or as a unilateral agreement.

In the bilateral contract where there is no consideration other than each party's counter promise the requirement that both parties must be bound (the promise of one party must support the promise of the other party) demands mutuality of obligation.

3. Offer and Acceptance

Offer and acceptance is implicit in every contract. Acceptance may be made by act, as in the unilateral contract, or by promise, as in the bilateral contract. Acceptance itself ordinarily implies a promise to perform. It makes no difference whether the agreement has been reduced to an integrated written contract or grows out of the correspondence of the parties, or is implied from their conduct and oral promises. In the option supported by consideration, the acceptance of the consideration by the optionor implies a promise on his part to hold the offer contained in the instrument open for the time indicated.

An offer intended for the benefit of a particular person is personal to that offeree and not assignable. A contract ordinarily is not binding upon the offeror [promisor] executing it if a third party has been substituted for the offeree [promisee] and executes the contract, the substitution being made without the approval of the offeror. But an offer need not be made to a particular person. An offer to pay a reward is an example. It may give rise to an obligation on the part of the offeror to any party within the class to which the reward was offered.

Although the offer is not assignable, a contract executed by both parties ordinarily is assignable unless otherwise provided in the agreement itself, or unless it calls for some particular quality or skill of the promisor charged with performance, or is prohibited by statute or public policy as manifested by judicial pronouncement, or where the integrity or solvency of one of the parties is relied upon.

Generally speaking, an option is assignable unless the solvency, the integrity or the credit of the assignor is of significant importance to the other party, or where personal skill or trust is involved.

Looking at the matter from a very practical point of view, the simple bilateral contract usually results from one of two or three methods of dealing. If the contract is oral it results from the mutual agreement and understanding between the parties growing out of consummated negotiations. If the contract is in writing it results either from some correspondence in writing between the parties in which an offer is made and an acceptance communicated. In more involved contracts, an agreement is prepared by an attorney who reduces to an integrated written contract the mutual understanding of the parties.[7]

A contract created in any of the above ways is known as a parol contract. The language (or the acts) of the parties binds each to perform certain obligations agreed to be assumed by him under the terms of the contract.

In the unilateral, as well as the bilateral contract, the offer may be oral unless there is some statutory provision or rule of law enforced by the courts requiring it to be in writing.

Many litigated business contracts grow out of an exchange of letters and telegrams in which are to be found offers and acceptances developed by the parties in the course of their correspondence. This manner of creating a contract is largely responsible for the volume of contract law which has shaped itself around the concepts of OFFER and ACCEPTANCE, so expressed.

EXAMPLE: "X Company" wires "Y" as follows: "We offer you one thousand pounds of Yel-0 cheese at 25¢ a pound, f.o.b. San Francisco to be shipped not later

than August 3, 1969. We must have your acceptance by wire within 24 hours your receipt of this
offer."

"Y" wires "X Company" within the 24-hour period
stipulated, as follows: "Your offer one thousand
pounds Yel-0 cheese at 25¢ a pound, f.o.b. San
Francisco to be shipped not later than August 3,
1969, accepted."

Here is an enforceable contract in which the offer and the acceptance stand
out clearly. However, in every contract there is an offer and an acceptance,
expressed or implied. The offer may, as in the unilateral contract, be found
in the promise of the promisor, and the acceptance implied in the act of the
promisee. In the bilateral, integrated written agreement the offer is found in
the promise of the promisor. The acceptance is found in the counter promise
to perform a demand of the promisor, or in a mere statement of agreement.

**OFFER AND AC-
CEPTANCE IN THE
UNILATERAL AND
THE BILATERAL
CONTRACTS: HOW
EFFECTED**

**OFFER MUST BE
CERTAIN, DEFINITE
AND COMMUNI-
CATED**

The offer must be certain, definite and communicated to the offeree. It
may be communicated directly to the offeree, or to his authorized agent. This
is demonstrated by the fact that "A"'s offer to sell "B" his typewriter and "B"'s
offer to buy "A"'s typewriter are not the basis of a binding contract if they
cross in the mail. "A"'s offer requires a specific acceptance by "B," and "B"
must know that such an offer has been made to him by actually receiving the
offer, either personally or through his agent. In short, the offer must be communicated to "B" before "B" can accept it.

**DELIVERY TO CAR-
RIER FOR TRANS-
MITTAL TO OF-
FEROR SUFFICIENT**

To effect a binding contract the offer must be accepted in the manner
prescribed by law. The offer may indicate the manner in which the acceptance
is to be communicated, i.e., by mail, by telegraph, by telephone, etc., and
this method must be adopted by the offeree to bind the offeror. If no particular
manner is prescribed, then any usual or reasonable mode of communication
may be adopted. The rule is that when the offeree puts his acceptance in the
course of transmission to the offeror he has done all he is required to do to
bind the contract. Delivery of the acceptance, in such case, to the United
States Post Office, or to the telegraph company's office for transmittal, would
be sufficient delivery to the offeror, unless some statutory rule otherwise
provides.

**REJECTION OF
OFFER**

An offer may be rejected positively, or by a counter offer, or by a qualified
or conditional acceptance. In any of such cases it cannot be afterward accepted
so as to bind the offeror, without his consent.

**REVOCATION OF
OFFER**

An offer may be revoked at any time before acceptance. It may be so
revoked even when a time certain is fixed in its language for acceptance. However, if the offer is made upon consideration given by the offeree it cannot be
revoked before the expiration of the specified time.[8] The general rule is that
the revocation must ordinarily be communicated to the offeree in the same
manner in which an offer is communicated.[9]

**THE CONTINUING
OFFER**

A continuing offer is an offer made for either an indefinite or for a fixed
period of time. It may or may not be supported by a consideration. An exam-

ple of a continuing offer supported by consideration is the OPTION. When an option is not supported by consideration it is a mere continuing offer which may ordinarily be revoked at any time before acceptance. Unless withdrawn, it continues as an offer for a reasonable time if there is no time limit fixed, or if a limit is fixed, until such limit is reached. If it is supported by a consideration it cannot be withdrawn until the limit fixed by its terms is reached.

THE OPTION DISTINGUISHED FROM MERE CONTINUING OFFER

The continuing offer may be accepted at any time before it is withdrawn, and before its expiration date. If there is no expiration date, then it may be accepted at any reasonable time before it is withdrawn.

CONTINUING OFFER WHEN MAY BE ACCEPTED

A continuing offer unsupported by consideration, sometimes called an option, which has not been "exercised" is by operation of law revoked by the death or insanity of the optionor. If the option is supported by a consideration given by the optionee, it is a binding contract, and binds the optionor's successors after his death. It is not revoked by the optionor's death.

CONTINUING OFFER UNSUPPORTED BY CONSIDERATION REVOKED BY DEATH OR INSANITY OF OFFEROR

Some offers [as in auctions] are mere invitations to bid and cannot be accepted to form a contract. The bid of the person wishing to purchase is the offer, which may be accepted only by the auctioneer. When so accepted there is a contract of purchase and sale.

WHEN NOT REVOCABLE

AUCTIONS INVITATIONS TO BID

The same rule prevails in advertisements for bids for public work. Here, the bid of the contractor is the offer. The award to the successful bidder is the acceptance, and consummates the contract.

ADVERTISING PUBLIC WORK FOR BIDS

4. Contract Made Where Last Act of Execution Performed

A contract is generally considered made at the place at which the last event occurs necessary to make it a binding agreement. This is usually at the place where it is executed and delivered, or where the offer is accepted.

CONTRACT WHERE MADE

Ordinarily, the acceptance of an offer made by letter is deemed to have been given when the letter containing the acceptance is deposited in the United States Post Office at the place from which it is sent. Likewise, had the offer been made by telegraph, the acceptance would ordinarily be deemed to have been given at the place from which the telegram of acceptance had been sent.

In both the last two supposed cases the contract would be considered made at the place where acceptance occurred.

5. Execution and Delivery

The execution of a written contract consists of more than affixing the signatures of the parties. It also implies a delivery of the instrument, but delivery does not necessarily mean its physical transfer. If the parties understand themselves to be bound, and the agreement operative, delivery is presumed.

DELIVERY ACTUAL AND CONSTRUCTIVE

The contract takes effect upon delivery. It may be delivered conditionally; in which case it does not become a binding obligation until the condition is met upon which it is to become effective.

CONTRACT TAKES EFFECT UPON DELIVERY

6. Law and Appellate Decisions Are Part of Contract

LEGISLATION PRE-
SUMED PART OF
EVERY CONTRACT

INCLUDES APPEL-
LATE DECISIONS

WHEN   LAWS
FORM NO PART
OF CONTRACT

A part of every contract are all pertinent and apposite laws and appellate court decisions in existence at the time the contract is made. These include provisions of the state constitution, statutes, codes, county and city charters and administrative regulations. These mandates the parties are presumed to have had in mind when they executed the contract.

The passage of laws subsequent to the execution of the contract will not be allowed to impair the obligation of the contract created at the time of its execution. Therefore, such laws form no part of the contract, unless the parties stipulate therein their intention to be governed thereby.

7. Minors

The rule that the capacity of parties to contract is usually determined by the law of the place where the contract is made applies also to minors. Minors, or infants as the law calls them, are persons under twenty-one years of age; but the capacity of minors to contract may be enlarged or restricted by statutory provision in the several states.

By statute and court decision, contractual acts of a minor fall into three general classes: [1] those which are void AB INITIO (void from the beginning); [2] those which are VOIDABLE; and [3] those which are BINDING upon the minor.

There are definite legal rules relating to contracts in each of these classifications that depend, in character and effect, upon the laws of the particular state in which the infant intended a contractual obligation. In many states the common, or unwritten law, is the general rule to be followed. But special statutes will alter that law. It is necessary, therefore, that the statutes and court decisions of a particular state be examined before dealing with minors in contractual matters.

SUGGESTED
CLASSES OF
MINORS CON-
TRACTS TO BE
CHECKED AGAINST
STATE LAW

For the purpose of determining whether a minor's contract is void, voidable or binding the reader should keep in mind whether the contract involves [1] a delegation of power; [2] an agreement relating to real property or an interest in real property; [3] an agreement relating to personal property not in the immediate possession or control of the minor; or, [4] agreements of minors for necessaries. This is not an inclusive checklist, but it does point the direction for the intelligent consideration of the contracts of minors.

8. Grounds for Rescission

No extended treatment of duress, menace, fraud, undue influence or mistake will be undertaken in this HANDBOOK. However, since these affect the freedom, or reality of consent essential to the enforceable contract, a brief comment on the nature of each will be made.

Statutes and judicial decisions in the several states may enlarge or restrict the area of conduct involved, yet the central idea of the wrongful or mistaken act may be understood by what follows.

A. Duress

The modern trend of decided cases is to find duress to be that intimidation which wrongfully subjugates the will of the party acted upon to the will of the acting party.

DURESS

B. Fraud

The elements of fraud which will prevent the consent, or mutual assent, of the parties to a contract from being real or free may vary in the several jurisdictions. However, for the purpose of establishing a guideline, the California statute defining actual fraud is a comprehensive statute and suggests what conduct ought to be avoided.

FRAUD

Actual fraud in that state consists in any of the following acts, committed by a party to the contract or with his connivance, with intent to deceive another party thereto, or to induce him to enter into the contract: [1] The suggestion, as a fact, of that which is not true, by one who does not believe it to be true; [2] The positive assertion, in a manner not warranted by the information of the person making it, of that which is not true though he believes it to be true; [3] The suppression of that which is true, by one having knowledge or belief of the fact; [4] A promise made without any intention of performing it; or [5] Any other act fitted to deceive.[10]

C. Undue Influence

Undue influence is defined as consisting in the use, by one in whom a confidence is reposed by another, or who holds a real or apparent authority over him, of such confidence or authority for the purpose of obtaining an unfair advantage over him; in taking an unfair advantage of another's weakness of mind; or in taking a grossly oppressive and unfair advantage of another's necessities or distress.

UNDUE INFLUENCE

D. Mistake of Fact or Law

Mistake of fact and mistake of law, in proper circumstances, are grounds for relief.

MISTAKE OF FACT OR LAW

Mistake of fact is a mistake not caused by the neglect of a legal duty on the part of the person making the mistake, and consisting in an unconscious ignorance or forgetfulness of a fact past or present, material to the contract. It may also consist in a belief in the present existence of a thing material to the contract which does not exist, or in a belief in the past existence of such a thing which has not existed.

A mistake of law may be the basis for relief under circumstances specified in the several state jurisdictions. A rule finding support in a number of states allows relief when the mistake arises from a misapprehension of the law by all parties to the contract, all supposing that they knew and understood it, and all making substantially the same mistake as to the law. Relief is likewise given when there is a misapprehension of the law by one party, of which the others are aware at the time of contracting, but which they do not rectify.

E. The Remedy of Rescission

THE REMEDY OF RESCISSION

When consent is obtained by means of one of the foregoing causes, and it appears that the party would not have given his consent had such cause not existed, he may rescind the contract.

ORDINARILY RESCINDING PARTY MUST RESTORE VALUE RECEIVED UNDER CONTRACT

EXCEPTION

A contract is extinguished by its rescission. Subject to certain delays allowed by the law, to effect a rescission a party to a contract must, upon discovering the facts which entitle him to rescind, promptly give notice of rescission to the party against whom he rescinds. He must, ordinarily, restore to that party everything of value which he had received from him under the contract. Or, he must offer to restore the same upon condition that the other party do likewise, unless the latter is unable or positively refuses to do so. But the rule is not absolute, equitable principles being involved. If the party against whom the rescission is directed refuses to restore everything of value he has received under the contract, the rescinding party is relieved of the necessity to restore what he has received of value. The parties are entitled to offsets, one against the other.

The established procedures for effecting a rescission are outside the scope of this book.

QUESTIONS AND ANSWERS

1. What are the principal divisions of informal contracts?

   Answer: Unilateral and bilateral contracts.

2. Briefly define a unilateral contract; a bilateral contract.

   Answer: A unilateral contract is a promise for an act; a bilateral contract is a promise for a promise. In the unilateral contract there is one promisor and one promisee. In the bilateral contract each party is both promisor and promisee.

3. How may unilateral and bilateral contracts be classified with respect to performance?

   Answer: Executory and executed.

4. With respect to creation?

   Answer: Oral and written; express and implied.

5. What contracts may be oral?

   Answer: All contracts except those required by statute to be in writing.

6. What is an express contract?

   Answer: One in which the terms are stated in words, either orally or in writing.

7. Explain "executory" and "executed" contracts.

   Answer: All contracts are to some extent executory; when there has been full performance by all parties the contract is said to be fully executed.

8. When the conduct of the parties obligates them contractually, what kind of contract is said to result?

   Answer: An implied contract.

9. Name the essentials of a contract.

   Answer: Parties capable of contracting; consent, or mutual assent; a lawful object; the promise, express or implied; sufficient consideration.

10. Who are capable of contracting?

    Answer: Generally speaking, all persons except minors, persons of unsound mind, and persons deprived by law of their civil rights.

11. Is it essential that the parties to a contract should exist and be identifiable?

    Answer: Yes.

12. What quality and attributes of consent are required by an enforceable contract?

    Answer: Consent must be free, mutual and communicated.

13. When is consent not free?

    Answer: When it is obtained through duress, menace, fraud, undue influence or mistake.

14. How is the intent of the parties to a contract tested, or determined?

Answer: By a reasonable interpretation of their acts and the language of their contract.

15. What kind of test is this known as?

Answer: The objective test.

16. May the secret intentions of the parties be shown to determine their intent?

Answer: Not in most jurisdictions.

17. May the "offer" prescribe the medium of "acceptance"?

Answer: Yes, and if acceptance is not so communicated it is ineffective.

18. If no medium of acceptance is demanded by the offer, how may acceptance be communicated?

Answer: In any reasonable or usual manner.

19. What qualification must the object of a contract meet?

Answer: It must be lawful, possible of performance and ascertainable.

20. What must every contract contain?

Answer: At least one promise made by at least one promisor.

21. Is a promise to be implied in the "offer" and in the "acceptance"?

Answer: Yes.

22. Name a marketing contract in which the "offer" and "acceptance" is found?

Answer: The "deposit receipt" used in the real estate transaction of purchase and sale.

23. Is performance of, or the promise to perform an act a man is presently bound in law to perform sufficient consideration to support a counter promise or act?

Answer: No, not ordinarily.

24. Define "consideration."

Answer: Consideration sufficient to support a promise or an act is a detriment suffered by the promisee, or a benefit received by the promisor.

25. In the bilateral contract may it be said that a promise is sufficient consideration for a promise?

Answer: Generally speaking, by the weight of authority this is so, but the character and quality of the promise may be inquired into.

26. What does "mutuality of obligation" mean?

Answer: That mutual promises must effect binding obligations, each promise sufficient consideration to support the counter promise.

27. Is there mutuality of obligation in the unilateral contract?

Answer: Mutuality of obligation is inapplicable to the unilateral contract.

28. Must there be mutuality of obligation in the bilateral simple contract?

Answer: Yes. Both parties must be bound.

29. May an offer be assigned without the consent of the offeror?

Answer: Not ordinarily.

30. Is a contract signed by all parties assignable?

Answer: Ordinarily it is, unless otherwise provided therein, or personal skill or trust is involved.

31. Is an option assignable?

Answer: Ordinarily it is, unless otherwise provided therein, or unless the solvency, integrity or credit of the assignor is of significant importance to the optionor, or where personal skill or trust is involved.

32. What is a parol contract?

Answer: Any contract not a specialty or a formal contract.

33. In what kind of contracts are "offers" and "acceptances," so phrased, usually found?

Answer: In contracts growing out of correspondence by letter or wire or some other medium of commercial communication.

34. What are the requisites of an offer?

Answer: It must be certain, definite and communicated.

35. When is an offer communicated?

Answer: When it reaches the offeree or his authorized agent.

36. When is an acceptance communicated?

Answer: When it is put in an authorized course of transmission to the offeror, i.e., deposited in the United States Post Office, or with the telegraph company or other commercial medium for transmission to the offeror or to his authorized agent.

37. How may an offer be rejected?

Answer: By a positive rejection, a counter offer, or a conditional acceptance.

38. When may an offer be revoked?

Answer: At any time before acceptance, unless supported by consideration, in which case not until the expiration of the time allowed for acceptance.

39. How is revocation communicated?

Answer: In the same manner an offer is communicated.

40. What is a continuing offer?

Answer: An offer made to continue for a definite or an indefinite period of time.

41. Give an example.

Answer: An option unsupported by a consideration, with or without an expiration date.

42. When may an option unsupported by consideration but having an expiration date be withdrawn?

Answer: At any time before its acceptance.

43. When may an option supported by consideration be withdrawn?

    Answer: Not before the expiration date fixed by its terms.

44. When may an option unsupported by consideration and having no expiration date be withdrawn?

    Answer: At any time before acceptance.

45. If an option has no expiration date, how long does it continue as an option?

    Answer: For a reasonable time, if not sooner withdrawn.

46. Does the death or insanity of the optionor revoke an option unsupported by consideration?

    Answer: Yes.

47. Does the death of the optionor revoke an option supported by consideration?

    Answer: No. It is binding upon his successors in interest.

48. Give an example of mere invitations to bid.

    Answer: The "offers" of an auctioneer at an auction. The bid of the prospective purchaser actually is the offer which the auctioneer may accept or reject.

49. Where is a contract considered made?

    Answer: Ordinarily, at the place where acceptance is effected.

50. Where is an offer made through the mail, accepted?

    Answer: Ordinarily, when the letter containing the acceptance is deposited in the United States Post Office addressed to the offeror, and postage prepaid, the contract is considered made at the place where the letter was so deposited.

51. When is such a contract made?

    Answer: At the time the acceptance was so deposited.

52. If the offer had been made by telegraph or other medium of communication requesting a like acceptance, where would it be accepted?

    Answer: At the place where the message of acceptance had been given to the office of the communicating medium for transmission to the offeror.

53. When is such a contract made?

    Answer: At the time the acceptance is given to the communicating medium for transmission to the offeror.

54. Does the execution of a contract ordinarily import its delivery?

    Answer: Yes, physical delivery is not always necessary.

55. When does a written contract take effect?

    Answer: Upon delivery and acceptance.

56. May a contract be delivered conditionally?

    Answer: The instrument may be delivered conditionally, but it is not a binding contract until the condition upon which it is to become effective is met.

57. In what kind of transactions are contracts usually delivered conditionally?

    Answer: Frequently in "escrow" transactions.

58. What things not written into a contract are considered in law a part of it?

    Answer: The constitutions and laws affecting the contract, including the federal constitution, state constitution, statutes, codes, county and city ordinances, administrative regulations and judicial precedents existing at the time of its execution.

59. At what place is the capacity of parties to contract usually determined?

    Answer: Ordinarily, at the place where the contract is made.

60. Does this rule apply to minors?

    Answer: Yes.

61. May the parties stipulate in their contract what state law is to govern the validity of the contract?

    Answer: Ordinarily, they may do this.

62. Name four grounds for rescission of a contract.

    Answer: Duress, fraud, undue influence and mistake.

63. What is the effect of rescission upon the contract?

    Answer: It extinguishes the contract.

64. Who are minors?

    Answer: All persons under 21 years of age.

65. What three general classifications do the contracts of minors fall into?

    Answer: 1—Those which are void *ab initio;* 2—Those which are merely voidable, and 3—Those which are absolutely binding upon the minor.

66. Is the term "executed" sometimes used in a different sense than when "executed" and "executory" contracts are spoken of?

    Answer: Yes. When it is said that a contract is "executed" and delivered, it simply means that it is signed by all parties and delivered as an effective instrument.

67. Does an executed contract supercede all agreements, stipulations and negotiations preceding its execution?

    Answer: Yes. Ordinarily this is so.

68. Will an illusory promise support a counter promise?

    Answer: No. It is not a sufficient consideration.

69. If a promise is not a valuable promise will it support a counter promise?

    Answer: No. If a man gave a dollar to support a promise for a dollar, he would have no cause of action. There is here neither detriment nor benefit.

70. What is "the obligation of contract"?

    Answer: It is the binding force of law acting upon the promises of the parties to a contract. The law must sanction the object of the contract and give its approval before there can be an enforceable contract.

71. When a contract has been completely executed what might it then be said to be?

    Answer: It is evidence of what the contract between the parties was, and could be introduced in evidence for that purpose.

CHECKLIST

A. Check to determine if this contract is enforceable in your state.

B. Check to determine if this contract must be in writing in your state.

C. Check to determine if this contract requires a seal in your state.

D. Check to determine if this contract requires court approval in your state.

E. Check to determine if the object of this contract is lawful in your state.

F. Check to determine if any licenses or permits are required by law in your state to effect the object of this contract.

G. Check to determine if there are any local statutes, or ordinances or administrative regulations in your state which prescribe a particular form, or the inclusion of certain provisions in this contract to give it validity or enforceability.

H. Check to determine if the consideration as expressed by each promise is sufficient in your state to support the counter promise, or the act to be performed.

I. Check to be sure that the language of this contract is intended to, and does clearly express the final and conclusive undertaking of the parties, so far as it is intended so to do; that is to say, be sure this contract evidences, by the language therein employed, the complete understanding and mutual assent of the parties.

J. Check to be sure that the intention of the parties is expressed in the language of the contract itself, and that it will not be necessary to go outside of the four corners of the contract to understand what the parties intended.

K. Check to be sure that this contract is possible of performance.

L. Be sure there has, to your knowledge, been no duress, fraud, undue influence or mistake of fact or of law, involved in the negotiations or handling of this contract.

M. Be sure the parties to this contract understand its terms and conditions, and their legal implications.

N. Check to determine if all the parties to this contract are competent, under the laws of your state, to enter into this contract.

O. Check to determine if the signatures of the parties to this contract, under the laws of your state, must be acknowledged or otherwise verified, or witnessed.

P. Check to determine if any party to this contract is signing as an agent, and if so, that he is lawfully authorized to so act.

Q. Be sure that the consent of the parties has been given freely.

R. Check to determine if the rights of minors are involved in this contract, and if so, see to it that any such have been properly dealt with under the laws of your state.

S. Check to determine if the signatures of minors appear on the contract, and if so, determine if this contract is of such a character the laws of your state permit to be executed by minors of the particular class involved.

T. Be sure the contract is properly executed and delivered, if you are going to be responsible for the consummation of the transaction.

U. Be sure all alterations, additions and deletions have been initialed by all of the parties to the contract.

FOOTNOTES

1 The promise under seal, or the sealed covenant, is the product of the Common Law of England. In many of the states of the United States of America the distinction between sealed and unsealed instruments has been abolished, in others the effect and significance of the seal limited and confined to certain instruments.

2 A recognizance is a contract of indemnity which is taken in legal proceedings for the performance of an obligation imposed or declared by the tribunal, or court. It is sometimes said to be a *judicial* covenant as distinguished from a *private* covenant.

3 See Chapter 9, Bills and Notes.

4 An example of an unenforceable contract would be where the Statute of Limitations had run against a promise contained in the contract to pay a sum of money to the promisee. Such a contract is not void; there is still a moral duty to pay the money, but the obligation cannot be enforced because of the statute. However, in an action to collect the sum due, the statute not being pleaded, the court will enforce the contract. A similar situation occurs when bankruptcy is filed. The bankrupt may, after being decreed a bankrupt, promise without new consideration to pay the debt, and will be bound to do so in such event. In both cases a moral obligation exists which the law in proper circumstances will recognize.

5 This is the contract implied in *fact*, as distinguished from the contract implied in *law*, which latter is properly called a quasi-contract.

6 In dealing with infants, insane persons, intoxicated persons, married women, spendthrifts, and aged persons, the laws of the state where transactions involving such persons take place, as well as the laws of the state where performance is contemplated, should be carefully examined before definitive action is taken.

7 All but the simplest contracts should be handled in this manner.

8 The subject is treated more fully in Chapter 5 of the Handbook. This rule of contract law is of great significance in connection with the use of the real estate Listing Agreement.

9 But see California Civil Code §§1587.1, 1581, 1583 which permit revocation to be accomplished by puting notice in the course of transmission to the offeree; the same method which allows the communication of acceptance.

10 California Civil Code §1572.

2

Real Property

1. The Property Concept

A. Property Related to Ownership

PROPERTY is that thing of which there may be OWNERSHIP. It may be tangible or intangible or a right or interest in a thing. It is land and that which is affixed to land. It is also that which is appurtenant to land. It embraces all inanimate things which are capable of appropriation or manual delivery, and includes all obligations, products of labor or skill and generally speaking, all other things of value.

PROPERTY IS ANYTHING WHICH MAY BE OWNED

Because the term "property" includes anything which may be the subject of ownership, its meaning in a given instance, and whether or not limited in application must be known by determining the sense in which it is used.

All property has an owner, whether that owner is the state, and the property public, or the owner an individual and the property private. The state may also hold property as a private proprietor.

ALL PROPERTY HAS AN OWNER

In those states which follow the common law rule the state is the owner of all land below tidewater, and below ordinary highwater mark brodering upon tide-water within the state; of all land below the water of a navigable lake or stream; of all property lawfully appropriated by it to its own use; of all property dedicated to the state; and of all property of which there is no other owner.

STATE-OWNED PROPERTY

The common law restrictions on the right of aliens to acquire and dispose of real property have been abated in many of the states. Treaty provisions have likewise mitigated the common law rule. Where the restrictions are enforced a distinction is usually made between the acquisition of property by DESCENT and by PURCHASE.[1]

OWNERSHIP OF REAL PROPERTY BY ALIENS

The 14th Amendment to the Constitution of the United States prohibits a state from denying a person within its borders the equal protection of the law. The prohibition is against a state, not an individual. Hence it has been held that the failure of a state to prohibit the making and exercise of a dis-

THE 14TH AMENDMENT TO THE U.S. CONSTITUTION

criminatory racial covenant is not such "state action" as will come within
the amendment. However, any state action, such as the judgment, or order,
of a court of law, which sanctions a discriminatory racial covenant by enjoin-
ing, or restraining, the violation thereof, or by awarding money damages for
a breach of the covenant, is prohibited by the amendment.

B. Real and Personal Property

Of those things in which property is recognized, two classes have long been
the subject of English jurisprudence. These are:

THE IMMOVABLES
AND THE
MOVABLES

Land, and certain things attached to the land
which the law deems a part thereof—the IMMOV-
ABLES; and
Things or articles of a movable character—the
MOVABLES.

This division was early recognized by the common law of England, from
which a major part of our own law has been derived.[2] It marks the distinction
between REAL [the immovables] and PERSONAL [the movables] property.

2. Real Estates

A. Modern Law Estates

ESTATES OF FREE-
HOLD AND LESS
THAN FREEHOLD

Estates in real property are either freehold or less than freehold.[3] Each
of these divisions is further divided, with respect to the duration of the enjoyment of the estate, into the following subclasses. These subclasses of freehold
and less-than-freehold estates are the principal estates in land.

PRINCIPAL ES-
TATES IN LAND

Estates of Freehold
  Fee Simple
    Absolute
    Defeasible
  Life Estate
    For the Life of the Grantee
    For the Life of Another
Estates of Less than Freehold
  Estate for years
  Periodic estate
  Estate at will
  Estate at sufferance

DOWER AND
CURTESY

Because common law dower consummate after assignment, and curtesy,
are life estates, they are here mentioned. Dower is the life interest acquired,
in some states, by a married woman in her deceased husband's real estate.
Curtesy is the life interest acquired, in those states where the right is recog-

nized, by the husband in his deceased wife's real estate when children have been born of the marriage. These estates are created by operation of law, and are known as "legal" estates as distinguished from "conventional" estates, or those created by the parties.

While the institutions of dower and curtesy are recognized in a number of the states,[4] the common law form has been much altered by statute. There is a modern tendency to provide a distributive share of the decedent's assets to the surviving spouse in lieu of these estates,[5] or to effect a community interest in property acquired by husband and wife.[6]

MODERN DISTRIBUTIVE-SHARE LEGISLATION

The statutes of those states recognizing dower or curtesy or community property should be consulted when these institutions become important in any real estate transaction.

Estates of freehold are either estates of inheritance, or estates not of inheritance. Estates of inheritance are those capable of passing to the heirs of the owner. Those estates of inheritance which were recognized by the common law were the fee simple, which could pass to both collateral and lineal heirs, and the fee tail, which passed only to lineal heirs. The freehold estate not of inheritance was the life estate.

ESTATES OF INHERITANCE AND NOT OF INHERITANCE

Because the conventional estate in fee tail is allowed in some of the states,[7] it must be mentioned here. The reader is advised to review the decisions of the courts of his state if the fee tail is recognized there. The fee tail is not favored in American jurisprudence.

THE FEE TAIL

The fee simple absolute is the greatest interest which may be held in real property. The fee simple can be a defeasible fee, that is to say, it may come to an end by special limitation,[8] condition subsequent[9] or by an executory limitation.[10]

THE FEE SIMPLE ABSOLUTE

THE DEFEASIBLE FEE

Estates for life are of two kinds; an estate limited upon the life of the grantee, and an estate limited upon the life of another. Neither estate is one of inheritance. There is nothing the heirs of a tenant, who has an estate only for his own life, can inherit upon the death of their ancestor. Nor is there anything such a tenant can devise to his heirs. When he dies his life estate ceases to exist.

The situation is somewhat different, however, in the case of an estate for the life of another. Here, when the tenant holding the estate for the life of another dies, and the third person upon whose life the estate is limited is still living, the estate has not terminated. It not being an estate of inheritance, how will it be handled? Modern law recognizes the DESCENDIBLE FREEHOLD, which permits the life estate to pass to the heirs or successors of the deceased tenant for the remainder of the term.

THE DESCENDIBLE FREEHOLD

The estate for years is an estate of less than freehold. It is for a fixed term, but not necessarily for a definite number of *years*, as its name would imply. It may be for any fixed period of time, such as six months, or even a month, if the term is limited, or is capable of being limited by computation.

THE ESTATE FOR YEARS

A CHATTEL REAL DISTRIBUTED AS PERSONALTY

An estate for years is governed generally by the law which channels the distribution of personal property. It is ordinarily referred to as a CHATTEL REAL. But by statute in some states leases for a term of years are regarded as real estate.

THE PERIODIC ESTATE

A periodic tenancy is one which continues from period to period, as from week to week, month to month, or for longer periods. The term of the estate is not fixed. The tenancy continues from period to period unless terminated. The period for which the tenancy continues until terminated is usually estimated by the period for which rent is agreed to be paid. Notice to terminate the tenancy is required. The character of the notice will differ in detail in the several states. In some states the term of the tenancy is made to end and recommence at the expiration of each period for which the rent is paid.

THE ESTATE AT WILL

PRINCIPAL CHARACTERISTIC

An estate at will may be defined as a tenancy for an uncertain time to continue so long as both lessor and lessee permit it. Either party has the right to put an end to the estate. By statute notice to terminate the estate is frequently required. If the tenancy is entered into with the express understanding that but one named party, either the lessor or the lessee, shall have the right to terminate it, it is not an estate at will. The principal feature of the estate is its uncertainty of duration, and its continuing permissive status.

DEATH TERMINATES ESTATE

An estate at will terminates upon the death of either lessor or lessee.

HOW CREATED

CONSENT TO POSSESSION

The estate is created in a number of ways: by express agreement; by failure of the grantor to yield possession after a conveyance; by going into possession under a void or unenforceable instrument of sale or lease. In all of the foregoing instances the lessee at will is in possession with the approval and consent of the lessor. This circumstance marks the distinction between an estate at will and one at sufferance, the lessee at sufferance remaining in possession against the will and without the consent of the lessor.

CONVERSION TO PERIODIC TENANCY

Ordinarily an estate at will may be converted into a periodic tenancy by the payment of rent, particularly if there is a reservation of rent in the lease agreement for holding over.

TENANT AT WILL LIABLE FOR RENT

The tenant holding under a tenancy at will is usually liable for rent.

TENANCY NOT ASSIGNABLE BUT TENANT MAY SUBLET

The estate is not assignable, although it has been held that the tenant at will may sublet the premises.

THE ESTATE AT SUFFERANCE

PERMISSIVE POSSESSION WRONGFULLY HELD

An estate at sufferance is distinguished in one aspect from a tenancy at will by the fact that it is held, in most cases, against the consent of the owner of the premises, while the tenant at will has the permission, expressed or implied, to remain in possession. This estate is created much in the same manner as an estate at will, except that some lawful factor has usually intervened which gives the owner of the premises the right to possession, the tenant at sufferance wrongfully continuing in possession against the will and consent of the owner.

POSSESSION WITHOUT CONSENT

A tenancy at sufferance may also occur where possession is obtained without the owner's consent.

In the absence of statute, the tenant at sufferance is not liable for rent, but he is liable for the value of the use and occupation of the premises. Likewise, in the absence of statute, he is not entitled to a notice to quit. He may be ejected. However, his holding is not wrongful, and before an action of trespass may be brought against him, the owner must ordinarily re-enter or take such other steps as will render the tenant's possession wrongful.

LIABLE FOR VALUE OF USE AND POSSESSION

NOT ENTITLED TO NOTICE TO QUIT

3. The Ownership Concept, Its Incidents and Forms

A. Definition of Ownership

Ownership and property are two tightly integrated concepts of modern law. Ownership of a thing is the right of one or more persons to possess and use it to the exclusion of others. Property is the thing of which there may be ownership. It is also the bundle of rights incident to ownership. If the totality of enforceable legal sanctions incident to this integrated concept is kept in mind, the idea is clear enough. To get the proper picture, however, emphasis must be placed upon a RIGHT rather than upon a physical thing. One may have property in an idea and ownership of it. One may also have property in, and ownership of, a parcel of land.

RIGHT TO EX- CLUSIVE POSSES- SION AND USE

B. Incidents and Forms of Ownership

The ownership of property is either absolute or qualified. It is absolute when a single person has the absolute dominion over it, and may use or dispose of it according to his pleasure, subject only to general laws. It is qualified when it is shared with one or more persons, when the time of enjoyment is deferred, or when the use is restricted.

ABSOLUTE OR QUALIFIED OWNERSHIP

An interest in property is perpetual when it has a duration equal to that of the property itself, and is limited when the duration is less than that of the property.

PERPETUAL OR LIMITED

In the absence of statute to the contrary, the owner of land in fee has the right to the surface and to everything permanently situated beneath or above it. Except where the grant under which the land is held indicates a different intent, the owner of the upland, when it borders on tidewater, takes to ordinary highwater mark; when it borders upon a navigable lake or stream, where there is no tide, the owner takes to the edge of the lake or stream at low water mark; when it borders upon any other water, the owner takes to the middle of the lake or stream. An owner of land bounded by a road or street is presumed to own to the center of the way; but the contrary may be shown. Modern conveyancing has lessened the importance of these rules.

BOUNDARIES

Each coterminus owner is entitled to the lateral and subjacent support which his land receives from the adjoining land, subject to the right of the owner of the adjoining land to make proper and usual excavations on the same for

LATERAL AND SUB- JACENT SUPPORT

purposes of construction or improvement. Such adjoining owner must, however, comply with the requirements of state law with respect to making such excavations.

This field of law, due to the constant growth of urban and suburban communities, is today largely statutory. Familiarize yourself with the statutes of your state if you are likely to be concerned with the problem of excavating land.

Interests in land are either present or future interests. A present interest entitles the owner to the immediate possession of the property. A future interest entitles the owner to the possession of the property only at a future time.

In the ordinary practice of the real estate business one is not going to be called upon to distinguish between the several kinds of future interests. Nevertheless, to round out the picture of estates, or interests in real property, a few words will be said about the REVERSION and the REMAINDER. The reader should know what they are.

A reversion is the residue of an estate left, by operation of law, in the grantor. It is a present estate, but commences in possession in the future upon the

RESIDUE AFTER
GRANT OF PAR-
TICULAR ESTATE
OF FREEHOLD OR
LESS THAN FREE-
HOLD.

determination of a PARTICULAR[11] ESTATE granted or devised, whether it be freehold or less than freehold.

> *EXAMPLES:*   John Doe, seized in fee simple, grants to Richard Roe for life.
> John Doe now holds an estate in reversion to take effect in possession in himself or his successor upon the death of Richard Roe.
> John Doe, tenant for a term of ten years, sublets to Richard for a term of five years.
> John Doe now holds an estate in reversion to take effect in possession in himself or his successor upon the expiration of the five-year term.

There are other reversionary interests in property, but the two examples serve to point out the nature of a reversion without introducing distinctions beyond the scope of this book.

A remainder, unlike a reversion, is never vested in the grantor. It is that portion of the fee which will pass to the remainderman upon the termination of the particular estate granted, both particular estate and remainder being created by the same instrument, or grant. A remainder is vested or contingent.

Statutory regulation of these estates has altered the common law rule in many particulars, relaxing the strictness of the old common law conventions. State statutes should be consulted.

The modern view, as expressed by the Property Restatement, classifies these future interests upon the basis of determinative factors now generally recognized by the courts in determining the validity of vested and contingent remainders. Under the Property Restatement classification remainders are said to be those INDEFEASIBLY vested, those vested SUBJECT TO OPEN, those vested SUBJECT TO COMPLETE DEFEASANCE, and those SUBJECT TO A CONDITION PRECE-DENT. The last is a contingent remainder.

EXAMPLES: John Doe, seized in fee simple, conveys to Richard Roe for life, remainder to Allen Poe and his heirs. Allen Poe has an indefeasibly vested remainder.

John Doe, seized in fee simple, conveys to Richard Roe for life, remainder to the children of Allen Poe, Allen Poe having children at the time of the limitation.

The children living at the time of the limitation take a vested remainder subject to open up as the class increases.

John Doe, seized in fee simple, conveys to Richard Roe for life, remainder to Allen Poe and his heirs, subject to any appointment Richard Roe may make by will.

Allen Poe takes a vested remainder subject to complete defeasance upon the exercise of the power of appointment given to Richard Roe.

John Doe, seized in fee simple, conveys to Richard Roe for life, remainder to the child of Allen Poe first to attain the age of 21 years. Allen Poe has two children living, both under the age of five years.

The remainder is subject to a condition precedent,—contingent upon one of Allen Poe's children reaching the age of 21 years.

SOLE OR SEVERAL OWNERSHIP

The ownership of property by a single person is designated as a sole or several ownership. An estate in severalty is one held by a sole or single tenant in his own right, as distinguished from an estate held in co-tenancy or any other joint or shared ownership.

CO-TENANTS

When persons have joint interests in real property they are said to hold as co-tenants. Interests in which ownership is shared are joint tenancy, tenancy in common, partnership interest and the community interest of husband and wife. Co-tenants may hold in joint tenancy or tenancy in common, but these two interests are separate and distinct interests in real property. The old common law interest of coparcenary has, under modern law, been resolved into tenancy in common and so treated. And the common law co-ownership of tenancies by the entireties, while existing probably in half of the states, has real significance in fewer that that.[12]

TENANCY IN COPARCENARY

BY THE ENTIRETIES

JOINT TENANCY THE FOUR UNITIES

The common law, effective in all jurisdictions where no statute has changed the rule of law, requires, as an essential to the creation of a joint tenancy, four unities: the unity of interest, unity of title, unity of time and unity of possession. These four unities must spring from a single instrument creating the estate.

RIGHT OF SURVI-
VORSHIP

The distinguishing characteristic of the joint tenancy is the right of survivor-ship.[13] Upon the death of one of the joint tenants the remaining tenants are the sole owners of the entire property, not by right of descent, but by right of survivorship under the instrument creating the joint estate.

PRESUMPTION:
AN INSTRUMENT
CREATES A
TENANCY IN
COMMON UNLESS
CONTRARY INTENT
APPEARS

Under the early common law of feudal times, the creation of concurrent ownership was presumed to be in joint tenancy. This presumption has been reversed in most of the states. The modern point of view is that a tenancy in common is intended.[14] Nevertheless, joint tenancy is often preferred, and is here considered as developed in a state where the presumption is in favor of an estate in common.

UNITY OF INTER-
EST AND POSSES-
SION

EQUAL SHARES OF
SAME DURATION
AND QUANTUM

ONE ESTATE

Unity of interest means that the joint tenants must have an equal interest in the estate; that is to say, their shares must be equal. And because there is but one estate involved in a joint tenancy, the shares of the joint tenants must all be of the same duration and quantum. There can be no exclusive posses-sion by one joint tenant. If one tenant were to hold a one-half interest and each of two others a one-quarter interest, they would all be tenants in common, not joint tenants.

However, if John Doe were to convey an undivided one-half interest in Goldacre to Richard Roe, and a one-half undivided interest in the same Gold-acre to Allen Poe and Cecil Coe, as joint tenants, Allen Poe and Cecil Coe would hold a joint tenancy in a one-half undivided interest in Goldacre. And they would hold a one-half undivided interest in common tenancy with Richard Roe.

ESTATE DISTIN-
GUISHED FROM
REAL PROPERTY

Unity of interest does not refer to an interest in the particular piece of real property, but rather, to the ESTATE held by the joint tenants in that real property. In the foregoing example there were two estates carved out of Goldacre, one an undivided one-half interest in Richard Roe and one an un-divided one half interest in joint tenancy in Allen Poe and Cecil Coe. These two estates may be limited for different durations. For example, the estate granted to Richard Roe may be for life, while that granted to Allen Poe and Cecil Coe may be in fee simple. The life tenant could not destroy the interest in common. Upon its termination it would either revert, or a new like estate in remainder take effect. The balance between the joint tenants and their co-tenant in common would remain undisturbed.

ESTATES OF DIF-
FERENT LIMITA-
TIONS OUT OF
ONE PARCEL OF
REAL PROPERTY

UNITY OF TITLE
AND TIME

CALIFORNIA RULE

Section 683 of the California Civil Code provides that a joint tenancy may be created by a transfer "from a sole owner to himself and others," or "from tenants in common," or "from a husband and wife," "to themselves or to themselves and others or to one of them and to another or others." Any one of such transfers would have destroyed the old common law unity of title and time. One who already has title in himself cannot, it is submitted, convey the same or any part thereof, to himself, for he already has title which he acquired at some time in the past. Therefore there is neither unity of time, nor unity of title, properly speaking. While he may include someone else in the title, his own title springs not from the present conveyance, but from that time he first acquired the title he presently holds. Yet Section 683 clearly indicates that a joint tenancy may be created by such a conveyance, when it is expressly declared in the transfer to be a joint tenancy.

Prior to the amendment of Section 683 it was customary for the owner of property who wished to hold it in joint tenancy with others to first convey all of his interest to a third person (strawman), who then conveyed to the owner and others in joint tenancy. In such a maneuver the unity of both title and time, as well as of interest and possession, combined in the act of transfer.[15]

THE STRAWMAN MANEUVER

The incident of survivorship can lessen the cost and inconvenience of probate proceedings. There is some advantage, too, to the surviving joint tenant in that he will hold the entire estate free and clear of all debts of the deceased joint tenant, and of any liens on his interest in the estate. A judgment lien ceases when the judgment debtor, being a joint tenant, dies prior to the levy of execution. The surviving joint tenant holds the estate discharged of the lien.

SOME ADVANTAGES AND DISADVANTAGES OF JOINT TENANCY

There are some disadvantages, however. The joint tenant dying first has no opportunity to dispose of his interest by will. Upon his death the surviving tenant, or tenants, succeed to the entire joint tenancy. There is nothing left that the tenant first dying could have passed by will. There may be some disadvantage, too, taxwise.

Other advantages and disadvantages exist in the joint tenancy, but those mentioned are probably of the greatest concern. Advantages and disadvantages must be balanced, one against the other, in the light of attendant circumstances. If the matter warrant it, the advice of competent counsel should be sought.

Whenever property held in severalty is considered for conversion into joint tenancy, one's last will and testament should be carefully reviewed to determine if any particular devise or bequest will be ineffective, or destroyed by reason of the conversion, and some heir unintentionally injured.

JOINT TENANCY AND THE LAST WILL AND TESTAMENT

A tenancy in common is one owned in co-tenancy by two or more persons. By statute in many states an interest created in favor of several persons in their own right is an interest in common, unless acquired by them in partnership, for partnership purposes, or declared in its creation to be a joint interest. Likewise if it is acquired as community property, or held in one of the other common law tenancies such as coparcenary or tenancy by the entireties, it will not be a tenancy in common.

TENANCY IN COMMON

While there is unity of possession in both joint tenancy and tenancy in common, the unities differ in character. The unity of possession in tenancy in common is a SEVERAL unity. The unity of possession in joint tenancy is a JOINT unity. A several unity permits the alienation of one co-tenant's interest without destroying the character of the co-tenancy. The alienation of one joint tenant's interest destroys the joint tenancy. Unlike tenants holding in joint tenancy, tenants holding in common tenancy need not hold shares in identical quantum. One such co-tenant may hold a one-half interest, while four other

UNITY OF POSSESSION A SEVERAL UNITY IN TENANCY IN COMMON

A JOINT UNITY OF POSSESSION IN JOINT TENANCY

co-tenants may each hold a one-eighth interest in the estate. In the tenancy in common there is no right of survivorship.

PRESUMPTION
FAVORS TENANCY
IN COMMON

The usual presumption today is that property is held in common tenancy unless some other intention be indicated, or unless otherwise provided by statute. Joint tenancy may be shown by the language of the conveyance.

TENANCY BY THE
ENTIRETIES

In those states which still recognize tenancy by the entireties, a conveyance to a man and woman described therein as husband and wife would be deemed to create such a tenancy.

LAW OF COM-
MUNITY PROPERTY

The law of community property is derived from the civil law coming down through the laws of Spain and Mexico to those states adopting the system. It has been influenced by the common law and modified by statute and court decision in the several states where it is recognized. Although it will differ in particulars in each jurisdiction, the central idea is a community interest of husband and wife in property acquired during the marriage and by their joint and several efforts. The general presumption is that property so acquired is community property. Yet each spouse may own and acquire during coverture separate as well as community property. How the property is acquired is important in determining its status. The character of the property is often fixed by statutory provision.

STATUTORY LAW

CALIFORNIA STAT-
UTES

Community property law is largely statutory law. The reader is cautioned to consult the statutes of the state in which a question of community property arises. In California the law of community property has been extensively developed. The code of that state provides that a husband and wife may hold property as joint tenants, tenants in common, or as community property.[16] It is further provided that all property owned by the wife before marriage and acquired by her after marriage by gift, bequest, devise or descent, with the rents, issues and profits thereof, is her separate property. The same provision is made on behalf of the husband. All other real property situated in the state and acquired during the marriage by a married person while domiciled in the state, is community property. Whenever any real property is acquired by a married woman by an instrument in writing the presumption is that the same is her separate property, and if acquired by such married woman and any other person the presumption is that she takes the part acquired by her as tenant in common, unless a different intention is expressed in the instrument. There is an exception to the presumption. Whenever any such property is acquired by husband and wife by an instrument in which they are described as husband and wife, unless a different intention is expressed in the instrument, the presumption is that such property is the community property of said husband and wife.

PRESUMPTIONS
WITH RESPECT TO
CHARACTER   OF
PROPERTY

Under the foregoing rules of law and presumptions as recognized in this community property state, the following propositions evolve:

TO HUSBAND AND
WIFE   DESCRIBED
AS SUCH IN DEED

> Property conveyed to John Doe and Jane Doe, husband and wife: presumption, community property both as to husband and wife.

Property conveyed to John Doe and Jane Doe: presumption tenancy in common, one-half interest to the wife as her separate property; one-half interest to the husband as community property.

Estates by the entireties, dower and curtesy are the common law approaches to the problems sought to be solved by the institution of community property.

Like joint tenancies the four unities of interest, title, time and possession are necessary to the creation of the tenancy by the entireties. There is survivorship which, unlike the usual joint tenancy, cannot be destroyed by a conveyance by one of the tenants to a stranger.

The conveyance usually takes the form of a transfer "to John Doe and Jane Doe, husband and wife." Under the old common law rule the parties had to be in fact husband and wife, and actually described as such in the deed. In modern law the marital status may be proved off the face of the deed.

A marked difference between joint tenancy and tenancy by the entireties is that the latter allows only one share to the husband and wife when the conveyance is to such husband and wife and a stranger. Thus, in the conveyance "to John Doe and Jane Doe, husband and wife, and Allen Poe, a single man," the husband and wife would take a one-half interest between them in tenancy by the entireties, and Allen Poe would take the other one-half interest in the property as tenant in common with John and Jane Doe. This follows because of the common law traditional position that husband and wife are but one person.

As we have seen, in the absence of statute, when a married person wished to create a joint tenancy in himself and spouse it was necessary to convey to a third person, who in turn conveyed to the husband and wife, observing the rules applicable to the creation of this tenancy. Such a procedure is also necessary in a number of states when an attempt is made by the husband to create a tenancy by the entireties in himself and wife. The procedure is not necessary in many of the states recognizing tenancies by the entireties either because of statutory provision, or as a result of the decided cases.

The Uniform Partnership Act has been adopted in thirty-three states.[17] A partnership under the act is defined as "an association of two or more persons to carry on as co-owners a business for profit." Under the act partnership property may be acquired in the partnership name. All property originally brought into the partnership stock or subsequently acquired by purchase or otherwise, on account of the partnership, is partnership property. Any estate in real property may be acquired in the partnership name. Title so acquired can be conveyed only in the partnership name. A conveyance to a partnership in the partnership name, though without words of inheritance, passes the entire estate of the grantor, unless a contrary intent appears.

The reader dealing with a partnership would do well to familiarize himself with the law of partnership in his state before making any irretrievable commitment.

ALLODIAL LAND   ALLODIAL land is usually spoken of as land which a person possesses in his own right, in absolute ownership. The concept is usually set off against the idea of feudal tenancy, where land was held from a superior to whom service or rent was rendered for its possession or use.

4. Fixtures

A. Relationship of the Parties

In determining whether or not a chattel is deemed in law to be a fixture the court will give consideration to; [1] the legal relationship of the parties [such as those shown in the following examples] and [2] which party within that relationship placed the chattel on the real property.

The decided cases point to a number of situations arising from such relationships. Some situations in which a particular chattel may or may not be deemed a fixture are given in the examples that follow.

The question of whether a chattel is to be considered a fixture may arise between

> An owner of the real property, who placed the chattel on the property, and
>> his vendee; or
>> his mortgagee or beneficiary under a deed of trust;
> An owner of the real property, who did not place the chattel on the property, and
>> his defaulting conditional vendee who placed the chattel on the property; or
>> his conditional vendee's chattel mortgagee; or
>>> [Landlord and Tenant]
>> his terminating or defaulting tenant who placed the chattel on the property; or
>> his tenant's chattel mortgagee.

BETWEEN OWNER PLACING CHAT-TELS ON PROP-ERTY, AND HIS VENDEE

EXAMPLE: John Doe sells his hotel to Richard Roe. It is a cash sale. Nothing in the agreement of sale is said about fixtures. John Doe is in the process of moving out stoves, refrigerators, carpets, bathroom and light fixtures, and curtain rods, which he had placed on the property. Richard Roe objects, claiming these chattels to be fixtures passing with the real estate under the conveyance.

Under the general rule, John Doe would not be allowed to remove the chattels. They would be considered fixtures passing with the land.

EXAMPLE: John Doe borrows money from Allen Poe and gives Poe his note secured by a first mortgage on his hotel. Nothing is said about fixtures. Later a dispute arises between John Doe and his mort-

gagee, Allen Poe, as to whether certain chattels,
to wit, storm windows, a bathtub, electric motor
and a gas range, are or are not fixtures. Some of
the chattels were annexed to the property after
the execution of the mortgage.

Under the general rule John Doe would not be allowed to remove any of
the chattels placed on the property by himself either before or after the execution of the mortgage. They would be considered fixtures annexed to the land.
His mortgagee, having a mortgage on the real estate, would have a mortgage
lien on the land and fixtures.

BETWEEN OWNER PLACING CHATTELS ON PROPERTY, AND HIS MORTGAGEE

EXAMPLE: John Doe sells his house to Richard Roe under an
executory contract of sale. Richard Roe annexes
a fountain to the land in the front court with a
cement base buried in the ground and connected
with water pipes and drain. He defaults in his
payments on the house, moves off the property but
attempts to take the fountain with him. John Doe
objects, claiming the fountain as a fixture, and
denying Richard Roe's right to remove it.

BETWEEN OWNER NOT PLACING CHATTELS ON PROPERTY AND HIS DEFAULTING CONDITIONAL VENDEE

Under the general rule Richard Roe would not be permitted to remove the
chattle, as it had by annexation become a fixture and a part of the real estate,
title to which was in John Doe. This would also be the rule where a chattel
had been annexed by a lessee of the vendee under an executory contract of
purchase and sale, even though it was annexed by the lessee under an agreement with the vendee that it was to be considered a trade fixture as between
themselves.

EXAMPLE: John Doe sells improved property to Richard Roe
under an executory contract of purchase and sale.
Richard Roe buys an oil heating system and
installs it on the premises giving the seller a chattel
mortgage to secure payment. Later Richard Roe
defaults in his payments to John Doe, who takes
back the property. The question then is, is the
heating system part of the realty? Is it a fixture
which cannot be removed either by Richard Roe
or his chattel mortgagee?

BETWEEN OWNER NOT PLACING CHATTEL ON PROPERTY AND HIS DEFAULTING CONDITIONAL VENDEE'S CHATTEL MORTGAGEE

Ordinarily, John Doe would be entitled to hold the chattel as a fixture.

EXAMPLE: Landlord and tenant

In this area the relationship between the parties is that of landlord and
tenant where the rules are much relaxed, not only in recognition of trade
fixtures, but chattels annexed for ornamental or domestic use.

BETWEEN LANDLORD NOT PLACING CHATTEL ON PROPERTY AND TERMINATING TENANT

John Doe leases a dwelling house to Richard Roe
for a term of years. Richard Roe installs a glass

> mirror in the entrance hall capable of being
> removed without material damage to the premises.
> Just before termination of the lease Richard Roe
> removes the mirror. John Doe objects, claiming
> the mirror as a fixture and part of the real prop-
> erty.

The tenant may remove such ornamental chattels, or those placed on the premises for domestic use, as shall not materially damage the lessor's property by the act of removal. He must remove them during the term of the lease or, in some jurisdictions, within a reasonable time after the expiration of the term.[18]

BETWEEN LAND-LORD NOT PLAC-ING CHATTEL ON PROPERTY AND DEFAULTING TENANT

EXAMPLE: John Doe leases a dwelling house to Richard Roe
for a term of years. Richard Roe installs a glass
mirror in the entrance hall capable of being
removed without material damage to the premises.
He defaults in the payment of rent, forfeiting his
interest under the lease. John Doe enforces the
forfeiture. Richard Roe attemps to remove the
mirror. John Doe objects, claiming Richard Roe
has lost his right to remove the chattel.

By the weight of authority a defaulting tenant who has forfeited his interest under the lease loses his right to remove annexed chattels.

EXAMPLE: John Doe leases a dwelling house to Richard Roe
for a term of years. Richard Roe buys a mirror on
time, giving the vendor a chattel mortgage on it
to secure the purchase price. Richard Roe installs
the mirror in the entrance hall of the leased house.
He defaults in the payment of rent, forfeiting his
interest under the lease. John Doe enforces the
forfeiture. Richard Roe's mortgagee attempts to
foreclose the chattel mortgage. John Doe objects,
claiming the chattel as a fixture and part of the
real property, and asserting his ownership thereof.

BETWEEN LAND-LORD NOT PLAC-ING CHATTEL ON PROPERTY AND HIS DEFAULTING TENANT'S CHATTEL MORTGAGEE

In this example Richard Roe, having forfeited his interest in the leasehold, is not entitled to remove the chattel. His mortgagee, in the absence of some agreement with John Doe to preserve the chattel character of the mirror, has no greater right than Richard Roe to remove it from the real property of John Doe.

There are other relationships, to which the law of fixtures applies. These may be explored further in any comprehensive work on fixtures should the reader find it profitable to do so.

CHARACTER OF CHATTEL STAND-ING ALONE NOT CONCLUSIVE

That a particular chattel has been adjudged a fixture in one relationship does not mean that it would be held to be a fixture in another relationship. What may be deemed a fixture in the relationship of vendor and purchaser,

or mortgagor and mortgagee, may not be a fixture in the relationship of landlord and tenant.

B. Determinative Factors

The determinative factors are the intention of the parties as manifested by
the objective test, the physical facts, the character of the annexation and the
use for which the chattel is designed—each group of factors to be judged within
the relationship of the parties.

Where the fixtures have been installed by a purchaser under a land contract, it has been held that he will not be allowed to remove them, although he
may have removed them as trade fixtures had he been a tenant under the
landlord-tenant relationship. Those things which are essential to the enjoyment
of the premises for the use they are intended, and which have been annexed
before the contract of sale, would probably be considered fixtures and would
pass under the conveyance, unless expressly excepted from the grant. Many
chattels in a house in some way annexed to it are considered fixtures. They pass
with a sale of the premises in spite of the fact that these same chattels would
not have become the property of the landlord upon the termination of the
lease, had the relationship been that of landlord and tenant, and the tenant
had attached the fixtures himself.[19]

In much of the real estate business a fixture will be determined in the vendor-
purchaser relationship. This will cover most sales of improved property, and
all dwelling houses where the question often arises as to just what part of the
furnishings is included in the sale, the parties being silent in the matter.

There is a distinction between the character of the annexation of a chattel
attached to those premises devoted to commercial and industrial uses and one
attached to a dwelling house, or to premises not used in commerce or industry.[20]
There may be mere *constructive* annexation in those premises used in commerce
and industry. In such premises unattached fixtures [machinery, special
equipment, etc.] are said to be constructively annexed as a part of a functioning
whole undertaking, for which the premises have been acquired.

Ordinarily, those fixtures which cannot be shown to be trade fixtures or
ornamental chattels, or chattels adapted to domestic use, or concerning which
there is no agreement between the parties to treat as personal property, or to
remove from the premises, are part of the realty, and cannot be removed or
treated as personal property.

The cases ought to be read to understand fully the reasoning behind the
conclusions reached by the courts in adjudicating the rights of the parties to
this class of chattels. In determining their character the court will consider
the setting in which it finds them. It will then determine what the legal relationship is between the parties. Next, it will find the character of the chattel
in that relationship and decide what the parties intended. Finally, the court
will determine the degree of integration of the chattel with the real estate.

DETERMINATIVE
FACTORS

CONSTRUCTIVE
ANNEXATION
WHEN PART OF
COMMERCIAL OR
INDUSTRIAL UN-
DERTAKING

5. Easements Appurtenant and in Gross

A. Definition

EASEMENT APPUR-
TENANT

For practical purposes an EASEMENT APPURTENANT may be defined as the right to a limited use or enjoyment of another's land (called the SERVIENT TENEMENT) by the owner of land benefited by such use or enjoyment. The benefited land is called the DOMINANT TENEMENT. The easement is APPURTENANT TO the dominant tenement, and is LAID UPON the servient tenement as a burden.

EASEMENT IN
GROSS

An EASEMENT IN GROSS is likewise the right to a limited use or enjoyment of another's land. It is, however, personal to the owner and held by him independently of any land owned by him. Unlike an easement appurtenant it is not incident or appurtenant to any dominant tenement.

AFFIRMATIVE AND
NEGATIVE EASE-
MENTS

Easements are affirmative or negative with respect to the acts or demands of the owner of the easement. If the owner has a right to perform an act, either on his own land or on the servient tenement, which creates a burden on the latter tenement, he has an affirmative easement.[21] If the easement gives its owner a right to prevent the owner of the servient tenement from doing some act or thing on the servient tenement which, were it not for the easement, he would have a right to do, the easement is said to be a negative easement.[22]

PROFIT À PRENDRE

A *profit à prendre* is similar to an easement, and may be appurtenant or in gross. It lies in grant, as does an easement. It is a right to take something from the land of another, such as grass by the pasturing of cattle, or to cut and remove timber, or to take minerals from the ground, and to take other things. A modern example of a *profit à prendre* would be the rights of a lessee under an oil and gas lease to drill for, take and carry away oil and gas. It carries ancillary easements to use the surface of the ground to reach and carry away the profit taken.

B. Easements by Express Grant

EASEMENT AN
INTEREST IN LAND
NOT AN ESTATE

An easement is an interest in land. Inasmuch as it cannot vest in possession it is not an estate in land, although it is sometimes so spoken of in the books. A true estate in land consists of a possessory interest in land, or of an interest that may, although it need not necessarily, vest in possession. The interest in land created by an easement, however, is limited in respect to duration in ownership, and this duration will mark its character as a freehold or less than freehold interest. It cannot, ordinarily, last longer than the servient estate. An easement may be either a non-possessory freehold interest, or a non-possessory less than freehold interest in land, measured in fee, for life or for years.

DURATION UNLESS
OTHERWISE PRO-
VIDED MEASURED
BY LIMITATION OF
SERVIENT ESTATE

EASEMENT MAY
BE CREATED BY
EXPRESS GRANT

An easement may be created by an express grant. By statute in most states it must be in writing, and in some states under seal. But today seals have either been abolished or not required for the grant of an easement in approximately thirty-five states.[23] Nevertheless it is safer to say that, except as otherwise provided by statute or the decided cases in any particular jurisdiction, an easement by express grant is required to be in writing and under seal.

C. Implied Easements

An easement may also be created by implication Two types of easements created by implication should be noticed; that which is implied in grant, or reservation, in the nature of a way of necessity, and that which is implied in grant, or reservation, growing out of a pre-existing quasi-easement.

These last two types of easements, namely, those created by implied grant or by implied reservation growing out of quasi-easements existing on land before its partition, severance or sale of separate parcels, are set forth for clarification in Exhibits 2–1, 2–2, 2–3 and 2–4. The type of easement created by implied grant or reservation in the nature of a way of necessity is shown in Exhibits 2–5 and 2–6.

There is a code provision in California which gives statutory support to those implied easements growing out of quasi-easements. It provides that a transfer of real property passes all easements attached thereto. It creates in favor of such transferred property an easement to use other real property of the transferor in the same manner and to the same extent as such property was obviously and permanently used by him for the benefit of the transferred property at the time when the transfer was agreed upon or completed.

IMPLIED EASE-
MENTS

IMPLIED EASE-
MENTS SPRING-
ING FROM QUASI-
EASEMENTS

THE WAY OF
NECESSITY

STATUTORY SUP-
PORT OF IMPLIED
EASEMENTS
SPRINGING FROM
QUASI-EASEMENTS

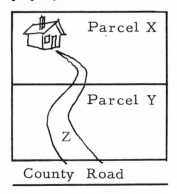

EXHIBIT 2-1

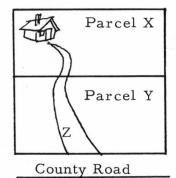

EXHIBIT 2-2

(1) Where the owner of two parcels of land sells one of them, the grantee takes the one sold subject to all obvious and permanent benefits and burdens which at the time of the sale seemed to be enjoyed by it, or laid upon it.

(a) Easement by implied grant growing out of pre-existing quasi-easements. Owner holding two parcels of land sells non-access parcel.

John Doe owns Parcels X and Y. Doe lives on Parcel X. Parcel X is reached by a road, z, which is obvious and permanent, and which leads to the county road. Doe sells Parcel X, nothing being said about easements. The purchaser takes Parcel X together with the right to use road z on Parcel Y, which now springs, by implied grant, into an easement appurtenant to Parcel X, which now becomes the dominant tenement, Parcel Y becoming the servient tenement.

(b) Easement by implied reservation growing out of pre-existing quasi-easements. Owner holding two parcels of land sells access parcel.

John Doe owns Parcels X and Y. Doe lives on Parcel X. Parcel X is reached by a road, z, which is obvious and permanent, and which leads to the county road. Doe sells Parcel Y,

IMPLIED GRANT

**IMPLIED RESERVA-
TION**

nothing being said about easements. The purchaser takes Y burdened with the road z, which now springs, by implied reservation, into an easement appurtenant to Parcel X, which becomes the dominant tenement, Parcel Y becoming the servient tenement.

In passing, it might be said that in the foregoing two cases a right of way by necessity does not arise, as it well might have, had there been no road z, in which case the purchaser of Parcel X could have had a right of way by necessity over Parcel Y, if he could in no other way reach the county road without going over the property of some other party.

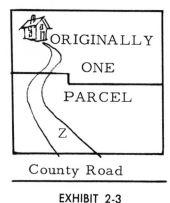

EXHIBIT 2-3

IMPLIED GRANT

**IMPLIED RESERVA-
TION**

(2) Where the owner of one parcel of land sells a part of it, the grantee takes the part sold subject to all obvious and permanent benefits and burdens which at the time of the sale seemed to be enjoyed by it, or laid upon it.

(a) Easement by implied grant; (b) Easement by implied reservation; both growing out of pre-existing quasi-easements. Owner holding one parcel of land sells a part of it. John Doe owns a parcel of land. Doe's house is set back some distance on the property from the county road. The house is reached by a road, z, which is obvious and permanent. Doe sells that part of the land on which his house is built, nothing being said about easements. The purchaser takes the parcel sold together with right to use road z over the land retained by the owner, which road now springs, by implied grant, into an easement appurtenant to the parcel sold, said parcel now becoming the dominant tenement, the other parcel becoming the servient tenement.

John Doe owns the before-mentioned piece of land on which his house is set back some distance from the county road reached by the road z. Doe sells that part of the land closer to the county road (on which the house does not set), nothing being said about easements. The purchaser takes the parcel sold burdened with the road z, which now springs into an easement by implied reservation, appurtenant to the parcel retained by the owner which now becomes the dominant tenement, the purchaser's parcel becoming the servient tenement.

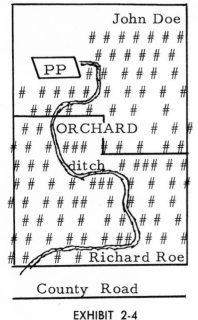

John Doe

PP

ORCHARD

ditch

Richard Roe

County Road

EXHIBIT 2-4

(3) Where co-tenants sever their joint interests each takes his estate subject to all obvious and permanent benefits and burdens which at the time of the severance may have been appurtenant to or laid upon it for the benefit of the whole estate before partition, to the end that each of the now separate tenements might enjoy the benefits that part of the whole estate previously enjoyed when held in co-tenancy.

CO-TENANTS PARTITIONING

(a) Easement by implied grant growing out of previously existing quasi-easement. Co-owners partitioning co-tenancy, each taking separate parcels of land.

John Doe and Richard Roe held a parcel of land in co-tenancy. They sever the co-tenancy, each taking a particular parcel of the land. While in co-tenancy the ditch ran across the land as indicated in Exhibit 2–4 by which the whole parcel benefited. A well and pumping plant was on the northwest section of the land, from which the ditch ran. John Doe took the north portion of the co-tenancy, Richard Roe, the southern portion. Richard Roe took by implied grant an easement to use the well and pumping plant and to take and conduct through the ditch on the northern portion to his own land a like amount of water formerly applied to the southern portion. The southern portion then became the dominant tenement, and the northern parcel the servient tenement.

IMPLIED GRANT

We have been talking about quasi-easements in the foregoing illustrations. We have shown how true easements spring out of quasi-easements under certain circumstances. We have been obliged to speak of certain permanent practices or uses established by the owner of land as quasi-easements because a servitude cannot be held by the owner of the servient tenement on that tenement. The burdens laid upon his land by himself and co-owner, or by himself for the benefit of a renter or occupant of part of his property do not create easements. They are in the nature of an easement, and may, as we have seen, spring into easements by implied grant or implied reservation. But they are not themselves true easements.

D. The Way of Necessity

A way of necessity may arise by operation of law, or by the implied intent of the parties.

THE WAY OF NECESSITY

Under the theory of an implied intent of the parties, an easement of a way of necessity appurtenant to the purchaser's parcel arises when the grantor has retained land surrounding the parcel granted, or when the granted parcel is surrounded by the grantor's land and that of a stranger. These would be cases of easements by implied grant. Were the grantor to sell all of his land except a landlocked parcel, he would have a way of necessity to this landlocked parcel by implied reservation.

IMPLIED GRANT AND IMPLIED RESERVATION

STRICT NECESSITY

If the grantee claims a way of necessity, he must show that it is a strict necessity. He cannot demand merely a more convenient way across the grantor's property. However, once the strict necessity is shown it is generally held that the way should be a convenient one, due regard being had to the interests of both parties.

A conveyance of the dominant tenement carries with it a way of necessity appurtenant thereto.

WAY OF NECESSITY BY IMPLIED GRANT: SOMETIMES SAID BY OPERATION OF LAW

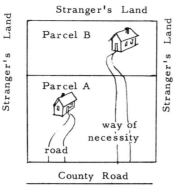

EXHIBIT 2-5

John Doe owns land composed of Parcels B and A. He carves out parcel B and sells it to Richard Roe, nothing being said in deed about a right of way to the county road. It is evident that Richard Roe has no access to the county road except over the land of John Doe or that of strangers to his title. He is entitled to a way of necessity across the land of John Doe, his grantor, and unless he and Doe can get together on some convenient way, he will be permitted by law to establish a way of necessity, taking into consideration the best interests of himself and his grantor. Whether this is said to be accomplished by operation of law, or by the implied intent of the parties is quite immaterial so far as the net result is concerned. Probably a way of necessity by implied grant is the modern way of looking at it.

WAY OF NECESSITY BY IMPLIED RESERVATION

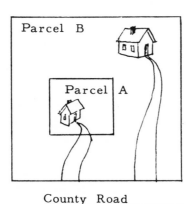

EXHIBIT 2-6

John Doe owns land composed of Parcels A and B. He carves out Parcel A for himself and sells the balance of his land, Parcel B to Richard Roe. This entire acreage at the time of the sale is unimproved land. Later both John Doe and Richard Roe build houses. Richard has access to the county road over his own land. John Doe, having cut himself off from the county road, is nevertheless entitled to have a way of necessity across Richard's land to the county road. This is generally looked upon as an easement of necessity by implied reservation, nothing having been said about a right of way in the deed.

6. Adverse Possession and the Prescriptive Right

A. General

When all legal verbiage is cleared away and the ideas of ADVERSE POSSESSION and PRESCRIPTION are reviewed practically, ADVERSE POSSESSION may ordinarily be established by showing that the adverse claimant's title is adverse (as defined by the decided cases in the particular jurisdiction) in its nature and occupancy, and has been so adverse for a longer period of time than within which the prevailing statute of limitations permits an action to be maintained for the recovery of land. PRESCRIPTION is established by showing that the *user* (the use of the property) has been exercised by the prescriptive claimant for a period of time the law requires for such use of the property to ripen into a RIGHT OF USER, or PRESCRIPTIVE RIGHT. Usually this is equal to the period of time fixed by the statute of limitations barring an action for the recovery of land.

> TITLE BY ADVERSE POSSESSION

> TITLE BY PRE-SCRIPTION

The thing sought to be acquired by adverse possession is ordinarily a corporeal hereditament, a fee simple absolute. That sought to be acquired by prescription is an incorporeal hereditament, as for example, an easement. In adverse possession *possession* is the key word, while in prescription *user* is the key word.

> POSSESSION AND USER KEY WORDS

B. Adverse Possession

To identify adverse possession one looks for a claim of right to a fee simple estate in land held in exclusive possession adversely for the statutory period either under color of title, or by a mere naked claim. The possession must be open, notorious and visible, wrongful and hostile to the title of the owner, and continuous. There must be no subordination to the rights of the owner.

> WHAT TO LOOK FOR IN ADVERSE POSSESSION

C. Prescription

To identify prescriptive user one will look for substantially the same elements as are found in adverse possession. Instead of an adverse *possession* an adverse *use* will be sought. The claimant need not establish an exclusive use in himself. The use may be shared by the claimant, the owner of the fee and/or third persons. Although the use must be hostile to the rights of the owner of the servient tenement, the use is yet a peaceable use continued because of the acquiescence of the owner. It must not, however, be in subordination to his rights.

> USE, NOT OWNER-SHIP, SOUGHT

The objective of the prescriptive claimant is not to obtain possession and ownership of the fee, but only to acquire a right to a limited use of the land of another.

7. Covenants Running with the Land and Equitable Servitudes

A. Running with the Land: Meaning of

MUST TOUCH OR CONCERN THE LAND

A covenant is said to RUN WITH THE LAND when in legal effect it binds, independently of privity of contract, subsequent transferees of the estate conveyed. The covenant must "touch or concern" the land as an incident of the land; that is to say it must not be a convenant only collateral to the land.

LANDLORD AND TENANT OR GRANTOR, GRANTEE

The practical problem is to determine when the benefit or the burden of the covenant runs with the land. The cases divide themselves, generally, into two classes, that of landlord and tenant and that of grantor and grantee. A third situation arises between the owners of separate parcels of land.

PRIVITY OF ESTATE

For the convenant to run, the general rule is that there must be PRIVITY OF ESTATE between the covenantor and covenantee. The question of the running of the covenant does not arise until there has been an assignment or transfer of an estate or interest in the land by one of the original parties, the grantor or grantee, or the landlord or tenant. When this occurs, in order that the covenant may run, in the absence of statutory provision, and in most jurisdictions, there must be privity of estate between the transferee of the covenantor and the covenantee. This means that the transferee must take the entire estate the transferor acquired from his covenantee. When the covenant runs with the land it runs because of this privity, not because of any privity of contract.

WHEN PRIVITY OF CONTRACT

As between the original grantor and grantee and their assignees who have assumed the obligation of the covenant, it is immaterial that the covenant run with the land. They will be bound because of the PRIVITY OF CONTRACT.

What constitutes privity of estate so as to permit a covenant to run has been a debated question of law for a long time. However, whatever conflict of opinion might appear in other areas of the transfer of estates in land, in the area of landlord and tenant there is presently no doubt of the presence of

IN LANDLORD— TENANT SITUA- TION: ALWAYS PRIVITY OF ESTATE

privity of estate. In the landlord and tenant relationship privity of estate means the simultaneous ownership of an interest in the land by both landlord and tenant. Example: a reversion in the landlord; an estate for life or for years in the tenant.

GRANTOR— GRANTEE SITUA- TION: WEIGHT OF AUTHORITY PROBABLY WITH " SUCCESSION " RULE

As between grantor and grantee there is still conflict of opinion. Some states follow the so-called Massachussetts rule, which restricts privity of estate to situations in which there is the simultaneous existence of separate interests held by each of the parties in the same land.[24] The weight of opinion, however, is with those jurisdictions which hold that the grant or other transfer of an interest in the land is enough, that is to say, "succession" supplies the necessary privity of estate.

B. Equitable Servitudes

THE EQUITABLE SERVITUDE

In the area of restrictive covenants where the doctrine of covenants running with the land will not support a general development program of residential neighborhoods thought socially desirable, THE EQUITABLE SERVITUDE plays an important role.

The weight of authority supports these equitable servitudes, or equitable easements, in the burdened land, which are said to be appurtenant to the benefited, or "dominant," land. Generally, covenants in deeds executed in furtherance of a general plan for the improvement and development of a residential building program containing restrictive covenants for the benefit of all lot owners in the tract will be enforced against each lot owner. Ordinarily, to enforce these equitable servitudes it must appear that the restrictive covenants are designed for the benefit of the lot owners in the tract; that there is "dominant," or benefited, land; that there is a general scheme or plan of improvement or development embracing all of the land; and that the covenants are intended as restrictions on the land conveyed and incident to its ownership, the purchaser accepting the lot subject to that burden.

FOUR PRINCIPAL ELEMENTS IN THE CREATION OF EQUITABLE SERVITUDES IN THE SALE OF LOTS IN SUBDIVISION WHERE DEED CONTAINS RESTRICTIVE COVENANTS WHICH DO NOT RUN WITH THE LAND

8. The Homestead Exemption

Homestead exemptions are creatures of statute the provisions of which, while all looking to the protection of the home against the demands of creditors, are not uniform in character in the several states and raise a variety of questions.

THE HOMESTEAD EXEMPTION

Only a limited aspect of these laws is here considered, namely, that segment which permits a good, commercial title to homesteaded property to be conveyed. This can only be determined with any reasonable degree of safety by the examination of pertinent statutes in the jurisdiction in which the property is situated.

The laws of one state are here briefly reviewed, giving a helpful pointer to what may be found in other states.

In California, the homestead consists of the dwelling house in which the homestead claimant resides, together with outbuildings and the land on which the same are situated.

DWELLING HOUSE

If the homestead claimant is married the homestead may be selected from the community property, the quasi-community property, the separate property of the husband, or, subject to Civil Code §1239, from the property held by the spouses as tenants in common or in joint tenancy, or from the separate property of the wife.

MARRIED CLAIMANT SELECTION

When the claimant is not married, but is the head of a family the homestead may be selected from any of his or her property. If the claimant be an unmarried person, other than the head of a family, the homestead may be selected from any of his or her property. The property here intended includes any freehold title, interest, or estate which vests in the claimant the immediate right of possession, even though such a right is not exclusive.

NOT MARRIED BUT HEAD OF FAMILY

UNMARRIED PERSON NOT HEAD OF FAMILY

FREEHOLD INTEREST

Homesteads may be selected and claimed by head of a family, or any other person, of not exceeding a sum fixed by law.

EXEMPTION

SELECTION OF CALIFORNIA HOMESTEAD

In order to select a homestead, the husband or other head of a family, or in case the husband has not made such selection, the wife, must execute and acknowledge, in the same manner as a grant of real property is acknowledged, a declaration of homestead, and file the same for record. The declaration must contain a statement showing that the person making it is the head of a family, and if the claimant is married, the name of the spouse. When the declaration is made by the wife, it must show that her husband has not made such a declaration and that she therefore makes it for their joint benefit. There must be a statement that the person making it is residing on the premises, and claims them as a homestead. A description of the property must be included, and an estimate of its actual cash value. These are the "musts." The declaration may contain a further statement of the character of the property showing the improvements which have been affixed to it, with sufficient detail to show that it is a proper subject of homestead, and that no former declaration has been made, or, if made, that it has been abandoned. If the declaration contains such further statement and is supported by the affidavit of the declarant, annexed thereto, that the matters therein stated are true of his or her own knowledge, such declaration, when properly recorded, shall be *prima facie* evidence of the facts stated, and conclusive evidence in favor of a purchaser or encumbrancer in good faith and for a valuable consideration.

EXEMPTONS AND EXCEPTIONS

The homestead, to the extent of the exemptions heretofore indicated, is exempt from execution or forced sale, except as hereinafter noted. It is subject to execution or forced sale in satisfaction of judgments obtained [1] before the declaration of homestead is recorded, and which, at the time of such recordation, constitute liens upon the premises, [2] on debts secured by mechanics, contractors, subcontractors, artisans, architects, builders, laborers of every class, materialmen's or vendor's liens upon the premises, [3] on debts secured by encumbrances on the premises executed and acknowledged by husband and wife, by a claimant of a married person's separate homestead, or by an unmarried claimant, [4] on debts secured by encumbrances on the premises, executed and recorded before the declaration of homestead was filed for record.

MUST BE RECORDED

The declaration of homestead must be recorded in the office of the recorder of the county in which the land is situated.

WHEN EFFECTIVE AS HOMESTEAD

UPON DEATH OF ONE SPOUSE PROPERTY VESTS IN SURVIVOR

EXCEPTION

FREE OF LIABILITIES

From and after the time the declaration is filed for record, the premises therein described constitute a homestead. If the selection was made by a married person from the community property, or from the quasi-community property, or from the separate property of the spouse making the selection or joining therein (the surviving spouse not having conveyed the homestead to the other spouse by a recorded conveyance which failed expressly to reserve his homestead rights as provided by §1242 of the California Civil Code) the land so selected, on the death of either of the spouses, vests in the survivor except in the case of a married person's separate homestead. Upon the death of the person whose property was selected as a homestead, it shall go to the heirs or devisees, subject to the power of the superior court to assign the same for a limited period to the family of the decedent. But in no case shall it, or the products, rents, issues or profits thereof be held liable for the debts of the owner, except as provided in the Civil Code dealing with homesteads. Should the homestead be sold by the owner, the proceeds arising from such sale to the extent of the value allowed for a homestead exemption as provided in the Civil Code shall be exempt to the owner of the homestead for a period of six months following such sale.

A person other than the head of a family may record a declaration of homestead. The contents of such declaration is practically the same as in the case of a head of a family, and it must be similiarly recorded. The land becomes a homestead upon recording the declaration.

Section 1243 of the California Civil Code determines how a homestead may be abandoned. Except where one or both spouses are incompetent, a homestead can be abandoned only by: [1] A declaration of abandonment executed and acknowledged by the husband and wife, jointly or by separate instruments, if the claimant is married; [2] A declaration of abandonment or a conveyance by the claimant if unmarried; [3] A declaration of abandonment or a conveyance by the grantee named in a conveyance by which one spouse conveys the homestead to the other spouse without expressly reserving his homestead rights; [4] A conveyance or conveyances by both spouses as provided in Section 1242; [5] A declaration of abandonment or a conveyance by the claimant alone in the case of a married person's separate homestead.

NEITHER HOMESTEAD, RENTS, ISSUES OR PROFITS CAN BE SOLD FOR DEBTS OF OWNER

PROCEEDS FROM SALE OF HOMESTEAD EXEMPT FOR SIX MONTHS

ONE NOT HEAD OF FAMILY MAY HAVE HOMESTEAD

ABANDONMENT OF HOMESTEAD

QUESTIONS AND ANSWERS

1. Does all property have an owner?

    Answer: Yes. Property is owned by the state or by private individuals or legal persons. The state holds it as public property, or may hold it as a private proprietor.

2. May a deed restrict land ownership to a particular racial, national or ethnic group?

    Answer: State law cannot so prescribe.

3. What is the "thing" of which there may be ownership?

    Answer: Every species of estate, real and personal, and everything which one person can own and transfer to another, including incorporeal rights, obligations and interests.

4. What is implied in the term "ownership"?

    Answer: The right of one or more persons to possess and use a thing to the exclusion of others.

5. Of what does real, or immovable property consist?

    Answer: Generally speaking, land; that which is affixed to land; that which is incidental or appurtenant to land; that which is immovable by law.

6. What is personal property?

    Answer: Every kind of property that is not real property. (One sometimes hears of "mixed" property which partakes of both real and personal property characteristics; example, heirlooms, fixtures, house keys, etc.)

7. Name two other terms for "real property" and "personal property."

    Answer: "Immovables," or real property; "movables," or personal property.

8. Of what does a man's estate consist?

    Answer: The bundle of movables and immovables and the rights and privileges attached thereto and growing out thereof make up his estate.

9. What are the principal "estates" in real property?

    Answer: Estates of inheritance, or perpetual estates; and estates of less than inheritance, or life estates, estates for years and estates at will.

10. What estates are freehold estates?

    Answer: Estates in fee simple, fee tail, for life of the tenant, for the life of another, dower and curtesy.

11. What are the principal estates of less than freehold?

    Answer: Estate for years, at will, periodic tenancy.

12. What are estates for years called?

    Answer: Chattels real.

13. What are estates at will called?

    Answer: Chattel interests.

14. Name two kinds of estates for life.

    Answer: Estates limited upon the life of the grantee; estates limited upon the life of a third person, known under the common law as an estate *pur autre vie*.

15. Is a life estate an estate of inheritance?

    Answer: No. The estate terminates upon the death of the grantee. There is nothing left for anyone to inherit.

16. Is the estate for the life of a third person an estate of inheritance?

    Answer: Not technically speaking; however it has been called a descendible freehold and allowed to pass to the heirs.

17. When is ownership absolute?

    Answer: When a single person has the absolute dominion over it subject only to general laws.

18. When is ownership qualified?

    Answer: When it is shared with one or more persons (legal persons); when the time of enjoyment is deferred or limited; when the use is restricted.

19. What is "several" or "sole" ownership?

    Answer: Ownership by a single person.

20. How may a person enjoy ownership other than in "severalty"?

    Answer: Broadly speaking, he or she may hold as "tenants in common," as "joint tenants," as "tenants by the entireties," as husband and wife in a "community" interest, as a partner in a "partnership" interest, and in a more limited sense where there is a contingent right such as dower inchoate and curtesy initiate.

21. With respect to time, what interest in property may a person have?

    Answer: Either a present interest, or a future interest.

22. When is an interest said to be a present interest in property?

    Answer: When the estate is held in possession.

23. When is an interest in property perpetual?

    Answer: When it has a duration for the life of the property.

24. When is an interest in property limited?

    Answer: When the duration is less than that of the property.

25. The owner of a fee estate has a right not only to the surface of the land, but to what other dimensions?

    Answer: To the surface and to everything permanently situated beneath or above it.

26. What protection are co-terminus owners of real property entitled to from one another?

Answer: Each is entitled to lateral and subjacent support from the other.

27. Is land held allodially in the United States?

Answer: Generally speaking, yes.

28. What is meant by land being held allodially?

Answer: Allodial land is that held in absolute ownership and independently of any rent, service or acknowledgment to a superior.

29. What is the opposite of allodial land?

Answer: Feudal land, or land held under feudal tenure.

30. Are reversions and remainders future interests in land?

Answer: In the sense that they are limited to begin in possession in the future.

31. Briefly define a reversion.

Answer: Briefly, a reversion is the residue of an estate left, by operation of law, in the grantor to take effect in possession upon the determination of the particular estate granted.

32. Briefly define a remainder.

Answer: Briefly, a remainder is an estate limited to commence in possession in the future immediately upon the determination of a particular estate.

33. May a remainder ever be vested in the grantor to take effect in the future?

Answer: No.

34. There are two kinds of remainders. Name them.

Answer: A VESTED remainder and a CONTINGENT remainder.

35. What are co-tenants?

Answer: When persons have a joint or common interest in property they generally hold as co-tenants.

36. What are the four unities of a joint tenancy?

Answer: Unity of interest, unity of title, unity of time and unity of possession.

37. What is meant by "unity of interest"?

Answer: That each joint tenant has an equal interest in the estate.

38. What is meant by "unity of possession"?

Answer: That there can be no "exclusive" possession by one joint tenant as of right.

39. Do these "unities" refer to an interest in a "parcel of land" or to an interest in an "estate" in a parcel of land?

Answer: Reference is to an interest in an "estate" in a parcel of land.

40. What is the distinguishing mark of a joint tenancy?

    Answer: The RIGHT OF SURVIVORSHIP.

41. What is this right?

    Answer: Upon the death of a joint tenant his interest in the joint tenancy passes by operation of law to the other joint tenant or tenants as the case may be. His interest does not descend to his heirs, nor can he devise it.

42. What is tenancy in common?

    Answer: An interest in common is one owned by several persons as co-tenants, not in any other co-tenancy.

43. May husband and wife hold property as tenants in common?

    Answer: Yes.

44. How is concurrent ownership in land presumed to be held today?

    Answer: In tenancy in common.

45. Is there a unity of possession in a tenancy in common?

    Answer: Yes.

46. How does this unity of possession in a tenancy in common differ from that unity of possession found in the joint tenancy?

    Answer: It is a several unity which permits alienability of the co-tenant's interest without destroying the character of the estate.

47. In an estate by the entireties is survivorship destroyed by conveyance by one tenant to a stranger?

    Answer: No. Not as it is in joint tenancy.

48. In a conveyance to a stranger and husband and wife by the entireties, what interest would the husband and wife take in the estate?

    Answer: A one-half interest, the husband and wife being considered one person in law.

49. Define a partnership.

    Answer: An association of two or more persons to carry on as co-owners a business for profit.

50. May property be acquired in the partnership name?

    Answer: Under the Uniform Partnership Act it may.

51. Broadly speaking, how many classes of "fixtures" are recognized in the law?

    Answer: Those which are permanently annexed to the land; those which are trade fixtures, are ornamental or annexed for domestic use; those which are agreed to be severed before sale or under contract of sale.

52. What is the general rule with respect to the character of fixtures as between vendor and vendee of real estate?

    Answer: The fixtures are generally considered part of the real property and pass with it, as against the vendor's attempt to remove them.

53. What is the rule with respect to fixtures installed by a defaulting purchaser under a land contract?

Answer: The defaulting purchaser cannot remove the fixtures he installed, unlike the situation presented by landlord and tenant.

54. What would the general rule be as between owner owning chattel and his mortgagee?

Answer: The owner would not ordinarily be permitted to remove the fixtures.

55. What would the general rule be as between owner not owning chattel and his defaulting conditional vendee?

Answer: The owner would ordinarily be permitted to retain the fixtures as part of the land.

56. Suppose the owner of real property mortgages it. Does the mortgage cover the fixtures?

Answer: The law would favor the mortgagee.

57. What would the general rule be as between the owner not owning the chattel and his conditional vendee's chattel mortgagee?

Answer: The owner would probably be permitted to hold the fixtures as part of the realty.

58. If fixtures cannot be shown to be trade fixtures, can they be removed in the absence of any agreement that they can be removed?

Answer: Generally not.

59. What is the general rule when a dwelling house is sold as to what things attached to the premises pass with the conveyance?

Answer: The rule is construed against the vendor. Things essential to the enjoyment of the premises will pass as fixtures, unless excepted out of the grant by agreement between the parties.

60. How does the court usually determine whether a chattel is a fixture?

Answer: The determinative factors are; intention of the parties as manifested by their acts; the character of annexation; the use for which the chattel was designed, all to be judged within the relationship of the parties.

61. What is referred to as "constructive annexation"?

Answer: It occurs where the chattel is a tool of industry or commerce and is a part of a functioning unit of property.

62. What distinction is made between premises devoted to commercial and industrial uses and those occupied as a dwelling house?

Answer: In dwelling houses there must be an actual attachment of the thing to the premises; while in commercial and industrial premises, there may be a constructive annexation.

63. What is an "easement appurtenant"?

Answer: For practical purposes it is a right to a limited use or enjoyment of another's land, called the servient tenement, by the owner of the dominant tenement.

64. Name five things appurtenant to land.

Answer: An easement for air or light; a right of way; the right to the flow of a stream; the right to flood land; the right to maintain a party wall.

65. If a "burden" or servitude" upon a parcel of land is not attached to another parcel of land, that is "appurtenant to it," but is held as a personal right unattached to any land, what is it called?

Answer: An easement in gross.

66. What is the parcel of land called to which an easement appurtenant attaches as a benefit?

Answer: The *dominant* tenement.

67. What is the parcel of land called upon which an easement is laid as a burden?

Answer: The *servient* tenement.

68. Is there a dominant tenement connected with an easement in gross?

Answer: No. The benefit attaches to a person as a personal right.

69. How are easements created?

Answer: By grant, express or implied; by reservation, express or implied, and by prescription.

70. What is an affirmative easement?

Answer: If the easement gives its owner a right to perform an act either upon his own land or that of the servient tenement, which creates a burden on the servient tenement, he has an affirmative easement. If it gives him the right to prevent the owner of the servient tenement from doing an act the owner of that tenement could do but for the easement, the owner of the easement has a negative easement.

71. What is a *profit à prendre?*

Answer: It is a right to take something from the land of another.

72. Give an example of a modern *profit à prendre.*

Answer: The right of a lessee under an oil and gas lease to take and carry away oil and gas from the land of the lessor.

73. Is an easement a true estate in land?

Answer: No, although it is sometimes spoken of as an estate.

74. If it is not an estate in land, how may it be described?

Answer: It may be described as an interest in land.

75. How is the life of an easement measured?

Answer: It is measured by the life of the estate of the servient tenement.

76. What is an appurtenance?

Answer: A thing is appurtenant to land when it is by right used with the land for its benefit.

77. What name is given to those so-called easements which are impliedly granted or reserved and have been "laid" upon the land by the owner himself?

Answer: Quasi-easements. A man cannot have an easement upon his own land. Therefore these quasi-easements only become true easements upon alienation of the owner's estate in the land.

78. What is a way of necessity?

Answer: It arises by operation of law to give a grantee access to a road from his property, when the property he purchases is shut off from access except over the land of the grantor or that of strangers. Such an easement also arises in favor of the grantor when he sells land land-locking the parcel he retains for himself.

79. What right is involved in a way of necessity?

Answer: The right to cut a way across the land of the grantor, or the land of the grantee, as the case may be, to a public road.

80. Must there be a strict necessity for a way of necessity?

Answer: Yes.

81. If a strict necessity for a way to a public road is found, may a convenient way be established?

Answer: Yes, the way may be convenient, but the interests of both grantor and grantee must be considered.

82. How is adverse possession established?

Answer: The adverse claimant's title is established by showing that his claim is "adverse" (as defined by the decided cases in the particular jurisdiction) in its nature and occupancy and has been so adverse for a longer time than within which the prevailing statute of limitation permits an action to be maintained for the recovery of land.

83. How is a prescriptive right established?

Answer: The prescriptive claimant's right is established by showing that he has adversely exercised the right of user he is seeking to establish, for a period of time the law requires for the perfection of such a right, which has been said to be equal to the period fixed by the statute of limitations barring the recovery of land.

84. What two words are key words in determining whether a claim is one of adverse possession or to acquire a prescriptive right?

Answer: The word "possession" in the case of adverse possession; and the word "user" in the case of the prescriptive right. "Adverse possession"; "Adverse user."

85. What is the object of the adverse possessor?

Answer: To obtain possession and ownership of the fee.

86. What is the object of the prescriptive claimant?

Answer: To secure a limited use of the land of another.

87. What is meant by a "covenant running with the land"?

    Answer: A covenant is said to run with the land when in legal effect it binds, independently of privity of contract, subsequent transferees of the estate conveyed.

88. Does a covenant run with the land because of any privity of contract?

    Answer: No. It runs because of privity of estate.

89. Is there any doubt of the privity of estate in the landlord-tenant situation?

    Answer: No. Here there is always simultaneous ownership.

90. Is there privity of estate in the grantor-grantee situation where the grant is of a fee simple?

    Answer: The weight of authority says there is privity of estate in mere "succession"; some states differ, requiring simultaneous ownership.

91. Does the benefit of the covenant run with the land?

    Answer: Yes, when there is privity of estate.

92. Does the burden run?

    Answer: Yes, when there is privity of estate.

93. Do both the benefit and the burden run with the land when there is an assignment of the leasehold?

    Answer: Yes. There is privity of estate by the weight of authority.

94. Do both the benefit and the burden run with the land when there is an assignment of the reversion?

    Answer: Yes. There is privity of estate by the weight of authority.

95. Do both the benefit and the burden run with the land when there is both an assignment of the leasehold and assignment of the reversion?

    Answer: Yes. Either assignee may sue the other in the event of a breach of a covenant.

96. May the sublessee sue the lessor for breach of a covenant?

    Answer: Aside from statutory provision, ordinarily no. There is neither privity of estate nor privity of contract between the sublessee and the lessor.

97. What equitable concept plays an important part in the development of subdivisions?

    Answer: The "equitable servitude," which permits the enforcement of those restrictive covenants which do not run with the land.

98. To create an equitable servitude, what two important facts must appear?

    Answer: There must be *dominant* land to which the servitude is appurtenant; the restrictions must have been imposed for the benefit of all the lot owners, which should be manifested by a general plan of improvement. The servitude must be incident to the ownership of a *servient* tenement.

CHECKLIST

A. Be sure you understand the character of the estate you are dealing with, whether freehold or less than freehold.

B. Check the laws of your state to determine if the freehold estate you wish to create is recognized by that state.

C. Check the laws of your state to determine if the estate of less than freehold you wish to create is regulated as to character of land involved, or because of its location or ownership.

D. Check to determine if fixtures involved in the transaction you are handling will, by the laws of your state, be considered as unseverable from the land, or as trade or ornamental fixtures, and removable.

E. For the purpose of determining whether chattels may be removed from the property, check the legal relationship of the parties concerned, and determine which of the parties affixed the chattels to the property.

F. For the purpose of determining the rights of the owner, check to determine if you are dealing with an easement appurtenant to a dominant tenement, or an easement in gross.

G. Check to determine the nature of any easement laid upon a servient tenement you may be handling.

H. Check to determine the nature of any easements which may be appurtenant to a dominant tenement you are handling.

I. Determine if there are any covenants running with the land you are handling, and their several obligations.

J. Check to determine if there are any equitable servitudes laid upon the land you are handling, and what they are.

K. Check to determine if a way of necessity must be acquired from and to the property you are handling, and if such way may be acquired without purchase from some third party due to changing road conditions.

L. If you are concerned with a homestead exemption, check the laws of your state for statutory requirements.

M. Check to determine what real property estates are recognized in your state.

N. Check to determine if dower and curtesy are recognized in your state.

O. Check to determine if fee tail is recognized in your state.

P. Check to determine if community property is recognized in your state.

Q. Check to determine if tenancy by the entireties is recognized in your state.

R. Check to determine if the descendible freehold is recognized in your state with respect to the descent of an estate *pur autre vie*.

S. Check the laws of your state to determine how less than freehold estates are terminated; what notices must be given, the time required, etc.

T. Check the laws of your state to determine the law of co-tenancy as it relates to tenancy by the entireties, joint tenancy, tenancy in common, the community interest of husband and wife, dower and curtesy; particularly with respect to creation, presumptions and termination.

U. Check the laws of your state to determine if the strawman maneuver is required to create a joint tenancy or a tenancy by the entireties in certain situations where otherwise the four unities could not be effected.

V. Check local provisions and the laws of your state with respect to excavations in connection with lateral and subjacent support.

W. Always remember that your state may not follow the general rule. Check to make sure.

FOOTNOTES

1 In approximately a third of the states the common law disability has been removed.

2 The term REAL ESTATE grew out of the early English system of *writs*, coupled with the doctrine of estates. This doctrine of estates had its inception in the feudal system of tenures whereby the rights of a man to the possession and use of his land depended upon the quantum, or duration, of the estate he held; for example, a fee simple, an estate for life, or an estate for years. Under the feudal system a man's status, or estate, was a very important thing to him. He was said to have the estate, or the status, of a tenant for years, or for life, or in fee simple absolute. His position in society was measured, very largely, by the character of the tenure under which his main landholdings were held. These landholdings, together with his personal chattels, constituted his estate.

   In time the Roman civil law laid its influence upon the law of England so that a man's land holdings became known as his *real* estate as distinguished from his chattel interests.

   In order that the established forms of redress in the courts of the day might be obtained, certain juridical procedures had to be followed. These procedures were built upon writs, which channeled the form of the action to the remedy sought. One such writ, the *writ of right*, was sued out when the interest to be recovered was a man's land, or his real estate as opposed to his personal or chattel interests. The bundle of rights making up that part of his estate which consisted of his land became known in time as his REAL estate. Today one commonly speaks of a man's REAL ESTATE, meaning his real property holdings.

   While the genesis of the term real estate has its roots deep in the common law of England, yet the English law had borrowed the concept from the Roman or civil law. The Romans had a form of action which was devised to recover the THING itself. It was known in the civil law as an action *in rem* as distinguished from an action *in personam*. The action *in rem* asserted a right against the whole world to the thing demanded, i.e., the land claimed. The action *in personam* sought only to enforce a right against an individual to compel him to return a specific chattel, or being unable so to do, to pay the value of the thing to the rightful owner.

   Actions *in rem* were known as real actions. [*actiones realis*] They were actions by which things real were recovered under the Roman Law, and under the English common law the actions by which LAND was recovered. In time the thing recovered took the name of the action by which it was recovered. Land became known as "realty," and under the doctrine of estates the term REAL ESTATE emerged.

3 Corresponding respectively to the early common law of free and villein tenures.

4 While dower and curtesy, in one form or another, may be found in other states, they are associated with life estates in the following states: Alabama, Alaska, Arkansas, Delaware, Georgia, Hawaii, Kentucky, Maryland, Massachusetts, New Jersey, Ohio, Oregon, Rhode Island, Tennessee, Virginia, West Virginia and Wisconsin.

5 See statutory provisions in Florida, Kansas, Minnesota, New York, South Dakota, Wisconsin and other states.

6 See statutory provisions in Arizona, California, Idaho, Louisiana, Nebraska, Nevada, New Mexico, Oklahoma, Oregon, Texas and Washington.

7 See decisions in Delaware, Maine, Massachusetts and Rhode Island.

8 An estate on special limitation is one which terminates upon the happening of a named contingency before the estate in its nature would normally end. For example, an estate to B *for so long as he shall remain single.*

9 Example; an estate to B upon the express condition that he use the premises for a public garage, and providing that *should he discontinue such use* the grantor to have the right to enter and terminate the estate. The condition permits the termination of the estate at the option of the grantor, or his successors.

10 Where upon the happening of a specified event an estate in fee simple is to be divested before its normal expiration with a limitation over to a person other than the grantor, or his successors in interest, there is, in such event, created an estate in fee simple subject to an executory limitation. Example; A grants Goldacre to B but if B die without issue surviving him, then limitation over to C and his heirs. Here B holds an estate in fee simple subject to an executory limitation.

11 The term "particular estate" is significant as meaning only a small part of the whole inheritance, a *particula*, the residue of which is in some other person.

12 Alaska, Arkansas, Delaware, Florida, Indiana, Kentucky, Maryland, Massachusetts, Michigan, Missouri, New Jersey, New York, North Carolina, Oklahoma, Oregon, Pennsylvania, Rhode Island, Tennessee, Vermont, Virginia, Wisconsin and Wyoming.

13 The joint tenants together have but one estate; that estate by operation of law passes upon death to the survivor or survivors of the joint tenants.

14 Arkansas, California, Colorado, Delaware, District of Columbia, Idaho, Illinois, Indiana, Iowa, Kansas, Maine, Maryland, Massachusetts, Michigan, Minnesota, Mississippi, Missouri, Nebraska, Nevada, New Hampshire, New Jersey, New Mexico, New York, North Dakota, Rhode Island, South Dakota, Utah, Vermont and Wisconsin.

15 This idle act has been avoided in a number of states, both as to joint tenancy and tenancy by the entirety.

16 California Civil Code §161: Community property states are Arizona, California, Idaho, Louisiana, Nevada, New Mexico, Texas and Washington.

17 Alaska, Arkansas, California, Colorado, Delaware, Idaho, Illinois, Indiana, Maryland, Massachusetts, Michigan, Minnesota, Missouri, Montana, Nebraska, Nevada, New Jersey, New Mexico, New York, North Carolina, Ohio, Oregòn, Pennsylvania, South Carolina, South Dakota, Tennessee, Utah, Vermont, Virginia, Washington, West Virginia, Wisconsin and Wyoming.

18 See cases in Illinois, Massachusetts, Pennsylvania, Vermont, West Virginia.

19 This follows from the nature of "trade fixtures," and sometimes from statutory law.

20 In such cases, articles not physically attached to the dwelling house are usually not intended to become a part of the realty, whereas the "constructive" annexation of articles as integrated units of a factory or industrial plant are usually intended to be permanent accessions.

21 Such as to construct a road across the servient tenement, or to flood a portion of it.

22 Such as to require the servient owner to permit light to come to the windows of a building on the dominant tenement by refraining from constructing on the servient tenement anything which might shut out the light.

23 Alabama, Arizona, Arkansas, California, Colorado, Georgia, Idaho, Indiana, Iowa, Kansas, Kentucky, Louisiana, Michigan, Minnesota, Mississippi, Missouri, Montana, Nebraska, Nevada, New Mexico, New York, North Dakota, Ohio, Oklahoma, Oregon, Pennsylvania, Rhode Island, South Dakota, Tennessee, Texas, Washington, West Virginia. The statute of frauds in the several states will vary in its requirements. The requirement of a seal in the conveyance of an easement in those states which have not abolished seals arises today because of the ancient common law rule that corporeal interests, such as estates in land, lay IN LIVERY, while incorporeal interests, such as an easement, lay IN GRANT, the deed of grant requiring a seal. The present day rule is said to require a conveyance under seal, except as modified by statute. The reader must therefore examine the statutory and case law of his particular state to determine the law as applied in that jurisdiction.

24 This situation is found [in the Landlord-tenant relationship] in the reversion and particular estate; and [in the grantor-grantee relationship] where one of the parties had an easement in the land of the other. The general rule, however, or weight of authority, finds "succession" sufficient to create privity of estate.

3

Recordation of Instruments
and Title Insurance

1. The Recording Laws

A. The Rule of Priority

While the first recording statutes were the means of protecting present ownership in land, they very early were extended to establish a system of priorities for the protection of subsequent purchasers. Except in those few states following the old English Statute of Enrollments,[1] which made priority of recording the exclusive test of superiority of right, all of the states now protect the subsequent bona fide purchaser for value who has had no notice (either actual or constructive) of a prior conveyance. The extent of that protection and when it will be given will vary accordingly as the particular state statute makes the mere absence of notice of a prior conveyance, or the absence of notice plus absence of prior recordation the deciding factor.

A SYSTEM OF PRIORITIES

The right to record an instrument is purely statutory. It is within the province of the legislature to say what documents or instruments must be recorded. Statutes also provide what instruments may be recorded for the purpose of giving constructive notice of their contents. It is with this latter kind of instrument we are primarily concerned. The layman is not, ordinarily, going to be responsible for the decision as to whether a particular instrument may or must be recorded, or going to be aware of what the consequences of failure to record will be. The decision is for an attorney at law to make. Nevertheless, if the instrument is one commonly used in the real estate business, a person in that business having some competence, through experience, in handling it, should not hesitate to do what is requisite and proper in the premises. If there should be any doubt as to the legal consequences of recording, or failing to record the instrument, the principal should be advised to consult his attorney.

RIGHT TO RECORD STATUTORY

61

B. Instruments Which May Be Recorded and Which Give Constructive Notice of Their Contents

RECORDABLE IN-
STRUMENTS

By statutory provision and judicial interpretation the area of recordable instruments has been enlarged progressively. Today all those instruments affecting title to or possession of real property or any estate or interest therein, whether by way of creation, alienation, encumbrance or termination, when recorded, give constructive notice of their existence and of their contents.[2] Among such are deeds, leases, deeds of trust, mortgages and powers of attorney. It has been held that contracts, instruments creating equitable interests, and chattel mortgages on fixtures (which ought to describe the real property in the indices of the Recorder's office) are recordable and give notice of their contents.

NOTICE TO SUB-
SEQUENT PUR-
CHASERS AND
ENCUMBRANCERS
UNAUTHORIZED
INSTRUMENTS MAY
IMPART   ACTUAL
NOTICE

These recorded instruments are made to impart constructive notice of their contents to subsequent purchasers and encumbrancers.

If a particular instrument is not authorized by law to be recorded it is ineffective to impart constructive notice of its contents. It may, however, impart actual notice if it is actually seen in the records by the party to be charged with notice.

C. The Unrecorded Deed

The unrecorded deed is valid between the parties to it and those who have actual notice of it. This statement is not so reassuring as it sounds, for it does not mean that such a grantee can hold title to the property against a subsequent bona fide purchaser for value first recording an instrument of conveyance. The first grantee may lose the property should another grantee of the same property appear who can show that he took subsequently to the first grantee in the chain of title, but that he recorded his deed prior to the time the first grantee recorded his. He must, of course, in most jurisdictions, also show that he was a bona fide purchaser for a valuable consideration and without knowledge, either actual or constructive, of the prior conveyance, and that he did at all times act in good faith. Actually, his diligence has prevailed over the prior grantee's negligence, and has been rewarded. Had the prior grantee recorded his deed immediately upon its delivery to him, he would have experienced no difficulty in holding his property.

OF TWO INNO-
CENT PARTIES HE
WHO IS DERELICT
MUST SUFFER

It will be understood, therefore, that the recording laws give the subsequent bona fide purchaser substantial protection, justifiable, aside from any grounds of public policy, only on the ground that as between two innocent purchasers, he must suffer who, by his own dereliction (in failing to record his deed) brought about a situation in which one or the other must take a loss. The prior grantee could and should have recorded his deed upon its delivery to him, and thus have enabled the second grantee to have learned of the prior grant by examining the public records before he paid over his money to the grantor.

2. The Subsequent Bona Fide Purchaser

A. Defined

The subsequent purchaser in good faith and for a valuable consideration, without notice of a prior conveyance, is the SUBSEQUENT BONA FIDE PURCHASER spoken of in the books and the decided cases. He is not found full blown and named in the recording statutes. He is a creature born of statutory and decision-made law. To establish a bona fide purchaser it must be shown that such a person purchased the property, or acquired the interest he has, for a valuable consideration, in good faith, and without knowledge, actual or constructive, of the prior rights of third parties.

B. Subsequent Bona Fide Purchaser Situations

The simplest way to present the law as applied to the vesting of title when the issue of the subsequent bona fide purchaser is raised is to diagram a few factual situations which have from time to time been presented to the courts for adjudication, and to draw from the holdings of the court in such cases propositions of law applicable to the facts presented. These propositions, while actual case law in the states from which they have been taken, can represent only what appears to be an increasingly acceptable judicial point of view in the majority of jurisdictions.

The factual situations presented will, for clarity's sake, be stripped to elemental simplicity.

PROPOSITION 1:   In a contest between two grantees of a common grantor, both grantees being bona fide purchasers, the grantee who records first gets the title.

EXHIBIT 3-1

A conveys to B	12– 1–65
B records deed	12–15–65
A conveys to C	12– 8–65
C records deed	12– 9–65
C has title	

Proposition 1 is the simple case of prior recordation between two grantees from a common grantor. Both instruments are of record. The illustration supposes that C, whose deed was delivered to him seven days after the delivery of a deed to B by a grantor common to both of them, had no knowledge, either constructive or actual, of the prior conveyance. The proposition asserts that such a grantee, first recording, takes title.

PROPOSITION 2:   In a contest between the prior grantee of an unrecorded deed and the grantee of a subsequent bona fide purchaser, where the prior grantee of the unrecorded deed and the subsequent bona fide purchaser hold from a common grantor, the

PRESENTATION OF SUBSEQUENT BONA FIDE PURCHASER SITUATIONS

SUBSEQUENT BONA FIDE PURCHASER CHALLENGED BY PRIOR GRANTEE OF COMMON GRANTOR

GRANTEE OF SUBSEQUENT BONA FIDE PURCHASER CHALLENGED BY

grantee of the subsequent bona fide purchaser takes title discharged of the equities of the prior grantee, though he take with knowledge of the prior conveyance.

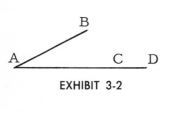

EXHIBIT 3-2

A conveys to B	12–1–65
B does not record	
A conveys to C	1–1–66
C is a bona fide purchaser	
C records	1–2–66
C conveys to D	2–1–66
D takes with knowledge of prior deed	
D records	2–2–66
D has title	

Proposition 2 presents a situation where a grantor has made two conveyances of the same property, one a month later than the first. The prior grantee has not recorded his deed. He is, therefore, a stranger to the record title. Subsequently the second grantee conveys to the present claimant, who before he received his deed learned of the conveyance to the prior grantee. That is to say, he had actual knowledge of the prior deed and is not a bona fide purchaser. Ordinarily, therefore, he could not prevail against the claim of the prior grantee. However, his grantor was in fact a subsequent bona fide purchaser. And the proposition says, in effect, that where the prior grantee is a stranger to the record title, such a bona fide purchaser can convey good title to another person notwithstanding such person has knowledge of the equities of the prior grantee.

PROPOSITION 3: In a contest between the prior grantee of a recorded deed and the grantee of a subsequent purchaser, where the prior grantee and the subsequent purchaser hold under a common grantor, the grantee of the subsequent purchaser takes title discharged of the equities of the prior grantee only in the event the deed of the subsequent purchaser is recorded prior to the deed of such prior grantee, and such subsequent purchaser had no actual knowledge of the prior conveyance and otherwise qualified as a subsequent bona fide purchaser; and it is immaterial that his grantee had knowledge, either actual or constructive, of such prior conveyance.

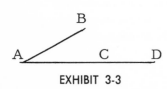

EXHIBIT 3-3

A conveys to B	12–1–65
B records	1–6–66
A conveys to C	1–1–66
C bona fide purchaser first recording	
C records	1–4–66
C conveys to D	2–1–66
D has constructive and actual knowlelge of prior conveyance	
D records	2–2–66
D takes title	

Proposition 3 is practically the same as proposition 2. Each asserts that a subsequent bona fide purchaser can pass good title to his grantee notwithstanding such grantee has, himself, knowledge, either constructive or actual, of the prior conveyance. In proposition 2 the prior grantee had not recorded his deed. The subsequent bona fide purchaser could not therefore be challenged on the ground of constructive knowledge. If he proved no actual knowledge and good faith his status was established. However, in proposition 3 whether he had constructive knowledge will depend entirely upon when the prior grantee recorded his deed. If the subsequent purchaser had no actual knowledge, acted in good faith, and recorded his own deed before the prior grantee had recorded his, his status of subsequent bona fide purchaser has been established, and his grantee, though having knowledge of the prior deed, will take good title.

Where the subsequent purchaser, in a similar situation, is unable to qualify as a subsequent bona fide purchaser, his grantee, in order to prevail over the prior grantee, must establish himself as a subsequent bona fide purchaser, as the following proposition 4 indicates.

PROPOSITION 4:	In a contest between a prior grantee and the grantee of a subsequent purchaser who cannot qualify as a subsequent bona fide purchaser, the grantee of such purchaser, in order to prevail over the prior grantee, must first establish himself as a subsequent bona fide purchaser first recording.	SUBSEQUENT BONA FIDE PURCHASER FIRST RECORDING, BEING GRANTEE OF SUBSEQUENT PURCHASER, TAKES GOOD TITLE

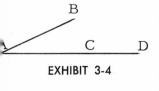

EXHIBIT 3-4

A conveys to B	12-1-65
B does not record	
A conveys to C	1-1-66
C not a subsequent bona fide purchaser	
C records	1-2-66
C conveys to D	2-1-66
D subsequent bona fide purchaser	
D records	2-2-66
D takes title	

Proposition 4 lays down the rule that a subsequent bona fide purchaser first recording, who takes from a grantee having knowledge of a prior conveyance, takes title notwithstanding his grantor's knowledge, discharged of the equities of the prior grantee. If, however, in this situation, B had recorded his deed prior to the time D recorded his, B would have prevailed even though D had neither actual nor constructive knowledge of the prior deed at the time C's deed was executed and delivered to him. B might well have recorded on February 1, 1966, either before or after D received his deed to the property, not leaving D much time for a race to the recorder's office.[3]

SUBSEQUENT BONA FIDE PURCHASER NOT CHARGED WITH CONSTRUCTIVE NOTICE OF RECORDED LEASE BY STRANGER TO RECORD TITLE

PROPOSITION 5: A subsequent bona fide purchaser is not charged with constructive notice of a recorded lease from a stranger to the record title.

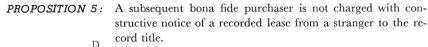

A leases to B	12–1–65
B does not record lease	
B sublets to C	12–5–65
C records lease	12–6–65
A conveys to D	1–1–66
D records	1–2–66
D has title free of leasehold	

EXHIBIT 3-5

Proposition 5 says that a subsequent bona fide purchaser takes title discharged of a lease of the property by his grantor when the lease is recorded only by a sublessee of the grantor, the original lease not having been recorded, and consequently the original lessee being a stranger to the record title.

SUBSEQUENT BONA FIDE PURCHASER NOT CHARGED WITH CONSTRUCTIVE NOTICE OF INSTRUMENT RECORDED BY HIS GRANTOR PRIOR TO ACQUISITION OF GRANTOR'S TITLE

PROPOSITION 6: In a contest between a mortgagee and a subsequent bona fide purchaser, both claiming from a common grantor-mortgagor, the subsequent bona fide purchaser is not charged with constructive notice of an instrument executed by his grantor and recorded prior to the date of execution of the instrument by which such grantor acquired title.

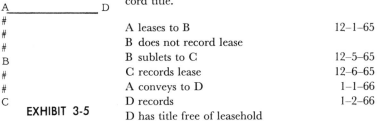

A executes land contract to B	12–1–65
B does not record	
B mortgages to C	12–6–65
C records	12–7–65
A conveys to B	1–1–66
B records	1–2–66
B conveys to D	1–3–66
D records	1–4–66
D has title free of mortgage	

EXHIBIT 3-6

Proposition 6 lays down the rule that a subsequent bona fide purchaser is not charged with constructive notice of an instrument executed by his grantor and recorded prior to the date of execution of the instrument by which such grantor acquired title. However, had the conveyance of the property from A to B on January 1, 1966, and recorded the following day, or the conveyance from B to D, referred to the mortgage, it would have put D upon notice and charged him with its contents, which would have destroyed his character as a subsequent bona fide purchaser. He would then have taken subject to the mortgage.

The foregoing examples establishing priority are based upon the presumption, which has not (to prevent confusion) been questioned, that the instruments were executed on the dates therein recited. But this presumption is rebuttable, which means that priority of right cannot always be determined upon the face of the record chain of title as to actual execution and delivery dates of the instruments involved. It might be that one instrument has been dated to show its execution prior or later in time to that of its actual execution and delivery. This being proved could well have the effect of forcing one of the parties in the record to qualify as a subsequent bona fide purchaser, and bring himself under the rules applicable thereto. Proposition 7 provides for this contingency.

PROPOSITION 7: The presumption that a deed is properly dated may be rebutted, and the challenged grantee forced into the position of qualifying himself as a subsequent bona fide purchaser.

Before proof:
C claims title

After proof:
Factual situation
of which C had
knowledge

A delivers deed to C dated	1– 1–66	
C records	2– 5–66	
A delivers deed to B dated	1–10–66	
B records	2– 7–66	**EXHIBIT 3-7**
A conveyed and delivered deed to C	1–12–66	
A conveyed and delivered deed to B	1–10–66	

In the example given, B having established the fact that C's deed was actually executed and delivered to him on January 12 rather than on January 1, 1966, and that C had knowledge of B's deed, B has done two things: first, he has shown that his own deed was the first executed and delivered; and second, he has shown that C is not a subsequent bona fide purchaser. Therefore, C cannot take advantage of the recording laws, for they protect only the subsequent bona fide purchaser in the situation in which the parties find themselves. It follows, then, that the fact he first recorded his deed means nothing. The situation now is viewed only with respect to the dates of execution and delivery of the two deeds, first in time being first in right.

The same proposition is applicable to instruments bearing the same date, one recorded before the other. The mere fact of early recordation does not necessarily establish priority of right. If prior execution and delivery, even on the same day, can be established one of the parties may be forced to prove himself a subsequent bona fide purchaser or encumbrancer.

C. Checking the Record

Sometime in January, 1966, let us suppose, E visits Goldacre, an unimproved acre of land in Lake County. Having decided to buy the property, he causes a title search to be run in the Recorder's Office of that county. This is done February 2, 1966. He finds that his grantor, C, has an apparently good and merchantable title to Goldacre, the chain of title being unbroken from the original U. S. patent. He finds that C holds a deed from A dated February 1, 1966, and recorded February 2, 1966.

E buys Goldacre, accepting delivery of a deed from C dated February 3, 1966, completes the transaction in the morning and records his deed the same day, February 3, 1966.

At the time E visited Goldacre there was no one in actual possession, nor had there been since, he having taken a last look just the day before accepting delivery of the deed.

March 1, 1966, he decides to build a home on Goldacre, and on March 10, 1966, has moved onto the property lumber and building materials preparatory to constructing a house.

D, a stranger, learns of E's activity on the property, and challenges his title to Goldacre, claiming ownership himself through a deed dated February 3, 1966, delivered to him by B, who had shown D a deed he, B, held to the property dated January 1, 1966, by which A had conveyed the property to B. E immediately re-examines the records, now finding a deed from A to B dated January 1, 1966, recorded February 4, 1966, just two days after A's deed to C, dated February 1, 1966, had been recorded. He then makes a complete check (more than he would ordinarily be required to make) of the records. Exhibit 3-8 reflects what he finds.

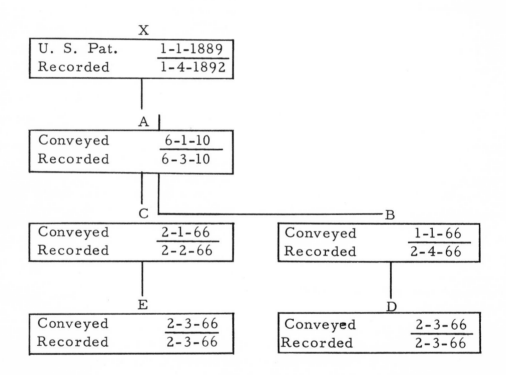

EXHIBIT 3-8

CHAIN OF TITLE

Where reliance is upon a paper title, the purchaser must trace his title either (1) to the Government; or (2) to a grantor in possession at the time of conveyance to the purchaser; or (3) to a source common to the chains of the purchaser and the party challenging his title.

SEARCHING   THE
RECORD

Following this procedure E checks back through the grantee index to find that C, his grantor, acquired title by conveyance from A dated February 1,

1966, and recorded February 2, 1966, which, of course, is what he found the first time he made the search before buying Goldacre. He then checks A in the grantee index to determine A's grantor, and so on, each owner being traced back through the grantee index to the source of his ownership. Now he runs each of these owners through the grantor index subsequent to the time such owner acquired title, in order to learn how each owner disposed of his land. From the patent down to A the chain is unbroken. He finds, however, that since he last checked the record, B has recorded a deed on February 4, 1966, the deed being dated January 1, 1966, by which A conveyed Goldacre to B. The record likewise shows that on February 2, 1966, C recorded a deed dated February 1, 1966, by which A conveyed the same property to C, E's grantor. This deed to B had not been recorded prior to the time C conveyed Goldacre to E, consequently when E made his first search of the record he had no knowledge of the prior grant to B. Now it appears that B holds a deed by which Goldacre was conveyed to him by A before the same property was conveyed to C, E's grantor. Running B through the grantor index he finds that B conveyed Goldacre to D February 3, 1966, and D recorded his deed the same day. From the record it appears that both E and D acquired Goldacre the same day, and likewise recorded their deeds the same day. Who, then, owns Goldacre?

E visits C to learn if C had any actual knowledge of the prior deed to B. C assures him he had not, that had he had such knowledge he never would have bought Goldacre. In his conversation with C, E is entirely satisfied that C bought the property in good faith and without any knowledge of, or reason to believe that A had previously conveyed the property to B.

After his talk with C, E calls upon D and both men discuss the matter. Being reasonable business men they agree to consult an attorney at law familiar with such matters, and to be guided entirely by what he advises.

After a consultation, the attorney advised them that, assuming the facts to be as they had been represented to him, under the recording laws of the state, E would most likely prevail if the matter reached the courts. He pointed out to them that C was a subsequent bona fide purchaser first recording and that such a purchaser could give good title to his grantee, and that D could have no greater rights than his grantor because he was not a subsequent bona fide purchaser for the reason that he had constructive notice of the C conveyance, that deed having been recorded February 2, 1966.

3. Title Insurance

The predecessors of the modern title insurance policy were the abstract,[4] the certificate of title[5] and the guaranty of title.[6]

These instruments were inadequate to an accelerating real estate business, and as protection against undisclosed title defects not apparent on the face of the record. There still remained a wide area of risk uncovered by any protection.

TITLE INSURANCE
THE ABSTRACT
THE CERTIFICATE OF TITLE
THE GUARANTEE OF TITLE

CONCEALED RISKS

Concealed within recorded documents and in their execution may be found fraud, forgery, lack of authority, failure of delivery, incompetence of the parties, mistaken identity and failure to comply with legal requirements. All develop defects in title. Off-record prescriptive easements and adverse possession, not appearing in the chain of title, may well defeat the object of a conveyance. There is, too, the possibility of error of judgment in the interpretation and construction of instruments in the chain of title.

THE MODERN TITLE INSURANCE POLICY

The modern title insurance policy has been developed to insure against these risks.

MAJOR SOURCES OF UNCERTAINTY

The risks actually insured develop from three major sources of uncertainty: [1] error in the search and examination of recorded instruments; [2] error in determining the legal effect of recorded instruments, and [3] lack of knowledge of facts outside of the records touching or concerning the title.

BUYER TITLE INSUR-ANCE STANDARD AND EXTENDED COVERAGE

Two types of buyer title insurance policies are in general use today, and are written for the average real estate transaction, to wit: [1] the standard policy, and [2] the extended coverage policy. The standard coverage policy usually insures "the insured," the heirs, devisees, personal representatives of such insured, or, if a corporation, its successors by dissolution, merger or con-solidation, against direct loss or damage (including costs, attorneys' fees and expenses which the company may become obligated to pay as provided in the conditions and stipulations of the policy) which the insured shall sustain by reason of (a) any defect in or lien or encumbrances on the estate or interest covered existing at the date of the policy and not particularly excluded; (b) unmarketability of title; (c) any defect in the execution of any mortgage or deed of trust shown in the policy securing an indebtedness, the owner of which is named as an insured, insofar as such defect affects the lien or charge of such mortgage or deed of trust upon the interest or estate covered; (d) priority of encumbrances over those acknowledged in the policy.

STANDARD RISKS INSURED AGAINST

EXCLUSION OF SPECIFIC RISKS

The standard coverage policy usually excludes specific risks such as: [1] taxes or assessments which are not shown as existing liens by the public records, or by the records of the properly authorized taxing or assessing authority; [2] any facts, rights, interests, claims, easements or encumbrances not shown on the public records but which could be ascertained by an inspection of property or by inquiry of persons in possession; discrepancies, boundary conflicts, area shortages, encroachments or any other facts which a correct survey would disclose, and which are not shown in the public records; reserva-tions or exceptions in patents or in Acts authorizing the issuance thereof, unpatented mining claims, water rights or claims or title to water; [3] those matters which have been expressly excluded from coverage in a schedule of the policy.

FURTHER EXCLU-SIONS

The policy under its "conditions and stipulations" clause makes further exclusions and fixes limitations upon the rights granted, and of course, the company's ultimate liability. Most of the risks not covered by the standard policy can be insured against by special endorsement by which the company undertakes further assurance.

The standard policy should be carefully examined for a proper understanding of its effectiveness as an instrument of title insurance.

The typical extended coverage policy enlarges the risk usually covered by the standard policy to include the rights of parties in actual possession of the property, off-record easements, unrecorded liens, rights and claims a correct survey or inspection of the land would show, mining claims, water rights, and reservations in patents. It ordinarily provides purchasers of real estate with the same protection the American Title Association Policy extends to lenders.

THE EXTENDED COVERAGE POLICY

ENLARGED RISK

These extended coverage policies, like the standard policy, ordinarily do not insure against unrevealed defects known to the insured at the time the policy was procured, nor against governmental regulations of occupancy or use.

In conclusion, it can be said that modern recording laws and title insurance offer the means of substantial and prompt protection of the investor in a business which has the urgency of the present-day real estate transaction.

QUESTIONS AND ANSWERS

1. Is the right to record an instrument governed by statute?
   Answer: Yes.

2. Name some instruments which may be recorded, and when recorded give constructive notice of their contents.
   Answer: Deeds, mortgages, deeds of trust, land contracts, leases and chattel mortgages on fixtures.

3. Generally speaking, what instruments may be recorded today and give notice of their contents?
   Answer: All instruments affecting title to or possession of real property or any estate or interest therein.

4. If an instrument not authorized by law to give constructive notice of its contents is recorded, can it ever give notice of its contents while in the public records?
   Answer: Yes. It can give actual notice of its contents to all who see it in the records.

5. Whom do the recording laws protect?
   Answer: Particularly subsequent bona fide purchasers as that term has been defined in the law. They likewise protect other persons having a present interest in property.

6. How does the law protect them?
   Answer: The instrument recorded is made to impart constructive notice of its contents to subsequent purchasers and encumbrancers so as to cut off any asserted rights of such persons, unless they are bona fide purchasers or encumbrancers, in which case, in the majority of states, the first grantee recording is protected.

7. What is the motivating public policy principle underlying the recording laws?
   Answer: There are a number of policy motivations, as for example, the policy of the law to keep real property marketable, transferable and valuable, etc.; but as between the parties involved, the recording laws favor the diligent over the negligent individual.

8. How is the diligent-negligent rule sometimes expressed?
   Answer: Often it is said that he who is derelict must suffer. It is also said that as between two innocent purchasers he must suffer who by his own dereliction brought about the situation in which one or the other must take a loss.

9. How did the concept of the subsequent bona fide purchaser come into being?
   Answer: Through equity, the decided cases and statutory law.

10. As between two grantees of a common grantor, when may the second grantee prevail?

Answer: Ordinarily, when he is a subsequent bona fide purchaser first recording. This would be the majority rule.

11. In a contest between the grantee of a subsequent bona fide purchaser and a stranger to the record title, who would prevail?

Answer: Ordinarily, the grantee of the subsequent bona fide purchaser.

12. As between a prior grantee and the grantee of a subsequent purchaser both deraigning title from a common grantor, who would prevail in a contest for title?

Answer: Ordinarily, the grantee of the subsequent purchaser first recording would take title discharged of the equities of the prior grantee only if the subsequent purchaser could be established as a subsequent bona fide purchaser.

13. In the foregoing situation, had the subsequent purchaser failed to establish himself as a subsequent bona fide purchaser, what would his grantee have to do in order to prevail in a contest between himself and the prior grantee?

Answer: Ordinarily, he would have to establish himself as a subsequent bona fide purchaser first recording.

14. Is a subsequent bona fide purchaser charged with constructive notice of a recorded lease from a stranger to the record title?

Answer: Ordinarily, he is not.

15. Is a subsequent bona fide purchaser charged with constructive notice of an instrument recorded by his grantor prior to the time that grantor acquired title to land conveyed to his grantee?

Answer: Ordinarily, he is not.

16. Is there a presumption that a deed is properly dated?

Answer: Ordinarily, this would be so.

17. May this presumption be rebutted?

Answer: Yes. It is a rebuttable presumption.

18. What do you suppose would be the object of challenging the date of a deed?

Answer: To force the challenged grantee into the position of qualifying himself as a subsequent bona fide purchaser to prevail in a title contest over the challenging grantee.

19. Of instruments bearing the same date, one recorded before the other, may it be shown that the one first recorded was executed subsequent to the one later recorded, and thus force the grantee of the first recorded deed into the position of a subsequent purchaser, and make him submit proof that he qualifies as a subsequent bona fide purchaser?

Answer: Yes; and if it can be shown that he took his deed with knowledge of the prior deed he cannot prevail as a subsequent bona fide purchaser, and his challenger would prevail.

20. If one relies upon paper title, to what must he trace his title?

    Answer: Ordinarily, either to the government, or to a grantor in possession at the time of the conveyance to the purchaser, or to a source common to the chains of the purchaser and the party challenging his title.

21. Briefly, what is a bona fide purchaser?

    Answer: One who purchases property, or acquires the interest he has therein, for a valuable consideration, in good faith and without knowledge, actual or constructive, of the prior equities of third persons.

22. Need the transferee of a subsequent bona fide purchaser be a bona fide purchaser himself to prevail over the claim of a prior grantee later recording?

    Answer: Ordinarily, he need not. The subsequent bona fide purchaser first recording should prevail over the prior grantee, and his grantee takes discharge of the equities of the prior grantee.

23. Between whom is an unrecorded deed valid?

    Answer: Between the parties thereto, and those who have knowledge thereof.

24. What are the three major sources of risks to be insured against?

    Answer: [1] Error in the search and examination of recorded instruments; [2] error in determining the legal effect of recorded instruments, and [3] lack of knowledge of facts outside of the records touching or concerning the title.

25. What two types of buyer title insurance policies are generally to be found?

    Answer: The standard coverage policy and the extended coverage policy.

26. What risks are ordinarily covered by the standard policy?

    Answer: Generally speaking, any defect in or lien or encumbrance upon the estate or interest covered existing at the date of the policy and not particularly excluded; unmarketability of title; any defect in the execution of any mortgage or deed of trust shown in the policy securing an indebtedness, the owner of which is named as an insured, insofar as such defect affects the lien or charge of such encumbrance; priority of encumbrances over those acknowledged in the policy.

27. What, ordinarily, are the exclusions?

    Answer: Such specific risks as [1] taxes or assessments which are not shown as existing liens by the public records, or by the records of the properly authorized taxing or assessing authority; [2] any facts, rights, interests, claims, easements or encumbrances not shown on the public records but which could be ascertained by an inspection of the property or by inquiry of persons in possession; discrepancies, boundary conflicts, area shortages, encroachments or any other facts which a correct survey would disclose, and which are not shown on the public records, reservations or exceptions in patents or in acts authorizing the issuance thereof, unpatented mining claims, water rights or claims or title to water; [3] those matters which have been expressly excluded from coverage in a schedule of the policy.

28. May most of the risks not covered by the standard policy be insured against?

    Answer: Yes. The extended coverage policy may include additional risks.

29. What does the typical extended coverage policy enlarge the risks to include?

    Answer: Rights of parties in actual possession of the property, off-record ease-
    ments, unrecorded liens, rights and claims a correct survey or inspection
    of the land would show, mining claims, water rights, and reservations in
    patents.

30. Do either the standard or extended coverage policies insure against unrevealed
    defects known to the insured at the time the policy was procured?

    Answer: No.

31. What has been the effect of the recording laws on the risks of title insurance?

    Answer: These laws have reduced the risks of title insurance.

32. What other risk is not insured against by both standard and extended coverage
    policies?

    Answer: Government regulations of occupancy or use.

CHECKLIST

A. Bear in mind that the right to record an instrument so that it imparts constructive notice of its contents is purely statutory. The recording laws of your state should be carefully examined.

B. Become familiar with the practice of searching the public records, but do not attempt to practice law by giving advice as to the construction and effect of the instruments in the record title. Let an attorney at law assume that responsibility.

C. Become familiar with the general principles discussed in the text to the end that you may intelligently discuss such matters.

D. Remember, there are many more "situations" of holders of the title to property than those discussed in the text. Those offered as examples have occurred sufficiently often to suggest an alertness to their reoccurrence.

E. If you observe a situation which appears to warrant further investigation, advise your principal to consult his attorney.

F. Familiarize yourself with the risks that ought to be insured against, and what type of title insurance policy will provide the protection you think advisable.

FOOTNOTES

1 Statute 27 Henry VIII, Chapter 16 [1536]

2 See California Civil Code §1215, reading: "The term 'conveyance,' as used in sections twelve hundred and thirteen and twelve hundred and fourteen, embraces every instrument in writing by which any estate or interest in real property is created, aliened, mortgaged, or encumbered, or by which the title to any real property may be affected, except wills."

3 The general rule is that protection is accorded to the bona fide purchaser first recording; although this is not the rule in some of the states which permit the bona fide purchaser priority irrespective of date of recordation.

4 Prepared by the conveyancer and the abstracter. These were either attorneys or lay "searchers of records" who made a living by searching records, drafting instruments of conveyance, and giving an oral or written opinion of the validity of the title conveyed.

5 Neither the opinion accompanying the abstract, nor the certificate of title indemnified the purchaser of real estate against loss. The liability of the company issuing these instruments was measured only by the degree of skill and competence possessed by others in a like profession. Negligence on the part of the companies had to be proved against them to make them liable in damages to the purchaser of the property, which might, of course, be a hard thing to prove.

6 A new departure from the abstract and the certificate of title. Title was guaranteed to be vested as shown by the record. Diligence or skill were no longer the yardsticks of company liability. The instrument was one of indemnity.

4

The Subdivision: Its Legal
Aspects in a
Representative State

1. Regulation Under the Police Power

Building zone laws began about the turn of the century. Until the first quarter of the 20th Century urban life was comparatively simple. With the great increase and concentration of population in urban centers since that time problems have developed, and constantly are developing, which require, and will continue to require, additional restrictions in respect of the use and occupation of private lands in urban and suburban communities. Regulations the wisdom, necessity and validity of which as applied to existing conditions are so apparent that they are now uniformly sustained by our courts, fifty or seventy-five years ago probably would have been rejected as arbitrary and oppressive. Such regulations are sustained and justified, because of the complex conditions of our day, under the police power of the state. And within reasonable limitations there is no inconsistency in this, for while the meaning of constitutional guaranties never varies, the scope of the application of these guaranties must expand or contract to meet the new and changing conditions which are constantly coming within the compass of their operation.

Under the first controls established, the police power was exercised for the protection and security of the health, safety and welfare of the community generally. But as building programs multiplied and large acreages of land were acquired by private promoters to be developed into the modern "subdivision," it soon became necessary to enlarge the scope of protection. This has been done by expanding regulation to prevent deception and fraud from being practiced upon individual buyers. Ultimately affirmative standards have been created for the business of selling, leasing and otherwise dealing in

INCREASE AND CONCENTRATION OF URBAN AND SUBURBAN POPULATION

REGULATION UNDER THE POLICE POWER OF THE STATE

HEALTH, SAFETY, AND WELFARE

TO PREVENT DECEPTION AND FRAUD

AFFIRMATIVE STANDARDS

79

subdivided land. Hence, the modern regulation by law of the acquisition, division and disposition of land in subdivided parcels, with its concomitant policy of full disclosure.

In an area of law where a plexus of rules is framed to produce a desired result limited to a particular field of activity, and where the fullness of objective demand may vary in the several states, broad general rules tend to become meaningless, especially when knowledge of procedure is required to understand the nature, character and extent of regulation. What is demanded is a review of the legal mechanics necessary to achieve the result. But this plexus of legal rules, both substantive and procedural, will vary in character and quality from state to state. Separate treatment would overrun the bounds of the HANDBOOK. To bridge the difficulty and yet provide the reader with valuable and informative material from which he may develop some idea of procedure to be checked against the practice in his own community, the regulatory laws affecting the subdivision of land indicative of the general modern trend in this area of the law will be examined in some depth. For this purpose the laws of a state representative of the direction in which regulation is moving will be considered in the following pages. A compass and a measuring rod are thus provided, and correspondence with or departure from the practices outlined may easily be checked in the reader's own jurisdiction.

2. Regulation of Subdivisions

A. Acts Regulating ; the Purpose and Governing Bodies

Subdivisions are regulated by the subdivision provisions of the Real Estate Law and by the Subdivision Map Act in the state of California. Those provisions of the Real Estate Law are administered by the Real Estate Commissioner, while the Subdivision Map Act is administered by the governing bodies of counties and cities.

These are two separate acts of the Legislature. The laws may be functionally differentiated. The basic purpose of the subdivision provisions of the Real Estate Law is to require full disclosure and prevent deception and fraud. The Final Subdivision Public Report, required to be obtained from the Real Estate Commissioner as a prerequisite to the sale or lease or financing of subdivided lands, was, prior to the 1963 amendments to the code, designed to prevent fraud by full disclosure of the risks that may be assumed by the prospective purchaser. But the law goes further than mere disclosure. The commissioner may prohibit transactions which involve misrepresentation, and may deny a Public Report upon a number of grounds set forth in the code, and for failure to meet the lawful demands of the commissioner. The effect of recent amendments to the code has been to create affirmative standards for the business of selling, leasing and otherwise dealing in subdivision properties.

The principal purpose of the Subdivision Map Act is to promote an orderly and wholesome community development in conformity with the MASTER PLAN adopted by the county and city governments. The act is administered by local county or city authorities. Every city and county is required to adopt an ordinance regulating and controlling the design and improvement of subdivisions.

THE SUBDIVISION MAP ACT

THE MASTER PLAN

While the state gives the administration of the act to local governing authorities through the adoption of local ordinances, such ordinances are valid only when they are supplemental to the Subdivision Map Act and are not in conflict with it, and bear a reasonable relation to its purposes and requirements.

The governing body referred to in the act is, of course, the board of supervisors in a county, and the city council in a city.

The act also provides for an "advisory agency," which term refers to an official or an official body designated by local ordinance and charged thereby with the duty of making investigations and reports on the design and improvement of proposed subdivisions. The Government Code of the state authorizes the legislative body of any county or city to designate the Planning Commission as the advisory agency with respect to the approval of subdivision maps. The Planning Commission may deal directly with the subdivider.

ADVISORY AGENCY

THE GOVERNING BODY

A subdivision under the subdivision provisions of the Real Estate Law is defined by a number of code sections. It is also defined by the Subdivision Map Act. With some exceptions land divided for the purpose of sale, lease or financing, whether immediate or future, into five or more lots or parcels is a subdivision and comes within the provisions of both acts. Under neither act is the limit within which sales, leases or financing may be made confined to any one year. Whenever the land is divided into five parcels it takes on the character of a subdivision.

SUBDIVISION 5 PARCELS OR MORE

B. The Notice of Intention to Subdivide, Questionnaire and Final Subdivision Public Report; the Preliminary Subdivision Public Report

Prior to the time when subdivided lands are to be offered for sale or lease, the owner, his agent or subdivider is required to notify the commissioner in writing of his intention to sell or lease such lands, and must supply the commissioner with certain information authorized to be demanded by him. Failure to comply with the requirements of the law may render any agreement for the sale of subdivided land voidable, in which event the purchaser may either affirm the agreement and perform according to its terms, or disaffirm and have any sums paid by him, less allowable offsets, returned. In addition, a failure to comply with the mandatory provisions of the law is a public offense. A

NOTICE TO COMMISSIONER

AGREEMENT VOIDABLE

broker who willfully disregards or violates any of the provisions of the Real Estate Law may have his license revoked or suspended.

After receiving a Notice of Intention to sell or lease subdivided lands, the commissioner may require such additional information concerning the project as he deems necessary, for which purpose he may prepare a Questionnaire for the owner, his agent or subdivider, to answer. In practice the Notice of Intention and Questionnaire are combined, it being an exceptional case in which the commissioner would waive the Questionnaire.

Unless there has been some previous discussion with a deputy commissioner, which is always advisable and time-saving, the filing of the Notice of Intention and Questionnaire could be the subdivider's first contact with the Division of Real Estate in connection with the development of the subdivision.

THE FINAL SUB-DIVISION PUBLIC REPORT

After the Notice of Intention and Questionnaire have been filed with the Division of Real Estate, the commissioner will, in due course, unless there are grounds for denial, issue to the subdivider a Final Subdivision Public Report authorizing the sale or lease of lots or parcels in the subdivision. The grounds for denial of such a report are set forth in the code. No person shall sell or lease or offer for sale or lease, or engage in financing of any lots or parcels in a subdivision without first obtaining a Final Subdivision Public Report from the commissioner, except as may be allowed under a Preliminary Subdivision Public Report. Nor shall an owner, subdivider, or agent demand or accept any deposit, money or other consideration, or accept a written offer to purchase or lease lots or parcels in a subdivision, until a copy of the Final Subdivision Public Report has been given to the prospective purchaser or lessee and he has been afforded the opportunity to read it, and his receipt taken therefore, except as provided under a Preliminary Report. This must be done prior to the execution of a binding contract or agreement for the sale or lease of any lot or parcel in a subdivision. Upon receipt of the Final Subdivision Public Report, the owner or subdivider may proceed to sell or lease lots or parcels in the subdivision.

THE PRELIMINARY SUBDIVISION PUBLIC REPORT

There are times, however, when the subdivider needs more time to complete the details called for by the approved Questionnaire, yet it is important for him to move forward in his sales program. This situation has been taken care of in the Regulations of the commissioner, which provide that a Preliminary Subdivision Public Report may be issued by the commissioner upon receipt of the filing fee and a subdivision Questionnaire which is complete except for some particular requirement, or requirements, which is or are at the time not fulfilled, but which reasonably may be expected to be completed. In the event a Preliminary Report is issued, the owner, subdivider or agent may accept a reservation to purchase or lease a lot or parcel in the subdivision under certain specified conditions.

Of course, a prospective purchaser is not likely to reserve a lot or parcel unless there is sufficient information in the Preliminary Report to enable him to get a fair idea of what rights he is acquiring and what restrictive burdens he must assume. Therefore, a copy of the Final Map, although not yet approved by the local governing body, should be made available to him, as well as the Declaration of Restrictions. The Preliminary Subdivision Public Report will, however, detail in what respect the requirements demanded of the subdivider are yet incomplete, which should caution the proposed purchaser to act with care in ascertaining how the incomplete requirements have been met before tieing up for too long a time his deposit or reservation money with the subdivider or his agent.

If, however, the prospective purchaser wishes to make a reservation he should see to it and any broker representing him, should demand that copies of the Final Map and Declaration of Restrictions as well as the Preliminary Report be handed to him at the time he is solicited to sign a reservation agreement. It would be wise for the broker himself to retain a copy of the receipt for the Preliminary Subdivision Public Report.

C. The Blanket Encumbrance

It is unlawful to sell or lease lots or parcels within a subdivision that is subject to a blanket encumbrance unless a release clause is contained in such encumbrance, or in some supplementary instrument, which provides for an unconditional transfer to the purchaser or lessee of the legal title or other interest contracted for, upon compliance with the terms and conditions of the purchase agreement or lease. This means that the holder of the blanket encumbrance must subordinate the lien of his mortgage, or his deed, and whatever rights he may have, to the rights of the contract purchaser. It is doubtful if a conventional lender would agree to any such clause. Only in the field of private finance and a close relationship between subdivider and lender could such a clause be expected.

BLANKET ENCUMBRANCE RELEASE CLAUSE

If such an unconditional release clause is not obtainable, the code provides that sales or leases of lots and parcels may yet be made upon compliance with any of several alternative provisions of the code which have for their purpose the protection of the purchaser under a contract of sale. Such alternative methods provide: [1] for impoundment of all funds in a neutral escrow, or so much as the commissioner may determine; [2] a bond ensuring return of purchaser's money. Each of these alternatives is conditioned upon a proper release of the blanket encumbrance. There is a third alternative which provides for the title to the subdivision to be held in trust under an agreement of trust acceptable to the commissioner until a proper release from such blanket encumbrance is obtained. The Regulations of the commissioner pursue the matter further. They should be consulted in connection with the corresponding sections of the Business and Professions Code for a more detailed understanding of the protection offered the contract buyer of subdivided land.

ALTERNATIVES TO SUBORDINATION

D. Advertising Material

DECEPTIVE
ADVERTISING
FORBIDDEN

The Final Subdivision Public Report may not be used for advertising purposes unless the entire report is used. Nor may any advertising indicate that the Division of Real Estate or the Real Estate Commissioner approves or recommends the subdivision project or its sale, beyond what the publication of the entire report might indicate. Nor may any advertising be used which tends to misrepresent the actual condition of the property and its amenities. Reference and illustrations which do not portray the property in its present state, without adequate qualifying phrases, are forbidden. The general purpose is to keep such advertising honest in all respects, and to prevent deception.

3. The Subdivision Map Act

As has been said, the principal purpose of the Subdivision Map Act is to provide for regulation and control of design and improvement of the subdivision with proper consideration of its relation to adjoining areas. While the administration of the act is placed in the hands of local authority through the enactment of ordinances, these ordinances must not be in conflict with the state act, and they must come, too, within the limitation of the act. Control of the design and improvement of subdivisions is expressly vested in the governing bodies of cities and counties. Every city and county must adopt ordinances regulating and controlling the design and improvement of subdivisions.

A. The Master Plan

THE MASTER PLAN
AND THE PLAN-
NING COMMIS-
SION

The Government Code provides that the legislative body of each city may, and of each county shall, by ordinance, create a Planning Commission. Each commission shall prepare and adopt a comprehensive, long-term general plan for the physical development of the city, county, area, or region, and of any land outside its boundaries which in the commission's judgment bears relation to its planning. Such a plan, upon its adoption by the legislative body, shall be officially certified as the Master or General Plan. The Master Plan is to be so prepared that all or portions of it may be adopted by the legislative body as a basis for the development of a city, county, area or region.

The Government Code provides that the Master Plan may include a community design element of the plan. This may consist of standards and principles governing the subdivision of land within the scope of the Subdivision Map Act. It should indicate recommended designs for community and neighborhood development and redevelopment, including sites for schools, parks, playgrounds and other uses.

Whenever a city or county Planning Commission has adopted a Master Plan which takes in land outside of its particular political jurisdiction but which it believes is necessary or proper for the full development of the plan, such plan must be certified to the Planning Commission of such outside jurisdictional entity. When the general concept of the Master Plan development program is kept in mind, the need for scrutiny of the tentative map of a proposed subdivision not only by the advisory agency of the city or county in which the subdivision is to be set up, but by the Planning Commissions of adjacent political units, is readily understandable. The purpose, of course, is to keep the general design and improvement of the subdivision in harmony with the general design and improvement of the Master Plan development program.

B. Design and Improvement

"Design" when considered by the Planning Commission refers to street alignment, grades and widths, alignment and widths of easements and rights-of-way for drainage and sanitary sewers and minimum lot area and width. It also includes land to be dedicated for park or recreational purposes.

DESIGN AND IMPROVEMENT

WHAT IS MEANT BY DESIGN

"Improvement" refers to only such street work and utilities to be installed, or agreed to be installed, by the subdivider on the land to be used for public or private streets, highways, ways and easements, as are necessary, for the general use of the lot owners in the subdivision and local neighborhood traffic and drainage needs as a condition precedent to the approval and acceptance of the Final Map.

WHAT IS MEANT BY IMPROVEMENT

C. The Tentative Map

A tentative map is a map made for the purpose of showing the design of a proposed subdivision and the existing conditions in and around it. It need not be based upon an accurate or detailed final survey of the property.

THE TENTATIVE MAP

The initial action in connection with the development of any subdivision is the preparation of a tentative map which shall show, or be accompanied by, such data as are specified in local ordinances, in addition to that required by the code. The subdivider must file a copy of this map with the Advisory Agency (Planning Commission) or with the clerk of the governing body if there is no Advisory Agency. If any adjoining city or county or the state Department of Public Works has filed a territorial map with the governing body of the city or county in which the subdivision is proposed, it must be given a copy of the tentative map in order that it may study it, and make recommendations with respect to the effect of the proposed subdivision upon the adjacent area of the city or county or upon any highway, or proposed highway route. These recommendations will be given consideration by the governing body, appeal board or Advisory Agency of the city or county having jurisdiction before action is taken upon the tentative map.

FILING OF THE TENTATIVE MAP

The Advisory Agency may approve the tentative map or disapprove it. The general practice, however, would seem to be a conditional approval leading to further discussion, adjustment and final approval. Of course, if the subdivider believes the the Advisory Agency has acted without authority, or has been unfair or arbitrary in the premises, he may appeal to the Appeal

ADVISORY AGENCY MAY APPROVE OR DISAPPROVE TENTATIVE MAP

Board, if one has been established by local ordinance, or if not, then directly to the governing body. If his appeal is to the Appeal Board, he may take the matter before the governing body if he is dissatisfied with the findings and decision of that board. From the governing body he may go to the courts.

WHAT TENTATIVE MAP MUST SHOW

Briefly stated, the tentative map will show design, improvement, layout and survey data of the subdivision, and in addition, show, or be accompanied by, such other data as are specified in the code or in local ordinances. In case there is a local ordinance, the subdivider shall comply with its provisions before the map or maps of a subdivision may be approved. In case there is no local ordinance, the governing body may, as a condition precedent to the approval of the map or maps, require streets and drainage ways, of adequate width, properly located.

TENTATIVE MAP FILED TO INITIATE STUDY

The tentative map is not recorded. It is filed with the Advisory Agency, or with the governing body of the city or county, for the purpose of, first, the initiation of a study by the proper public officials of the design and improvement of a proposed subdivision; and second, the pursuance of such a study and its ultimate completion as evidence by approval of the tentative map, either fully or conditionally, indicating compliance on the part of the subdivider with state law and local ordinance. When this point is reached the tentative map, upon approval of the Advisory Agency, or the governing body, as the case may be, (no appeal having been taken by the subdivider from any recommendations of the governing body or Advisory Agency) lays the foundation for preparation of the Final Map.

D. The Final Map

CERTIFICATE OF DEDICATION OF STREETS

The layout of streets will appear on the tentative map. The offer of dedication will take the form of a certificate on the Final Map. If there be offers of dedication for streets or other areas to public use there is required a certificate, signed and acknowledged by the parties having any record title interest in the land subdivided, offering certain parcels of land for dedication for certain specified public uses, subject to such reservations as may be contained in any such offer. In the event the streets, or any of them shown on a subdivision map, are not offered for dedication the certificate may contain a statement to this effect. If such statement appears on the map, and the map is approved by the governing body, the use of any such streets by the public shall be permissive

DEDICATION OF PARCELS INTENDED FOR PUBLICE USE

WAIVER OF ACCESS RIGHTS

only. However, a local ordinance may require as a condition precedent to the approval of any Final Map that any or all of the parcels of land shown thereon and intended for public use shall be offered for dedication for public use, except those parcels intended for the exclusive use of lot owners in the subdivision, their licensees, visitor, tenants and servants. Waiver of access rights to dedicated streets from property shown on the Final Map as abutting thereon, while heretofore not enforceable by local authorities, may now be made a condition precedent to the approval of any Final Map by local authorities.

Local ordinances may, under certain circumstances, require the payment of a fee as a condition of approval of a Final Map for purposes of defraying the actual or estimated costs of constructing planned drainage facilities for the removal of surface and storm waters from local or neighborhood drainage areas. And such ordinances may also require the dedication of land, the payment of fees in lieu thereof, or a combination of both, for park or recreational purposes as a condition to the approval of a Final Map, subject to certain provisions set forth in the code.

COSTS OF CONSTRUCTING DRAINAGE FACILITIES: FEE FOR

Whenever a local ordinance requires that a subdivider install sewers, drains, or other facilities for sewers and drains as a condition precedent to the acceptance of a Final Map, the governing body may, by contract with the subdivider, agree to reimburse and may reimburse the subdivider for such facilities. This arrangement may likewise be made when in the opinion of the governing body it is necessary that laterals or other facilities be constructed which can be, or will be, used for the benefit of property not in the subdivision, and such sewers, drains, or other facilities are dedicated to the public. Such contract shall provide that the governing body may collect from any person using such lateral or other facility for the benefit of property not within such subdivision a reasonable charge for such use.

REIMBURSEMENT OF SUBDIVIDER FOR COST OF FACILITIES OUTSIDE OF SUBDIVISION

Whenever the governing body has reimbursed or agreed to reimburse a subdivider for the construction of a lateral or other facility which can or will be used by persons for the benefit of property other than that being subdivided by such subdivider, such governing body may impose and collect for such use a reasonable charge.

The Final Map must conform to all of the provisions of the approved tentative map, and in addition the provisions of Section 11566 of the code. All certificates and acknowledgments required under the law must appear on the Final Map.

Provision is made in the law for handling tax and assessment matters so as to enable the Final Map to be filed with the governing body for approval.

When all the certificates which appear on the Final Map have been signed and, where necessary, acknowledged, the Final Map may be filed for approval.

WHEN FINAL MAP MAY BE FILED FOR APPROVAL

If the subdivision lies entirely within the territory of a city, the filing shall be with the governing body of that city; if entirely within the unincorporated area of a county, with the governing body of the county; and if partly within two or more of such territories, with the governing body of each.

WHERE FILED

The governing body shall at its next meeting or within a period of not more than ten days after the filing approve the map if it conforms to all the requirements of the code and of any local ordinance applicable at the time of approval of the tentative map or any rulings made thereunder.

APPROVAL OF FINAL MAP

The time limit for the approval of such map may be extended by mutual consent of the subdivider and the governing body. If no action is taken within such time or within the time to which it has been extended by such mutual consent, the map, if it conforms to all the requirements set forth, shall be deemed

CERTIFICATION OF APPROVAL BY CLERK

to be approved, and it shall be the duty of the clerk of the governing body thereupon to certify the approval.

ACCEPTANCE OR REJECTION OF IMPROVEMENTS OR ARRANGEMENTS THEREFOR

The governing body shall at that time also accept, subject to improvement, or reject any or all offers of dedication and, unless the streets and easements have been improved and accepted, shall as a condition precedent to the acceptance of any streets or easements, provide for the improvement of such streets or easements in accordance with standards established by such governing body by local ordinance applicable at the time of approval of the tentative map by requiring the subdivider (a) to enter into an agreement with the city or county upon mutually agreeable terms to thereafter improve said streets and easements at the subdivider's expense, or (b) to enter into a contract with the city or county upon mutually agreeable terms to thereafter initiate and consummate proceedings under an appropriate special assessment act for the financing and installation of all the improvements required by local ordinance.

Upon the execution by the subdivider of either one of the agreements or contracts and the posting of the required bond, or the deposit of the required money or negotiable bonds, provided for by the code, the map of such subdivision shall forthwith be approved and accepted for recordation.

AMENDING FINAL MAP

Any map of a subdivision that has been filed for record may be amended to correct an error in any course or distance shown or to show any course or distance that was omitted by the filing for record of an amending map of said subdivision. The amending map shall conform to the requirements of the code. The county surveyor shall examine such amending map and if such examination discloses that the only changes on the amending map are changes above provided for, he shall certify this to be a fact over his signature on the amending map. Thereafter the amending map shall be entitled to be filed in the office of the recorder in which the original subdivsion map was filed. Upon such filing, the recorder shall note upon the map thereby superseded the book and page reference to the amending map.

QUESTIONS AND ANSWERS

1. What authority underlies the regulation of subdivisions?

   Answer: The police power of the State.

2. Is there any uniform legislation covering the regulation of subdivisions in the several states?

   Answer: No. There is not. But in a majority of the states street-layout, drainage, sewers, water mains, lot size and certain amenities are frequently found to be regulated.

3. What has been largely responsible for regulation of the use of private lands?

   Answer: The increase and concentration of urban and suburban population is one of the main causes.

4. How is the regulation of land to the extent we have it today reconciled with the guaranties of the federal and state constitutions?

   Answer: The meaning of the constitutional guarantees never varies, but the scope and application of them expand to meet new and changing conditions.

5. What, broadly speaking, were the first controls limited to protecting?

   Answer: The health, safety and welfare of the people.

6. Do the controls reach beyond that now?

   Answer: Yes. Legislation may be found designed to effect full disclosure in subdivision development, financing, and in the sale or lease of lots therein. In fact, there has been recent legislation designed to create affirmative standards of business dealings in subdivision properties.

7. What two laws regulate subdivisions in California?

   Answer: The subdivision provisions of the Real Estate Law, and the Subdivision Map Act.

8. What is the basic purpose of the subdivision provisions of the Real Estate Law?

   Answer: To prevent misrepresentation and fraud by full disclosure of all risks which may be assumed by a prospective purchaser of lots in a subdivision, and to impose affirmative standards of business dealing in the development, lease and sale of subdivision properties.

9. What is the basic purpose of the Subdivision Map Act?

   Answer: To promote and further an orderly and wholesome community development in conformity with the Master Plan adopted by the city or county, by regulating and controlling design and improvement of the subdivision.

10. Who administers the subdivision provisions of the Real Estate Law?

    Answer: The Real Estate Commissioner.

11. Who administers the Subdivision Map Act?

    Answer: The governing bodies of cities and counties.

12. How is the administration of the Subdivision Map Act given to the local governing authorities by the state?

    Answer: It authorizes them to adopt local ordinances supplemental to, and not in conflict with, the provisions of the Subdivision Map Act.

13. What is the "governing body" referred to?

    Answer: The Board of Supervisors in a county, and the City Council in a city.

14. What body may be the "advisory agency" referred to in the code?

    Answer: The Government Code authorizes the legislative body of a county or city to designate the Planning Commission as the advisory agency.

15. May a separate Advisory Agency be set up other than the Planning Commission?

    Answer: Yes. The Business and Professions Code defines such as an "official" or "official body" designated by local ordinance and charged with the duty to make investigations and reports on the design and improvement of proposed divisions of land.

16. What is a subdivision under the Subdivision Provisions of the Real Estate Law?

    Answer: Business and Professions Code, § 11000, defines a subdivision. It should be consulted. Briefly, however, a subdivision, under this act, consists of improved or unimproved land or lands divided or proposed to be divided for the purpose of sale or lease or financing, whether immediate or future, into five or more lots or parcels.

17. What is a subdivision under the Subdivision Map Act?

    Answer: Business and Professions Code, § 11535, defines a subdivision. It should be consulted. Briefly, however, a subdivision, under this act, consists of any real property, improved or unimproved, or portion thereof, shown on the latest adopted county tax roll as a unit or as contiguous units, which is divided for the purpose of sale, lease or financing, whether immediate or future, by any subdivider into five or more parcels. There are exceptions.

18. May the Planning Commission deal directly with a subdivider?

    Answer: Yes.

19. To bring an operation under B & P Code, § 11000 or § 11535, must the area be divided into the prohibited number of parcels within one year, or may the division occur over any length of time?

    Answer: Whenever the land is divided into five parcels it becomes a subdivision.

20. What are the civil consequences of failure to comply with §§ 11011 or 11012 of the B & P Code?

    Answer: It renders the agreement for the sale of subdivided lands voidable at the option of the purchaser.

21. May a broker's license be suspended or revoked for a willful violation of the provisions of either the subdivision provisions of the Real Estate Law, or the provisions of the Subdivision Map Act?

    Answer: Yes.

22. In general practice are the Notice of Intention referred to in B & P Code, § 11010, and the Questionnaire referred to in B & P Code, § 11011, combined into one instrument?

    Answer: Yes.

23. Is it advisable to talk with the Real Estate Division before filing a Questionnaire?

    Answer: It is always advisable to contact the division before making the preliminary move in an application for a Public Report. It can be time-saving for all parties concerned, and it tends to show good faith in an honest attempt to comply with the law.

24. May lots be sold in a subdivision before issuance of a Final Subdivision Public Report?

    Answer: No. No person shall sell, lease, or offer for sale or lease, or engage in financing of any lot or parcel of ground in a subdivision in this state without first obtaining a final public report from the commissioner, except as may be allowed under a preliminary subdivision public report.

25. Must a Final Public Report first be given the prospective purchaser for examination before acceptance of a deposit or other consideration?

    Answer: Yes, and the prospective purchaser's receipt of the report must be also first obtained.

26. When may the owner of a subdivision begin to sell lots therein?

    Answer: Upon receipt of the Final Subdivision Public Report.

27. May the commissioner in a preliminary Public Report permit some negotiations to be started in respect of the sale of the subdivided property?

    Answer: Yes. Very limited negotiations, however.

28. Must there be a partial release clause in a blanket encumbrance, or some supplementary instrument, to permit the subdivider to sell lots in a subdivision?

    Answer: There must either be such a release clause, or compliance by the subdivider with certain code sections designed to protect the purchaser under a contract of sale or otherwise.

29. Name two or three alternative provisions.

    Answer: There is provision for impoundment of all funds in a neutral escrow, or so much as the commissioner may require; provision for a bond insuring return of the purchaser's money; provision for title of the subdivision to be held in trust acceptable to the commissioner, until such time as a proper release from such blanket encumbrance is obtained. The Regulations of the commissioner pursue the matter further. They should be consulted.

30. May the Public Report be used for advertising purposes?

    Answer: No. Unless the entire report is used.

31. Is advertising of subdivisions regulated by the commissioner?

    Answer: To the extent of preventing misrepresentation.

32. What is a tentative map?

   Answer: A preliminary map made for the purpose of showing the design of a proposed subdivision and the existing conditions in and around it.

33. Where is the tentative map filed?

   Answer: It is filed with the advisory agency of the city or county, as the case may be, usually with the Planning Commission. In certain cases it must also be filed with other bodies.

34. What is a "Master Plan"?

   Answer: A long-term general plan for the physical development of a city, county, area or region, and which may include a community design element consisting of standards and principles governing the subdivision of land within the scope of the Subdivision Map Act.

35. What does "design" refer to when considered by the Planning Commission?

   Answer: It refers to street alignment, grades and widths of easements and rights of way for drainage and sanitary sewers, and minimum lot area and width; also land for park or recreational purposes.

36. What does "improvement" refer to when considered by the Planning Commission?

   Answer: It refers to only such street work and utilities to be installed by the subdivider as are necessary for the general use of lot owners, as well as drainage needs.

37. Who approves or disapproves the tentative map?

   Answer: The advisory agency, usually the Planning Commission.

38. If the subdivider is dissatisfied with the ruling of the advisory agency, to whom may he appeal?

   Answer: To the "Appeal Board," if one has been established, or if not, then to the governing body. From the governing body he may go to the courts.

39. What should be shown on the tentative map?

   Answer: Briefly, design, improvement, layout and survey data of the subdivision, and such other data as prescribed by local ordinance.

40. How is dedication of streets indicated?

   Answer: The offer of dedication will take the form of a certificate on the Final Map.

41. To what must the Final Map conform?

   Answer: It must conform to all of the provisions of the approved tentative map, and in addition, the provisions of B & P Code, § 11566. All required certificates and acknowledgments must appear on the map.

42. When may the Final Map be filed for approval?

   Answer: When all certificates which appear thereon have been signed and when necessary, acknowledged.

43. With what body is the Final Map filed?

Answer: If the subdivision lies entirely within the territory of the city, with the governing body of that city; if entirely within the unincorporated area of a county, with the governing body of that county; if partly within two or more such territories, with the governing body of each.

44. How long has the governing body within which to approve the Final Map?

Answer: It must be approved at not more then 10 days after filing, if it conforms to all requirements.

If no action has been taken thereon within the time allowed, or any mutual extension thereof, the Final Map, if it conform to all requirements is deemed approved, and the clerk of the governing body shall certify the approval.

45. When may the Final Map be approved and accepted for recordation?

Answer: Upon compliance on the part of the subdivider with street and easement requirements as provided by the code, the Final Map shall be approved and accepted for recordation.

46. May a Final Map be amended to correct an error in a course or distance thereon, or to show an omitted course or distance?

Answer: Yes. An "amending map" must be filed.

CHECKLIST

A. Determine if there is a legislative enactment specifically regulating the creation, development and disposition of subdivided land in your state.

B. Determine if there is a legislative enactment specifically regulating the design and improvement of subdivided land in your state.

C. Determine if the subdivision of land is regulated only incidentally by health, safety and welfare statutes and local ordinance in your state, rather than by an integrated act directed specifically to the regulation of subdivisions.

D. Determine if your state has gone as far as the State of California in regulating subdivisions.

E. Determine what is required before lots may be sold, or leased, or financing undertaken in subdivision development in your state.

F. Become familiar with the definition of a subdivision in your state, and what laws and local ordinances are particularly applicable thereto.

G. Determine if there is legislative provision in your state for a Master Plan of community development.

H. Determine how subdivision regulations "tie in" with such a Master Plan, if there be one.

I. Determine from what state official you may obtain information with respect to the development and disposition of subdivided land in your state.

J. Determine if your principal has complied with all legal requirements before offering for sale or lease the property you are handling.

K. Determine if you have checked far enough into the transaction you are handling to be sure that your prospective purchasers are lawfully protected in the purchase or lease of the property offered them.

L. Determine if there is some requirement or instrument you are overlooking in initiating or concluding the transaction you are handling, and correct the oversight if such there be.

5

Legal Aspects of Real
Estate Forms

1. The Basic Forms

A. Principal Forms Employed

Many market and conventional instruments are employed in the real estate business. While these instruments may not be identical in content or wording in every jurisdiction, they are designed to effect pretty much the same objectives. In some jurisdictions they have become highly standardized.

In any jurisdiction, however, the more complicated the real estate transaction the more specialized and the less standardized will be the agreements creating the rights and obligations of the parties. The general run of sales, leases and exchanges of improved and unimproved real property in an active real estate market will be, in most cases, initiated and consummated with standard, printed forms. Although these may vary in language and scope, the most frequently employed will drop into one or more of the five classes indicated here. The name by which the class or form is herein designated is not of too much importance. It is intended only to indicate the character of the transaction involved, by whatever name the instrument itself may be called.

The first two forms listed are in the nature of market instruments. The next three are conventional dispositive instruments.

- The Listing Agreement
- The Deposit Receipt
- The Land Contract
- The Exchange Agreement
- The Lease

FORMS IN COMMON USE

The foregoing instruments are discussed in the following pages.

97

2. The Listing Agreement

A. An Agency Contract of Employment

LIMITED POWER OR AUTHORITY

The Listing Agreement is an agency contract of emplyment in which a broker is given a limited authority, or power, to act on behalf of his principal. The broker is employed to perform definite services for which he is to be paid a commission. His commission is contingent upon his performance within the terms of the agency created by the Listing Agreement.

BROKER'S AU-THORITY TERMS AND CONDITIONS OF SALE

It therefore becomes important to know exactly what he is required to do in order to earn his commission. And this depends upon [1] the authority granted him within which he must act, and [2] the terms and conditions set forth in the Listing Agreement upon which the principal is willing to sell his property or otherwise dispose of it as provided in the Listing Agreement.

If the broker is to produce a buyer ready, willing and able to purchase the principal's property for a sum certain, the broker has not earned his commission if he produces a buyer ready, willing and able to pay, something less than the sum demanded. The point is, that it is important that the Listing Agreement spell out in sufficient detail the offer the principal will accept from a buyer. The offer contained in the Deposit Receipt should conform to

BROKER'S BASIC OBLIGATION TO PRODUCE A BUYER READY, WILLING AND ABLE TO BUY OR OTHERWISE PERFORM

the terms and conditions set down in the Listing Agreement.

Of course the principal may accept less performance than originally intended, in which case the broker may have his commission, for the obligation of the broker under the ordinary agency contract is basically to produce a buyer ready, willing and able to buy upon the terms and conditions ultimately acceptable to the principal.

B. Types of Listing Agreements

There are six types of Listing Agreements in general use in the real estate brokerage business. These are:

COMMON TYPES OF LISTING AGREEMENT

The Exclusive Authorization and Right to Sell Agency Contract;
The Exclusive Agency Contract;
The Non-Exclusive Agency Contract with Commencement and Termination Dates;
The Open Listing Agency Contract;
The Multiple Listing Agency Contract;
The Net Listing Agreement.

Except to note, at this time, the outstanding feature which distinguishes these several agency contracts one from the other, all Listing Agreements will be treated together in the text, differentiation in terms, conditions, validity and effect of the agency scope and limitation being pointed out in the course of the discussion.

THE EXCLUSIVE AUTHORIZATION

The Exclusive Authorization and Right to Sell Contract is distinguished from the others by its EXCLUSIVE RIGHT TO SELL provision. As between the principal and the broker, the broker taking this contract has the sole right to sell the property listed. If the principal should sell the property himself, he would be liable to the broker for the commission agreed upon.

AND RIGHT TO SELL

The Exclusive Agency Contract, as between principal and broker, gives the broker taking the listing the EXCLUSIVE RIGHT AS AN AGENT TO SELL the property, and impliedly promises the broker that the principal will not during the term of the agency list the property with any other AGENT. The owner, not being an agent, may himself sell the property without obligating himself to pay the broker a commission on the sale.

THE EXCLUSIVE AGENCY

The Non-Exclusive Agency Contract with COMMENCEMENT and TERMINATION dates is very similar to the open listing, except that there is a definite termination date upon which the contract of agency terminates. The matter of a consideration to support a fixed term is also involved and is an important element to be considered in the revocation or other termination of this agency contract. The matter is discussed *infra* under powers and contractual rights.

THE NON-EXCLUSIVE AGENCY

The Open Listing requires no termination date. It may ordinarily be terminated at any time before performance without liability to the principal.

THE OPEN LISTING

The Multiple Listing Agency Contract is principally a device employed by groups of brokers to obtain a wider market for the sale of property. It is usually of the exclusive authorization and right to sell type.

THE MULTIPLE LISTING

The Net Listing is a convenient listing for a property owner who has determined what price he wants for his property, and is willing to let the broker make what he can on the sale. There has been a lot of criticism about this type of listing, but such criticism is largely directed to an assumed, whether jusifiably or not, inability of men and women to exercise a reasonably intelligent judgment in their business affairs, or to the dishonesty of the real estate broker, both of which assumptions can be greatly overworked in an era which leans heavily upon the State for direction and guidance. Unless the property owner has been badly mislead, and deliberately so, by the broker, as to the value of the property listed, there should be no ground for complaint. And if the broker is that type of man he should be quickly removed from the ranks of his colleagues.

THE NET LISTING

C. The Obligation of Contract and the Authority or Power

In the absence of statute the agency contract of employment between broker and principal need not be in writing. In many states, however, such an agreement must be in writing.

Irrespective of whether a writing is required, standard printed forms have been developed looking to an expeditious and standardized practice in the handling of real estate transactions. Hence the printed Listing Agreement and the printed Deposit Receipt as market instruments. In an active market this has almost become a necessity. If the forms prepared hew to the line of the decided cases and statutory law, they can be very useful in keeping transfers in real estate within the four corners of the law, and moving smoothly to a satisfactory conclusion.

THE PRINTED FORM

NO   PARTICULAR
FORM NECESSARY

The purpose of the listing agreement is to effect a binding and enforceable contract between the broker and his principal, and to comply with statutes in those states requiring a written instrument. It is not necessary that any particular form be used. Any agreement which would meet the requirements of a binding contract, even though it were an exchange of correspondence between a broker and his principal, would suffice.

UNDER ORDINARY
EMPLOYMENT
CONTRACT BRO-
KER MAY NOT
CONVEY PRINCI-
PAL'S PROPERTY

It has been held that the standard printed exclusive authorization and right to sell form is not worded so as to confer a power on the broker to execute a deed of conveyance of the property listed on behalf of the principal. However, there is no legal reason why the language of such a listing agreement might not be enlarged to that extent. But when it is intended to authorize the broker to make a conveyance of the property in the name of the owner, the words employed should leave no doubt of the power conferred.

THE   UNILATERAL
PROMISE: A PRO-
MISE FOR AN ACT

Under the ordinary right to sell contract the broker has a very limited authority. The promise of the principal to pay the broker a commission, is contingent upon the broker's performance. It is a promise for an act, and it is the performance of that act which binds the principal to pay the broker the commission agreed upon. In the ordinary printed form the broker makes no promise to sell the property. He merely agrees to use diligence in procuring a purchaser.

A broker employed to sell real estate may be required and authorized under the terms of the agency contract not only to procure a purchaser ready, willing and able to purchase the principal's property, but to effect an actual transfer, or to obtain from the purchaser a valid, written agreement binding him to purchase the property upon the terms and conditions set forth in the authorization. If this is the undertaking of the broker, he has not performed until a conveyance has been effected by him, or he has obtained from the purchaser an agreement to buy on such terms and conditions; or, as an alternative, the principal has accepted a less complete performance. Under the standard exclusive listing the broker is not required to effect a conveyance, for such an employment contract is generally construed not to authorize the broker to execute a conveyance or to close the bargain. A sale of land involves so many questions concerning which the seller presumptively would wish to decide for himself [such as the personality of the purchaser, the condition of the title, the kind and form of conveyance, the adjustment of the terms, the surrender of possession, and the like] that a mere authority to sell can hardly confer

"TO SELL" IN THE
ORDINARY LIST-
ING DOES NOT
MEAN "TO CON-
VEY "

power upon the broker to determine these matters for his principal so as to bind him. To give the mere words "to sell" such broad significance as would invest the broker with powers of that ample and discretionary a character, ordinarily conferred with caution, would be reading too much authority into them.

WHEN BROKER
PERFORMS

The rule laid down generally is that the broker has performed when he has procured a purchaser who is ready, willing and able to purchase the property upon the terms set forth in the listing agreement or if the exact terms are not therein specified, then upon terms acceptable to the principal. If the principal and the person procured by the broker are unable to agree upon the terms, the broker is not entitled to a commission.

In any event, the broker must be the efficient, procuring proximate or inducing cause of a transaction or sale between the principal and the prospective purchaser. His obligation is to bring the purchaser and the principal to an agreement. If this is not done he has not ordinarily performed and is not entitled to his commission, unless, of course, the acts of the principal have prevented performance on his part, or the principal by his conduct has waived or prevented complete performance. There are many cases supporting the rule that the broker is the procuring cause when he finds a purchaser ready, willing and able to buy the property on the terms fixed in the listing agreement and either obtains from that person a valid contract binding him to purchase the property, or brings the intended purchaser and the principal together so that they may enter into a binding agreement of purchase and sale.

BROKER MUST BE THE PROCURING CAUSE

In modern real estate practice where the Deposit Receipt is used to effect a purchase and sale transaction a great deal of uncertainty is removed from broker procurement activities. If the broker produces for the principal a Deposit Receipt signed by the prospective purchaser, accompanied by an earnest money deposit and consisting of an offer to buy the property upon the terms and conditions contained in the broker's employment contract, or listing agreement, which offer the principal accepts, there is a binding agreement between the principal and the purchaser. The broker is then in the absence of fraud or concealment on his part, entitled to his commission. It is a generally established rule that where the principal accepts the offer of the prospective purchaser produced by the broker, he thereby admits the readiness, willingness and ability of the purchaser to conclude the sale. By accepting the offer of the purchaser the principal, ordinarily, is not permitted to deny the readiness, willingness and ability of the purchaser to perform. No estoppel arises if the broker can be proved guilty of fraudulently representing the purchaser's financial integrity. On the other hand, if fraud or misrepresentation is traced to the conduct of the purchaser, the courts have differed as to whether or not the broker can have his commission. Some have said he can, while others have denied him the right to collect a commission.

THE DEPOSIT RECEIPT AND ACCEPTANCE BY PRINCIPAL

PRINCIPAL ACCEPTING OFFER ESTOPPED TO DENY PURCHASER'S READINESS, WILLINGNESS AND ABILITY TO PERFORM

Suppose the broker produces the Deposit Receipt mentioned in the preceding paragraph, executed by the purchaser in which the latter has made an offer to purchase the property, and the principal refuses to accept the offer. Has the broker earned his commission? Suppose the principal claims that the offer does not meet the terms and conditions upon which the broker was authorized to sell the property. It is to be remembered that the broker is the man who will actually fill out this Deposit Receipt which contains the offer of the purchaser.

THE IMPORTANCE OF CAREFUL AND KNOWLEDGEABLE PREPARATION OF THE DEPOSIT RECEIPT TO CONFORM TO THE TERMS AND CONDITIONS OF THE LISTING AGREEMENT

If the principal is wrong in his assertion that the terms and conditions contained in the Deposit Receipt are not what he presented to the broker, then no doubt the broker is entitled to his commission. He has done all he is obliged to do under his agency contract. But if there may be some doubt in the premises, then, the offer of the purchaser not having been accepted by the principal, and no estoppel arising, the matter of whether or not the broker has in fact performed resolves itself into a question of fact, to be proved, if necessary, in court. And right at this point the broker's success or failure in enforcing the payment of his commission will depend upon his ability and diligence to have gotten into the listing agreement full and complete and effective terms and conditions upon which the principal had agreed to sell his property, and in preparing the Deposit Receipt in conformity with such terms and conditions. The broker has no authority to procure a purchaser who offers to acquire the property upon different terms or conditions than those which have been set forth in the listing agreement. In the absence of acceptance by the principal of any such offer, the broker is not entitled to his commission.

LISTING AGREEMENT AND DEPOSIT RECEIPT SHOULD CONFORM AS TO TERMS AND CONDITIONS

The terms and conditions of sale must be detailed and clear enough as written in the listing agreement to express what the principal intended. The offer as set forth in the Deposit Receipt should strictly conform to such terms and conditions. There should be no room for a counter offer unless the principal intends to negotiate with a prospective purchaser.

TERMS AND CONDITIONS OF SALE SHOULD BE UNAMBIGUOUS

From the foregoing it ought to be plain that the greatest care should be exercised by the broker, not only to understand what the principal intends by his offer to sell, but to express this intent adequately and unequivocally in the listing agreement which the principal is asked to sign. The broker will ordinarily be the person drafting the terms of the listing agreement. The importance of writing an intelligent and legally adequate listing agreement and Deposit Receipt cannot be over-emphasized.

D. Continuance and Termination of Agency Contract and Revocation of Power, or Authority

FINAL TERMINATION DATE

Exclusive listing agreements have been required by statute to have definite, specific dates of final and complete termination. This is sound practice, as it avoids the uncertainties involved in determining what is a reasonable time within which the broker ought to have performed, and leaves the issue strictly to one of performance.

LISTING AGREEMENT HAVING NO TERMINATION DATE

The prevailing rule is that if the agency contract contains no termination date the agency status will continue for a reasonable time. The principal may, however, revoke the agency without liability at his pleasure unless to do so would amount to a prevention of performance already well under way, the principal having knowledge of such negotiations, and merely attempting to avoid paying a commission.

LIMITATION UPON AUTHORITY OF BROKER

If the agency contract contains a termination date the broker's position will depend upon at least two factors: Was the agreement supported by a consideration? and, What was the language creating the authority? If there is no consideration and the promise of the principal is to pay the broker a commission *if he perform within the time allowed* these dated listings are treated as open listings and revocable by the principal at any time before performance. In such an agreement the broker would not be entitled to commission if he produced a purchaser within the specified time, but after the principal had revoked the agency, for there is authority to the effect that such a promise of the principal is to be construed as *a limitation upon the authority of the broker*. If, however, the agreement is supported by consideration and the language is that the agency shall continue *during the period specified by the commencement and termination dates*, and that the broker shall have the right to perform within that time, such language will be construed as *a limitation upon the power of the principal to revoke the agency*, and the broker may recover his commission if he performs within the time limited although the performance be subsequent to revocation.

LIMITATION UPON POWER OF THE PRINCIPAL TO RE-VOKE AGENCY

The authority or power conferred upon the broker in the ordinary listing agreement is what is known in the law of agency as a NAKED, or BARE power. There is another kind of power, however, known as A POWER COUPLED WITH AN INTEREST. But an interest in the subject matter, as well as in the exercise of the power, is necessary to the existence of an agency in which there is a power coupled with an interest.

NAKED OR BARE POWER AND THE POWER COUPLED WITH AN INTEREST

The principal may at any time revoke a bare power, even though based upon a consideration. He cannot revoke a power coupled with an interest.

What is being revoked is the POWER, or the AUTHORITY, created by the agency status. This status is never dependent upon consideration. It rests upon principles of trust and confidence, leaving to the agent his constitutionally protected CONTRACTUAL RIGHTS arising out of the obligation of contract.

POWER NOT DE-PENDENT UPON CONSIDERATION BUT RATHER UPON TRUST OR CON-FIDENCE

The authority, or power, given a broker in a listing agreement is not the same thing as the contractual rights established by the agreement.

DISTINCTION BE-TWEEN POWER AND CONTRAC-TUAL RIGHT

> *EXAMPLES:* I give a broker authority to sell my house and promise him a commission. He promises me nothing.
> There is no contractual relationship between us. I have given him a naked power to act, which I may revoke at any time before he performs without becoming liable to him for a commission.
> I give a broker authority to sell my house and promise him a commission in exchange for his promise to diligently seek a buyer for my house upon the terms and conditions I have offered it for sale. I promise not to revoke his authority, or power, for a certain time.
> Here there is a power and a contractual right. I may still revoke his authority, but if I do I shall become liable for a breach of contract.

E. Summary of Legal Consequences of Revocation of Agency Contract

The agency contract is actually composed of two parts. First, there is an authority, or power, given the agent, or broker, by the principal. Secondly, there is an obligation of contract. A power, except in the case of a power coupled with an interest, as has been said, may always be revoked. A lawful obligation of contract, which implies a consideration, may not be avoided without liability. We therefore may summarize:

POWER COUPLED WITH INTEREST

A power coupled with an interest may not be revoked.

NAKED POWER MAY BE REVOKED ANY TIME

A naked, or bare, power may be revoked at any time.

WHEN PRINCIPAL IS NOT LIABLE, NO CONSIDERATION

If a bare power is revoked, and there is neither a termination date nor consideration to support a contract, the principal is *not* ordinarily liable to the broker for commission if the revocation is effected before the broker has produced a purchaser ready, willing and able to buy the property. Here is a unilateral offer revocable at any time before performance.

WHEN PRINCIPAL IS LIABLE, NO CONSIDERATION

If a bare power is revoked, and there is neither a termination date nor consideration to support a contract, the principal *is* liable to the broker for commission if the revocation is effected after the broker has produced a purchaser ready, willing and able to buy the property. Here is the performance of an act by the broker for a promise of the principal converting the unilateral offer into a unilateral contract and thus binding both parties.

WHEN PRINCIPAL NOT LIABLE, NO CONSIDERATION BUT A TERMINATION DATE

If a bare power is revoked, and there is a termination date, but no consideration to support a contract, the principal is *not* liable to the broker for commission if the revocation is before the broker has produced a buyer ready, willing and able to buy the property, notwithstanding the revocation is before the termination date, and whether the language of the agency is construed to be a limitation upon the broker's authority, or a limitation upon the principal's power of revocation, there still being no binding contract supported by a consideration. If the principal has used language which limits his power of revocation he does not make himself liable to the broker for commission unless there is consideration passing from the broker to himself to support such a limitation.

From the foregoing it would seem that liability of the principal for a commission to the broker arising from the revocation of the agency contract before performance on the part of the broker will largely depend, ordinarily, upon whether a bilateral contract has been entered into between the parties supported by sufficient consideration. Whether the language of the agency be construed as a limitation upon the principal's power of revocation, or a limitation upon the authority of the broker, would be of little significance unless an existing contract binding the parties could be shown. It is generally accepted law that where there is no consideration a bare power or authority may be withdrawn or revoked without liability if done before performance on the part of the broker. And this is so whether the language of the agency limits the principal's power of revocation, or limits the authority of the broker. Unfortunately the courts in this matter of liability involving fixed dates have often

IS THERE A CONTRACT?

IS THERE CONSIDERATION?

said nothing about consideration, but apparently have assumed the existence of a contract. In order to make the principal liable to the broker for commission for revocation of the agency before performance by the broker, and where the language of the agency contract amounts to a limitation upon the principal's power of revocation, the broker, ordinarily, ought to be able to show either that there was a binding bilateral contract between himself and the principal, or that the agency contract was in the nature of an option supported by consideration giving the broker the right to offer the property for sale for a fixed period of time, or, that the principal's unilateral offer has been accepted by the broker.

The partly performed unilateral agency contract bearing a termination date, is one which has given the courts some trouble. There are two lines of reasoning looking to a solution of the problem involved in these cases. Legal authorities are divided in their answers. Some take the position that the usual agency agreement, being in the nature of a unilateral offer calling for an act, or full performance on the part of the broker, may be withdrawn or revoked at any time before full performance. These authorities take the position that part performance is not full performance and will not prevent revocation by the principal if he is otherwise entitled to revoke the agency without liability. Others take the position that whatever the brokers' undertaking is, it requires a certain amount of time and certain preliminary acts to perform it fully, and that when the first of such acts is commenced the process of full performance is set in motion, and the principal cannot then revoke the agency without liability.

PART PERFORMANCE

However, when it can be said that a bilateral contract has been effected between principal and broker the aforementioned divergent views become reconciled. If, for example, the agency contract may be construed to contain an exchange of promises express or implied, whereby the principal promises to pay the broker a commission for listing and diligently undertaking to sell his property, doing all those things necessary and proper in the premises, and the broker promises that he will list the property and do and perform all and every thing requisite and proper to sell the property, a bilateral agreement emerges and the principal cannot revoke it without becoming liable to the broker for his commission. The courts have attempted in all part performance cases, particularly where there has been any show of bad faith on the part of the principal, to favor the broker and if possible to find consideration in the undertaking of the broker in initiating pursuance of full performance; such undertaking being looked upon as an acceptance of the employment contract by the broker, and his implied promise to continue to perform.

SHOW OF BAD FAITH ON PART OF PRINCIPAL

Under the usual modern Exclusive Authorization and Right to Sell listing agreement giving the broker the exclusive right to sell the property described therein, a sale by the principal or any agent appointed by him during the term of the listing or any extension thereof would render the principal liable for the broker's commission.

EXCLUSIVE AUTHORIZATION AND RIGHT TO SELL

The usual agency contract provides that if the principal withdraws from sale the property to be sold, or transfers it, or leases it during the term of the agency, or any extension thereof, the broker shall be entitled to his commission.

THREE-MONTH SAFETY PROVISION

In such an agency contract there is also a provision to the effect that if a sale, lease or transfer of the property is made within a three-month period, or some other fixed time, after the termination of the listing, or any extension thereof, to any party with whom the broker negotiated, and notified the principal in writing of such negotiations during the regular term, or any extension thereof, and before its termination date, the broker shall be entitled to his commission. This three-month safety provision protects the broker only when he has begun negotiations during the effective term of the agency contract and during that effective period has notified the principal of such negotiations and supplied him with the name of the prospective purchaser.

FINAL AND COMPLETE TERMINATION DATE

The Exclusive Authorization and Right to Sell listing has been required by statute to have a definite, specified date of final and complete termination. And while it has been held that the Real Estate Commissioner may, under such statute, institute disciplinary proceedings against the broker for not including a final date in such an agency contract, there are some exceptions to the rule which permit a broker to collect his commission in spite of the omission.

REVOCATION OF THE AGENCY

In those agency contracts where the limitation is upon the broker's authority, it is generally held that a notice of revocation is not required to terminate the agency, such revocation being implied from the acts of the parties, such as a sale of the property by the owner or another broker. Nevertheless, some courts have held that notice to the broker is necessary. Revocation by operation of law occurs upon the death or insanity of either party, destruction of the subject matter of the agency, or where the object of the contract becomes illegal by change in the law.

F. Acceptance of Deposit on Account of the Sale Price

ACCEPTANCE OF DEPOSIT BY BROKER

The Exclusive Authorization and Right to Sell listing agreement usually provides that the broker shall have the authority to accept a deposit on account of the sale price of the principal's property.

WHERE NO AUTHORITY IS GIVEN

Where no authority is given the broker to accept a deposit, the acceptance of such by him would place him in the position of holding it as the servant of the proposed purchaser, not as the agent of the seller, and a misappropriation of the deposit money would be the loss of the purchaser, not of the seller.

DEPOSIT OF FUNDS RECEIVED BY BROKER

However, under the terms of the usual exclusive agency contract the broker, being authorized to receive the money, would accept it from the purchaser as agent of the seller. What, then, must he do with it? Being in a fiduciary relationship with his principal, he must do what a trustee would be required to do under the circumstances, that is to say, he must deposit the money in a trustee account. Good practice would suggest that in those cases where a broker does not immediately place all funds entrusted to him by his principal or others in a neutral escrow depository or in the hands of his principal, he should maintain a trust fund account with some bank or recognized depository and place all such entrusted funds therein upon receipt. Such trust fund account ought to designate him as trustee and be of such character as to permit of withdrawal of the money without previous notice.

The broker should likewise keep a record of all trust funds received by him, **RECORD** including uncashed ckecks held pursuant to instructions of his principal. Such a record, to be adequate, ought to show the following information:

> The date the funds were received;
> From whom received;
> The amount received;
> With respect to funds deposited to trust bank account, date of such deposit;
> With respect to funds previously deposited to trust bank account, check number or date of related disbursement;
> With respect to funds not deposited in trust bank account, nature of other depository and date funds were forwarded;
> Daily balance of trust bank account. Each broker who maintains a formal trust cash receipts journal and a formal cash disbursement journal or other similar records, in accordance with sound accounting principles, should be deemed to have complied with the foregoing provisions.

The broker ought also to keep a separate record for each transaction, accounting for all funds noted therein which have been deposited to the broker's trust bank account. This record ought to set forth sufficient information to identify the transaction and the parties in interest.

Listing agreements ordinarily provide that the broker shall be entitled to **RETENTION OF** retain some proportion, usually one-half, [but not to exceed his commission] **DEPOSIT UPON** of a forfeited deposit. So long as the purchaser believes he has forfeited his **BREACH OF PER-** deposit and makes no demand for its return there is no problem. But should **FORMANCE** the purchaser demand the return of his deposit on the ground that it cannot be retained as liquidated damages, there might be some problem requiring a solution between the broker and his principal, particularly so if the principal had permitted the broker to retain any part of the deposit. The Deposit Receipt, under which the breach would occur and the deposit forfeited, being principally a market instrument, it is not too likely that the purchaser could recover the deposit.

While it appears to be the weight of authority and the general American doctrine that the seller may retain payments under a forfeiture clause where the purchaser has defaulted, and especially where provision is made in the contract for retention of a deposit as liquidated damages should the purchaser fail to complete the contract, yet a warning has been sounded in at least one jurisdiction against the use of "liquidated damage" clauses in contracts which preserve other remedies to the seller and thus thereby characterize such clauses as pure forfeitures or set-offs against actual damages.

G. Agency Contract by Ratification

AGENCY BY RATI-
FICATION

An agency may be created and an authority may be conferred either by a precedent authorization or a subsequent ratification. The principal, by accepting the offer of a purchaser who is ready, willing and able to buy, ratifies the acts of the broker procuring such a purchaser, and creates thereby an agency contract between himself and the broker by ratification.

It frequently happens that a broker is not able to obtain a listing of an owner's property, yet the property is for sale and the owner is willing to consider any reasonable, firm offer. Under such circumstances a broker may show the property to a prospective purchaser who later executes an ordinary Deposit Receipt and gives the broker his check as a deposit. The broker presents the offer and the check to the owner for acceptance.

Certainly, up to this point, the broker is not the agent of the seller. There has been no legally binding agency agreement between them. Should the seller accept the offer, by so doing he would be held to have ratified the acts of the broker and by agreeing to pay the commission (which agreement is usually a part of the acceptance in the ordinary Deposit Receipt) would have obligated himself to pay the broker a commission upon the consummation of the transaction.

SUBSEQUENT RATI-
FICATION VS PREC-
EDENT AUTHORI-
ZATION

An agency contract created by subsequent ratification is not as satisfactory a commission agreement as an agency created by a precedent authorization, because the only agreement to pay the broker a commission is found in the contract between the purchaser and the seller. And it has been held that where the only agreement to pay the broker a commission is found in the contract between his principal and the purchaser, the broker's right to commission is dependent upon performance of the contract between buyer and seller. If the buyer refuses to perform, or the contract is canceled or rescinded, the broker cannot ordinarily recover his commission.

3. The Deposit Receipt

A. Practice

THE DEPOSIT RE-
CEIPT
FIRM OFFER MADE
BY PROSPECTIVE
BUYER

Ordinarily when one has something to sell he offers it for sale at a price and upon certain terms and conditions, the purchaser accepting the offer and paying the price. In the sale of real estate under an agency contract, this procedure is somewhat reversed to facilitate handling. The prospective buyer makes the seller a firm offer through the Deposit Receipt device which is accompanied by an earnest-money deposit on account of the purchase price. The seller may accept or reject the offer.

THE OFFER AND
ACCEPTANCE

Actually, the common practice is for the owner of real property to enter into an agency contract with a broker in which contract the property to be sold is identified and the price, terms and conditions of sale set forth. With this supplied information, the broker seeks a buyer ready, willing and able to purchase the property upon the stipulated terms and conditions. The buyer then makes the owner an offer (by means of the Deposit Receipt) based upon the terms and conditions of sale the owner has authorized the broker to produce a buyer able to meet. If the owner accepts the offer the sale is consummated, an escrow is opened, the transaction is concluded and the broker is paid his commission. Often, however, in actual practice, the broker produces a buyer ready, willing and able to pay what he believes a fair price for the property, and bargaining begins, the owner and the prospective purchaser ultimately arriving at a price and terms mutually agreeable, and the broker adjusting his commission to the actual selling price. If the owner accepts the offer as adjusted by negotiation the transaction is escrowed, the sale is concluded and the broker is paid his adjusted commission.

B. Failure of Buyer to Perform

The ordinary Deposit Receipt may contain language similar to the following:

> "If the purchaser fails to pay the balance of the purchase price, or to complete the purchase as herein provided, the amounts paid hereon may be retained by seller as consideration for the execution of this agreement by Seller."

And there is usually the provision that:

> "The principal agrees to pay Broker to sell said property as commission the sum of $____ , or one-half of the amounts paid by purchaser in the event the same are forfeited, provided such one-half shall not exceed the full amount of said commission."

It should be noted, too, that the exclusive authorization listing agreement generally provides:

> "If deposit or amounts paid on account of purchase price are forfeited, broker shall be entitled to one-half of said amount or amounts, but not to exceed the amount agreed upon as and for commission."

We have seen that when the principal has accepted the offer of the prospective purchaser and thereby entered into a contract of purchase and sale with him, he is estopped thereafter to deny the ability of the purchaser to perform and, ordinarily, the broker has earned his commission. If the broker has already taken a deposit, under the commonly found provisions already noted, he is entitled to one-half of the deposit, not to exceed his commission, in the event the purchaser subsequently defaults and refuses or fails to consummate the transaction. There are exceptions to this rule, as where the broker has made misrepresentations to the purchaser concerning the property, or where the payment of commission is otherwise agreed upon between buyer and seller.[1]

IF PROVIDED IN AGENCY CONTRACT, BROKER IS ENTITLED TO SHARE WITH PRINCIPAL FORFEITED DEPOSIT

It is generally held that the financial inability of the purchaser to go through with the contract of purchase will not prevent the broker from collecting his commission. But there are decisions to the effect that the broker's commission will be denied in such cases on the ground that when he produced the purchaser he impliedly warranted his ability to pay, the principal relying upon the representations of the broker in the premises.

C. Conformity of Listing Agreement and Deposit Receipt

SHOULD BE NO
MATERIAL VARI-
ANCE BETWEEN
TERMS OF LISTING
AGREEMENT AND
DEPOSIT RECEIPT

There should be no material difference between the terms and conditions set forth in the listing agreement and those set down in the Deposit Receipt if performance of the broker is made to depend upon the principal's offer contained in the former instrument.

The Deposit Receipt contains the offer of the purchaser to buy the property. In this connection it is important to repeat that there should be no material variance in the terms set forth in that instrument with those proposed in the listing agreement if the broker intends the offer to lay the foundation for his commission.

4. The Land Contract, or the Executory Contract of Sale

A. Definition

One definition of a land contract which might be generally acceptable is that such a contract is a real property sales agreement wherein one party agrees to convey title to real property to another party upon the satisfaction of specified conditions set forth in the contract and which does not require conveyance of title within one year from the date of formation of the contract.

In considering any instrument which has for its purpose the transfer of an interest in real property the question of immediate concern to both seller and buyer is: What is the legal effect of the instrument, and how does it affect the title to the property it describes? The answer to this question is important not only from an ownership point of view, but from a tax point of view. In the Land Contract it is going to be extremely important to the seller, in case of a breach, to know the legal consequences, and the remedies of the parties.

B. Status of the Parties Under Land Contract and Usual Terms

The Land Contract is executory in nature. The seller holds the naked legal title in trust for the buyer. The buyer acquires an equitable ownership, and usually possession of the property under the terms of the contract. Upon conveyance of the property to the buyer the equitable and legal titles merge, the buyer's equitable title becoming absolute. Upon complete performance the buyer is entitled to receive the legal title from the seller.

The disposition of rents and profits should be controlled by express agreement in the contract. They may be retained by the seller, or prorated between the parties. In the absence of agreement between seller and buyer, growing crops are part of the realty and belong to the buyer in possession.

With respect to the payment of taxes the general rule, with some exceptions, is that the party in possession under a Land Contract is bound, in the absence of statute or contrary agreement, to pay taxes accruing after the execution of the contract and before a conveyance. This ordinarily would mean the purchaser. However, if the seller retains possession he would himself be liable for tax assessments. The Land Contract usually provides that the buyer shall pay all taxes and assessments assessed and levied against the property from the date of the contract, and that taxes for the fiscal year following such date shall be pro-rated. These provisions avoid controversy.

Both the seller and the buyer have an insurable interest in the improvements. The usual insurance provision in the contract recites that the buyer shall insure the buildings against fire with a fire insurance company to be approved by the seller, and that any loss shall be paid to the buyer and the seller as their respective interests may appear; that if the property is not so insured the seller may insure and charge the costs to the buyer; that all insurance policies shall be delivered to and held by the seller until the buyer has fully performed under the contract of sale.

Under the Uniform Vendor and Purchaser Risk Act the buyer in possession bears the risk of loss of improvements, and loss of land by eminent domain. Thus, when neither the legal title nor the possession of the property has been transferred, and all or a material part thereof is destroyed without fault of the purchaser, or is taken by eminent domain, the seller cannot enforce the contract, and the purchaser is entitled to recover any portion of the price that he has paid. However, when either the legal title or the possession of the property has been transferred, and all or any part thereof is destroyed without fault of the seller, or is taken by eminent domain, the purchaser is not thereby relieved of a duty to pay the price, nor is he entitled to recover any portion thereof that he has paid.

It is usually provided in the Land Contract that possession is to be delivered to the purchaser when the instrument is executed and delivered. In practice this occurs when the contract is delivered out of escrow and unconditionally to the purchaser, if there has been an escrow, otherwise if the parties understand the contract has been executed and is an effective, operating instrument, it will be considered delivered, notwithstanding there has not been a physical transfer of the document. The delivery must not be conditional if the contract is to impose a binding obligation.

The contract will ordinarily provide for delivery of a deed upon receipt of all payments due, and for title insurance showing a merchantable title free of all liens, encumbrances, assessments and taxes not otherwise provided for

RENTS, PROFITS AND GROWING CROPS

TAXES AND ASSESSMENTS

INSURABLE INTEREST

BUYER PAYS FOR INSURANCE

UNIFORM VENDOR AND PURCHASER RISK ACT

LIABILITY OF SELLER AND PURCHASER WHEN PROPERTY IS DESTROYED OR TAKEN BY EMINENT DOMAIN

DELIVERY OF POSSESSION

DELIVERY OF DEED, TITLE INSURANCE

in the contract. Title insurance may be paid for by either seller or purchaser as agreed. The seller must be able to deliver good title at the time provided for in the contract. Ordinarily he need not have any title whatsoever in the property at the time of the execution of the contract, and before the time for performance, provided no fraud or bad faith is involved.

FORFEITURE CLAUSE

A liquidated damage clause is sometimes inserted in the contract. This is a clause to the effect that in the event of default all payments may be retained by the seller in consideration of the execution of the agreement by seller, the seller thereafter being released from further performance in law or equity. The purchaser thereafter is made a tenant at the will of the seller, and waives all claims of title by reason of his possession.

STRICT ENFORCE-MENT OF RULE AGAINST FORFEI-TURES

In those states, such as California, which strictly enforce statutory provisions against forfeitures, and where legislation restricts the use of liquidated damage clauses, care must be observed in employing language of forfeiture. The above mentioned provision with respect to tenancy at will is intended to protect the seller from unwarranted claims against the property.

CONVERSION CLAUSE IN LAND CONTRACT

In some Land Contracts there is a provision that the seller shall have the right to deliver a deed to the property at any time during the term of the contract, and that in such event the purchaser shall accept such a deed in lieu of the contract, and shall concurrently with the delivery of the deed deliver to the seller his note, secured by a power of sale mortgage or deed of trust, for the balance of the purchase price. This provision enables the seller to convert the executory contract of sale into a conveyance of title and a security instrument. By this maneuver the seller has divested himself of the title to the property and relies upon the lien of the deed of trust, or mortgage, to protect his interest in the unpaid balance. The seller is, ordinarily, in a more desirable position after the conversion than he was before, should he have to foreclose to protect himself. However, federal and state tax angles should be considered before making the conversion.

DANGEROUS BUYER-REMEDIES AVOIDED BY CON-VERTING LAND CONTRACT INTO DEED AND SECU-RITY INSTRUMENT

The seller has by this simple device rid himself of some dangerous buyer-remedies, such as the buyer's right to restitution, and his statutory right to redeem after foreclosure, as well as the destruction of the benefit-of-bargain the seller ought to be entitled to. Such buyer-remedies are too often availed of by unscrupulous and irresponsible buyers gambling with the property of sellers and indifferent to their interests and peace of mind. By converting the contract into a conveyance, note and deed of trust, the seller has a more effective remedy in the event of the buyer's willful, stalling default. If, on the other hand, the buyer is not a willful defaulter, but has defaulted unavoidably, he still has under some statutes a reasonable time within which to reinstate himself.

ADDITIONAL PRO-VISIONS

Provision is made for the insurance of improvements by the buyer against loss by fire, with loss payable to buyer and seller as their respective interests may appear, the seller to hold the policies, and the seller having the right to insure and charge the cost to the buyer in the event the buyer fails to insure.

A provision against vitiation of covenants and conditions by waiver of any one or more of them from time to time by the seller, along with a covenant binding the heirs and successors of the parties, a "time is of the essence" provision, followed by a provision for the payment of attorneys' fees in the event seller must sue buyer to enforce the agreement, are likewise usually found in the Land Contract.

Where time is of the essence of the contract it is the duty of the purchaser to comply strictly with the provisions regarding time of payment.

TIME OF THE ESSENCE

C. Federal Income Tax Advantage of Sale Under Land Contract

A sale of property under a Land Contract does offer some flexibility taxwise.

Ordinarily if real property is sold on the installment plan with a down payment and a note for the balance secured by a purchase money mortgage, the seller is presumed by the Treasury Department to have received the entire amount of the sale price in the year of the sale, and will be taxed in advance on the assumed profit. Gains, profits, and income are to be included in gross income for the taxable year in which they are actually or CONSTRUCTIVELY received by the taxpayer.[2]

INCOME TAX ADVANTAGE

CONSTRUCTIVE CAPITAL INCOME TAXED

To postpone payment of the tax on the full taxable income, and thus adjust the tax to the actual taxable income received, the law allows two methods of reporting income, namely, by the Installment Method, and by the Deferred Payment Method.

We are not here concerned with the Installment Method of reporting taxable income, except to say that it is more demanding then the Deferred Payment Method.[3] We are concerned with the latter method.

Under the terms of the ordinary Land Contract title is retained in the seller until the purchase price is paid. Because title does not pass at the time of the sale the courts have held that the rights of the seller under the installment Land Contract are incapable of valuation, and that the sale may be reported on the Deferred Payment Method. This would not be possible were the security interest capable of valuation at the time of the sale, in which case the less flexible Installment Method might, if other prescribed conditions were met, be employed.[4] To enable the seller to report on the Installment Method he cannot have received in the year of sale more than 30% of the total sale price. This, however, is not so when reporting under the Deferred Payment Method.[5] If the seller is on the cash method of accounting he may adopt the Deferred Payment Method of reporting his income. The balance, after deducting cost basis and expenses of sale, will represent taxable gain. By using this method the seller may be sure that he is being taxed only on actual gain.

DEFERRED PAYMENT METHOD ADAPTABLE TO REPORTING INCOME FROM LAND CONTRACT

So long as the Land Contract remains an installment contract and title is not transferred, the down payment and all payments received by the seller in the year of sale may, under the Deferred Payment Method, exceed 30% of the total sale price. No gain will be taxed to the seller until the payments received shall exceed the basis of the property and the costs of sale.

This method is spoken of as the return of capital theory—contingent payments.

> *EXAMPLE:*　　　John Doe owns real estate which he sells to Richard
> Roe under a Land Contract for the price of
> $200,000. He takes $75,000 cash, the balance to
> be paid over a period of five years. His adjusted
> basis is $100,000. He pays a commission of
> $10,000 to the broker who sold the property for
> him; title search $100; and escrow and miscella-
> neous charges of $250.

Inasmuch as the cash payment in the year of sale is in excess of 30% of the sale price, the transaction does not qualify for the Installment Method of reporting capital income. The seller being on the cash method of accounting, and the payments contingent, he is permitted to report the sale on the return of capital theory, i.e., the Deferred Payment Method.

The transaction is set up as follows, to indicate the mechanics.

Selling price		$200,000
Adjusted basis	$100,000	
Selling expenses		
Commission	10,000	
Title search	100	
Escrow charges	250	
Return of capital and expenses allowed		110,350
Gross profit, adjusted		$ 89,650
Return of capital and expenses	$110,350	
Payments year of sale　(1966)	75,000	
Bal. untaxable return of capital	35,350	
1st installment　(1967)	25,000	
Bal. untaxable return of capital	10,350	
2nd installment　(1968)	25,000	
Taxable income　(1968)	14,650	
3rd installment　(1969)	25,000	
(all taxable)		
4th installment　(1970)	25,000	
(all taxable)		
5th installment　(1971)	25,000	
(all taxable)	$ 89,650	

D. Laymen in the Real Estate Business Should Not Give Legal Advice

While it is undoubtedly not the business of the real estate dealer to give legal advice with respect to the advantages of one instrument over another, there could be no objection to the occasional expression of a personal opinion based upon sound business experience. But the layman in the real estate business should refrain from using language which might be construed as professionally advising his principal of the legal effect and consequences of instruments employed in the consummation of a real estate transaction. In those states where real estate brokers are strictly regulated, conduct which might be construed as the unlawful practice of the law could result in the suspension or revocation of a real estate broker's license.

The term "practice of the law" includes not only doing or performing services in a court of justice, but also the giving of legal advice and counsel, and the preparation of legal instruments and contracts, by which legal rights are secured, although such matters may or may not be pending in a court. Particularly is this so if it can be proved that a charge was made for such services.

UNLAWFUL PRACTICE OF THE LAW

The law recognizes that the activities of real estate brokers must necessarily involve the preparation of moving papers and that there must be an area in which a sound discretion may be exercised with respect to the preparation of dispositive instruments. It is usually agreed that the filling in of blanks in printed forms (if the transaction is simple or standardized) by real estate brokers in the course of their business transactions will not ordinarily be considered as the unlawful practice of the law if no fee is charged for the service. On the other hand, a real estate broker was held to be guilty of unlawful practice of the law where he drew a trust deed to secure a loan, for which services he charged a fee, and the activity was not incidental to any real estate transaction handled by him.

LIMITATIONS ON THE PREPARATION OF INSTRUMENTS

Without laboring the point further, no intelligent person in the real estate business wants to involve himself in a situation where very serious consequences might result should he tamper with legal concepts he is not licensed to handle.

INSTRUMENTS SHOULD NOT BE DRAFTED BY THE BROKER

Deposit Receipts, Land Contracts, Leases, and in some cases, Escrow Instructions can be complicated and involved instruments, and must satisfy the requirements of the law. They should be drawn to stand up in court should litigation arise out of the real estate transaction. The fact that most "deals" are concluded without contest does not justify sloppy preparation, or excuse ignorance or negligence in drafting legal instruments. Except in the simpler transactions, the principal's attorney should assist in the preparation of all binding agreements. This practice would afford protection not only to the principal, but to the real estate broker handling the transaction.

ALL INSTRUMENTS SHOULD BE CAREFULLY PREPARED

5. The Exchange Agreement

A. Definition

Broadly speaking the Exchange Agreement is an instrument by which the parties thereto exchange properties, agreeing upon an exchange price for each property, and balancing their respective equities by additional consideration from the party with the smaller equity.

THE EXCHANGE AGREEMENT

Actually, "equity" is not quite the proper term to use, but it will suffice to indicate the use of the Exchange Agreement. The asking or selling price of a property is not always based upon value, properly speaking. Very often it is

THE EQUITY

based upon arbitrary demands, the property nevertheless selling for the "price" asked because of an appeal by some peculiar attribute of the property to the particular buyer, or for any number of other reasons not necessarily connected with value.

INFLATED EQUITIES

This element of inflated asking price is more common to exchange transactions than to sales transactions. If neither party is under compulsion to exchange and each is an intelligent, reasonable individual, the value or equity each has in his own property is much more likely to be adjusted by the good offices of the broker toward a true market value. In such cases the "equities" traded will approach a correspondence in value, and the cash payment made by the one party to bring the exchange into balance is likely to represent a nearly real difference in the value of the properties.

However, it often happens that difficult owners who have overpriced their respective properties on the market will be brought together in an exchange transaction. The price of each property is badly inflated. The broker finds little difficulty in determining the real value of the properties. He knows that a buyer for either property at the price asked would be extremely hard to find. The best thing he can do is to try to bring each property owner as nearly in line with value as he can without offense. The broker wants to make the trade, and the parties are ready, willing and able to do so.

INCREASED SEL- LING COMMIS- SIONS MIGHT WELL BE PENALTY FOR INFLATED SALE PRICE

If the inflation is about equal on both sides of the transaction the only persons to be hurt are the parties to the exchange themselves, by having to pay an increased commission on the properties they are selling. It is common practice for the broker to charge a commission on each property. The commission is based not upon the equity exchanged but upon the exchange price of each of the properties. A tax problem too, is involved.

B. Provisions of the Exchange Agreement

IS AN OFFER TO EXCHANGE

From the language of the usual Exchange Agreement it is evident that the instrument is set up as an offer to exchange properties described therein on the basis set forth in the agreement. The parties are required to procure preliminary title reports on their respective properties within a time specified; they must also execute and deliver [normally, into escrow] all instruments

NECESSARY ACTS OF PARTIES TO EFFECT EXCHANGE

necessary to transfer title to the property each intends to exchange. This must be done within a certain stipulated time after acceptance. The usual provision is made for evidence of a merchantable title free of all encumbrances save those particularly excepted.

CORRECTION OF ERRORS

A paragraph of the exchange agreement makes provision for the correction of errors in title. It sets the time limit within which to correct such errors usually at three months after acceptance of the offer, or within any additional time to which the parties might agree. If such error or errors cannot be corrected within the time limited, and the property is not acceptable subject thereto, the agreement provides for its termination. It is nevertheless continued in effect with respect to brokerage commissions.

Provision is made for the proration of all taxes, rents and other expenses. Insurance is also prorated if present policies are satisfactory to the party acquiring the property exchanged. All prorations are usually made effective as of the close of the escrow.

PRORATION OF FIXED CHARGES AND EXPENSES

If the printed form employed in the usual Exchange Agreement is to be in any way altered, changes would have to be written into some appropriate blank space in the agreement, or on separate sheets attached to the agreement and made a part thereof by incorporation therein. All alterations, additions or deletions should be initialed or signed by the parties. The printed provisions where altered or changed should be ruled out with a pen or typewriter and likewise initialed by the parties.

Where written and printed parts of an agreement are irreconcilable, the written parts prevail. Typewritten parts will prevail over printed parts. Nevertheless, to avoid the necessity of establishing repugnancy or irreconcilability if the contract is questioned, all printed matter changed by handwritten or typewritten insertions of the parties should be striken out with pen or typewriter, and the new handwritten or typewritten insertions, together with the stricken printed matter, initialed by all parties to the agreement.

INITIALING DELETIONS AND INSERTIONS

And finally, the party making the offer to exchange usually authorizes a designated broker to act on behalf of both parties and to accept commission from each. Provision is made for the release of the offeror from the payment of brokerage commission should the other party be unable to correct an error in his title, unless the offeror is willing to accept the property subject thereto. In the "acceptance" part of the Exchange Agreement similar provisions are contained with respect to commission.

AUTHORIZING BROKER TO ACT FOR BOTH PARTIES AND PAYMENT OF COMMISSION

As has been said, the Exchange Agreement is in the nature of an "offer" and an "acceptance." If the acceptance is signed by the party to whom the offer is directed, a binding contract results.

6. The Lease

A. Nature and Elements of the Lease

Estates, as we have seen,[6] are of freehold and of less than freehold. The lease for a term of years comes under the latter classification of estates. In theory leases may be for life, at will or for years. A lease for life, as well as a lease at the will of both parties, would be a rare, though possible, way of taking possession of land. Usually estates for life are created by deed or by devise. Estates at will are not expressly created. In the more complicated integrated document the parties are referred to as lessor and lessee, corresponding respectively in the ordinary lease-rental agreement to landlord and tenant.

LEASES FOR YEARS ARE ESTATES OF LESS THAN FREEHOLD

THE LESSOR AND LESSEE

**OPERATIVE
WORDS**

The operative words in a lease are "demise," "lets" or "leases," as for example: "John Doe demises and lets to Richard Roe all of that certain piece or parcel of land," etc., or "John Doe leases to Richard Roe," etc.

**LEASE PARTAKES
OF NATURE OF
BOTH CONVEY-
ANCE AND CON-
TRACT**

A lease partakes of the nature of both a conveyance and a contract. It gives rise to two basically different sets of rights and obligations, the one rested upon privity of estate, and the other upon privity of contract. Fundamentally, however, a lease is a conveyance in as much as it creates an estate in land. A contract cannot create a legal estate in land, although it might give rise to an equitable interest.

**LESSEE HOLDS IN
SUBORDINATION
TO RIGHTS OF
LESSOR**

The possession or occupancy under a lease must be in subordination to the rights of the lessor, or landlord, in the land. The lessor, or landlord must have a reversionary interest. In other words, if the lessor held an estate in fee simple in possession before the lease, by the lease he gives an estate in possession for a certain time to his lessee, retaining in himself a fee simple estate in reversion. The lessee holds in subordination to the lessor's greater reversionary estate.

**ESSENTIALS OF
LEASE AGREEMENT**

The essential requisites to the creation of a lease for a term of years may be said to be:

- Privity of estate;
- Privity of contract;
- A description of the property leased;
- Names of Lessor and Lessee, or Landlord and Tenant;
- A definite term, or a term which may be made definite by reference in the lease agreement to an event certain to happen;
- A reservation of rent payable upon specified terms; and
- A transfer of possession of the property leased to the lessee.

B. The Term of the Lease

**THE USUAL LEASE
FOR A TERM OF
YEARS**

The usual lease is for a term of years. The word "years" means any fraction of a year, or any fixed period of time expressed in terms of the calendar[7] or otherwise. A lease for a longer period than one year must, in most jurisdictions, be in writing. And because the statutes in most states require agreements not to be performed within a year from the making thereof to be in writing, a lease for a year, which itself would not be required to be in writing, would nevertheless be so required if by its terms it was to begin in the future, that is, subsequent to the date of its execution, and run thereafter for one year.

**STATUTORY LIMI-
TATION OF TERM
OF LEASE**

Leases of various types, such as for horticultural or agricultural purposes, oil and gas leases, leases of town and city lots, land held and leased by municipalities and other government agencies, for certain purposes, are in many jurisdictions limited as to term and purpose, and otherwise regulated. Statutes concerning such leases should be consulted in the several jurisdictions.

The terms of leases correspond to the limitations of estates discussed in an earlier chapter,[8] which might be well to review again.

C. The Contract of Lease

A lease contains contractual language fixing the terms and conditions of the leasehold estate conveyed. The rules of contract apply to this part of the lease.

Execution and delivery of the lease create a binding contract and establish privity of contract. The delivery of the lease creates the relationship of lessor and lessee, or landlord and tenant, and establishes privity of estate. Possession by the lessee may create a presumption of acceptance and delivery of the lease contract. But what makes the lease binding is the delivery and acceptance, actual or constructive. A formal written acceptance is preferable, but not absolutely necessary.

A lease to become effective must, therefore, be both executed and delivered. This is a general rule to keep in mind. It need be signed only by the lessor, if the lessee accepts it. Ordinarily the lessee is bound by the covenants contained in the lease if he accepts it, notwithstanding he has failed to sign it. Nevertheless diligence should be exercised to avoid such legal props upon which to support a real estate transaction.

As between the lessor and lessee the lease is an effective and valid instrument whether or not it is recorded. But as to subsequent bona fide purchasers and encumbrancers for value who first record, such an unrecorded lease is invalid. See chapter 3, where the subject of the bona fide purchaser is treated at some length.

Any alteration in the terms and conditions of the lease contract should be initialed by all of the parties thereto.

D. Provisions of the Ordinary Lease Contract

While all leases are similar in content, a discussion of the provisions found in the ordinary, printed form of lease will aid in understanding the character and scope of the instrument.

A paragraph of the lease will provide that the lessee shall pay the lessor the rent indicated in the manner prescribed; that he shall not let or underlet the whole or any part of the premises, nor sell or assign the lease; that this shall not be done voluntarily or by operation of law; that the lessee shall not permit the property to be occupied by any person contrary to the terms of the lease; that none of these prohibited things are to be done without the written consent of the lessor.

The provision with respect to "rent" is clear enough. The other provisions need some clarification. "To let" or "to underlet" may be rephrased "to lease" or "to sublease." One ASSIGNS a lease when the balance of the entire term is being transferred to the assignee, the lessee retaining no interest whatsoever

[Margin notes:]

THE CONTRACT OF LEASE

DELIVERY PRIVITY OF CONTRACT PRIVITY OF ESTATE

EXECUTED AND DELIVERED

SUBSEQUENT BONA FIDE PURCHASERS

ALTERATIONS

PROVISION FOR RENT AGAINST SUBLETTING OR ASSIGNMENT IMPROPER OCCUPANCY

DIFFERENTIATING ASSIGNING AND SUBLEASING

in the leasehold estate. A SUBLETING occurs when less than the entire balance of the term is being transferred to the sublessee. In other words, when one sublets the premises he does not transfer the entire balance of the term. But if the matter is stated this way, an entirely accurate understanding is not likely to be gained, as will appear by examining the five situations to be discussed hereinbelow.

AN ASSIGNMENT

The words of transfer are not important. It is the intendment in law the words imply which determines whether the instrument is an assignment or a sublease. If the entire term is transferred, there being no reversion or contingent reversionary interest remaining in the lessee, the transaction is an assignment. If there is preserved a reversionary estate in the transferor to take effect upon the termination of the estate transferred, or if by reserving the right of re-entry upon breach of condition, a contingent reversionary interest remains in the lessor, or the lessee where the transfer is made by the latter, the transfer

A SUBLEASE

is in most states, a sublease.

> Correctly stated the rules are:
> Assigning the entire balance of the term without reserving a right of re-entry for breach of condition—an ASSIGNMENT.
> Assigning the entire balance of the term but reserving a right of re-entry for a breach of condition—a SUBLEASE.
> Subletting the entire balance of the term but reserving the right of re-entry for breach of condition—a SUBLEASE.
> Subletting for a term of less than the balance of the original term, thus leaving room for a reversion in the sublessor, (original lessee), upon termination of the sublease—a SUBLEASE.
> "Subletting" the entire balance of the term without reserving a right of re-entry for breach of condition—an ASSIGNMENT.

PROTECTION AGAINST ASSIGNMENT BY OPERATION OF LAW

In the ordinary lease the lessor protects himself against assignment or subletting by a covenant to that effect. Without such covenant the lessee has the right to assign or sublet. It is to be noted that he is not only protected against a voluntary assignment or subletting, but against an assignment by operation of law. There are situations which arise between the lessee and third persons which at times give rise to this latter type of assignment. For example, the lessee permits the use of leased land by a partnership in the conduct of its business, the lessee being one of the partners. In such a case it has been held that there is an assignment by operation of law of an interest in the lease to the partnership. An assignment by operation of law occurs, too, in the case of the insolvency of the lessee resulting in bankruptcy, the assignment running to the trustee in bankruptcy.

HOW COVENANT AGAINST ASSIGNMENT OR SUBLETTING PROTECTS LESSOR

Of course, the advantage to the lessor of such covenants in the lease lies in the right given him in a subsequent paragraph of the ordinary lease to re-enter the premises, upon breach of covenant and to terminate the lease, or pursue such other remedies he may be allowed by law.

Provision in the lease will usually be found to the effect that the lessee shall keep the premises in good condition and repair, the usual wear and tear and damage of the elements excepted, and shall not alter the premises without the written consent of the lessor. A provision against waste is likewise included.

Use of the premises for any purpose other than that for which the property was leased is generally prohibited. In some states statutes in effect provide that when a thing is let for a particular purpose the hirer must not use it for any other purpose, and if he does so use it the contract of letting may be rescinded. The covenant in the lease against such use avoids controversy. This covenant is not, however, the usual covenant against illegal use of the property, or a use specifically prohibited by law.

The latter covenant generally provides against the use of the property for the sale of intoxicating liquors, or for any illegal or immoral purpose. A breach of such covenant is made grounds for forfeiture or termination of the lease.

In those states following the common law, without a covenant against illegal use of the premises, followed by a forfeiture clause, the lessor cannot, ordinarily, terminate the lessee's term. And in those states where the law makes the lease void if made for illegal purposes [such provision by operation of law becoming a part of every lease contract] a covenant against such use, and forfeiture for its breach, is necessary if *forfeiture* of the lease is what the lessor intends to demand, the lease not having been made for an illegal purpose, but such illegal use subsequently practiced upon the premises. Without such a covenant the lessor's remedy would ordinarily be for damages, or for an injunction. The usual lease provides the remedy of forfeiture or termination of the lease contract for violation of the covenant.

A covenant will also be found which gives the lessor the right to re-enter the premises and remove all persons therefrom upon failure of the lessee to pay the rent when due, or should he default in any of the covenants or conditions contained in the lease contract.

It is generally provided that should the occupancy of the premises by the lessee cause the present fire and liability insurance rates to be increased, the lessee shall pay the difference, and said difference shall be added to the rent reserved, and paid to the lessor upon demand.

Provision is made for compliance on the part of the lessee with all government laws and ordinances.

Under the common law of England, from which our own law is largely derived, the tenant took the premises as he found them. The landlord had no duty to repair or keep the premises in any particular condition of repair. And this rule of law applies pretty generally in the American states. There are statutes, however, which except from the rule buildings intended for human occupation. A provision is often found in a lease contract waiving such statutes, thereby actually reinstating the old English common law rule. The

MAINTENANCE OF PREMISES PROVISION AGAINST WASTE

COVENANT AGAINST USE OF PREMISES FOR PURPOSE OTHER THAN THAT FOR WHICH LEASED

COVENANT AGAINST UNLAWFUL USE

COVENANT AGAINST UNLAWFUL USE NECESSARY TO TERMINATE LEASE CONTRACT

RIGHT OF RE-ENTRY UPON BREACH OF COVENANT OR CONDITION

ADDED COST OF INSURANCE ADDED TO RENT

COMPLIANCE WITH GOVERNMENT LAWS AND ORDINANCES

NO DUTY TO KEEP PREMISES IN REPAIR UNDER COMMON LAW RULE: STATUTORY EXCEPTIONS law of the state in which the reader has his place of business should be checked to determine what the rule is in that state.

A covenant usually provides that the terms and conditions contained in the lease contract shall apply to and bind the heirs, successors and assigns of the respective parties, and that the waiver by the lessor of any covenant or condition in the lease shall not vitiate the same or any other covenant or condition of the lease.

The general rule is that a covenant or a condition may be waived by the conduct of the party for whose benefit it was made. Whenever the course of dealing between landlord and tenant may lull the tenant into concluding that the landlord will not require a strict compliance with the terms of a covenant or condition binding upon him, the landlord will ordinarily be estopped to claim a forfeiture. The covenant in the lease providing that waiver shall not vitiate any covenant therein contained settles the effect of waiver on present and future breaches, whether such covenants breached be dependent, independent, continuing or non-continuing covenants.

Ordinarily, waiver of a present breach by the lessee of a continuing covenant does not vitiate the future effectiveness of the covenant, which may be relied upon by the lessor in the event of a later breach by the lessee. The lessor's waiver of the present breach does not waive future performance of the covenant. On the other hand, the waiver of a breach of a non-continuing covenant waives all subsequent breaches.

The distinction usually made between these two kinds of covenants is that a continuing covenant is one that binds the covenantor to the performance of like periodic acts, while a non-continuing covenant is one that binds the covenantor to perform but a single act, such as to repair, to insure or not to assign. Examples of continuing covenants are, to pay rent by installments, not to sublet, to pay taxes, to keep the premises repaired or insured. Briefly stated, dependent covenants arise when the performance of the covenant of one party

is intended to depend upon the performance of another covenant whether made by the same or the other party. An independent covenant is one the performance of which is not dependent upon the performance of another covenant by the same or other party. For example, where the parties have not made the covenant to pay rent dependent upon the lessor's covenant to pay taxes, each covenant is independent of the other, and in such case the payment of the rent would not be a waiver of the obligation of the lessor to pay taxes. Again, a covenant of the lessor to repair and a covenant of the lessee to pay rent are independent covenants unless the covenant to repair is made a condition precedent to the payment of rent.

There is the usual provision that at the expiration of the term, or its sooner determination, the lessee shall peacefully quit and surrender possession of the premises in as good condition as reasonable use and wear thereof permit.

The tenant is bound, under the law, to surrender the premises to his landlord at the termination of the tenancy. But this covenant to surrender possession of the premises in good condition binds him in damages for the loss or injury to the property whatever the cause. The provision excepting reasonable use and wear is not intended to except damage resulting from carelessness on the part of the lessee. And he must ordinarily restore the premises to their original condition.

There is a provision that should the tenant occupy the premises at the expiration of the term with the consent of the landlord, either express or implied, he shall pay a stipulated monthly rent and the tenancy shall be deemed a tenancy from month to month. Were this provision not contained in the lease contract the tenant holding over might be either a tenant at will or a tenant at sufferance. The provision determines the tenancy at a specified monthly rental.

TENANT HOLDING OVER: MONTH TO MONTH TENANCY PROVIDED

Then follows the provision with respect to the payment by the lessee of costs and attorneys' fees in the event it should become necessary for the lessor to commence suit against the lessee for the collection of rent, for possession of the property or dispossession of the lessee. And finally the usual clause with respect to making all words used in the singular to include the plural, the present tense to include the future and the masculine gender to include the feminine and neuter.

PROVISION FOR ATTORNEYS' FEES AND COSTS

7. The Broker's Loan Statement

Statutory provision is found having for its purpose the prevention of excessive commissions, hidden charges and unfair demands upon borrowers offering their equities in real property as security for loans. Such legislation is not general and where effective applies only to "hard money" loans, that is to say, where the broker is lending a client's money on new notes secured by equities in real property. It has no application to purchase money loans.

HARD MONEY LOANS

In at least one state such legislation does not apply to any bona fide loan secured directly or collaterally by a first deed of trust, the principal of which is $10,000 or more, or to any bona fide loan secured directly or collaterally by any lien junior thereto, the principal of which is $5,000 or more. In that state, the maximum commission a broker may charge on such hard money loans is 5 per cent of the principal amount on a loan of less than three years, and 10 per cent of the principal amount on a loan of three years or more, provided such loans are secured by a first deed of trust. On junior deeds of trust 5 per cent of the principal amount may be charged by the broker as commission on loans of less than two years, 10 per cent on loans of two but less than three years, and 15 per cent on loans of three years or more. Costs of the loan are limited to 4 per cent of the principal amount of the loan, but in no

BROKER'S COMMISSION ON HARD MONEY LOANS

event to exceed $250, and such costs must be supported in fact. Ten per cent per annum is the maximum rate of interest that may be charged. Balloon payments are prohibited.

To control and facilitate the regulation of commissions, costs and charges connected with hard money loans, the broker is required to prepare and deliver to the borrower before the latter becomes obligated to complete the loan, a statement, to be signed by both borrower and broker, containing specific information. This statement is known as the Broker's Loan Statement. The statute prescribes what information must be shown on the statement.

The regulation of hard money loans in the manner set forth is not universal. The reader should check the statutes of his own jurisdiction to learn if such loans are regulated in his state, and if so, to what extent.

QUESTIONS AND ANSWERS

1. What five instruments are commonly employed in the real estate business?

    Answer: The listing agreement, the deposit receipt, the land contract, the exchange agreement and the lease.

2. What is a Listing Agreement?

    Answer: It is an agency contract of employment in which the broker is given a limited authority or power to act on behalf of his principal, usually in connection with the sale of real estate.

3. Basically, what is the obligation of the broker under the terms of the listing agreement?

    Answer: To produce a buyer ready, willing and able to buy the principal's property on the terms and conditions indicated in the listing agreement.

4. In what other market instrument should the terms and conditions set down in the listing agreement be in complete agreement?

    Answer: The Deposit Receipt.

5. Why is this important?

    Answer: For a number of reasons. But, among others, the Deposit Receipt will contain the terms upon which the buyer is offering to buy the principal's property. Unless they conform to the terms of the Listing Agreement, the broker has not produced a buyer ready, willing and able to buy the property upon the terms and conditions he was authorized to offer, and he will not have earned his commission.

6. If the principal accepts less performance than indicated in the Listing Agreement, is the broker entitled to his commission?

    Answer: Yes. The basic obligation is to produce a buyer ready, willing and able to buy upon terms agreeable to the principal.

7. How is the Exclusive Authorization and Right to Sell listing distinguished from the others?

    Answer: In this listing the broker has the exclusive right to sell the property. If it is sold by anyone else, including the owner, during the term of the employment, the broker may collect his commission.

8. How is the Exclusive Agency listing distinguished from the others?

    Answer: In this listing the principal in effect contracts that he will not sell the property through any other agent than the broker taking the listing. Should the principal sell the property through some other broker, the listing broker will be entitled to his commission. However, the principal, not being an agent, may sell the property himself, in which case the listing broker will not be entitled to any commission.

9. Do exclusive listings have commencement and termination dates?

Answer: Yes, they usually do. In some jurisdictions a definite and final termination date is required by law.

10. What is an "open" listing?

Answer: One that is not exclusive and usually has no final termination date.

11. May the principal list his property with any number of brokers if such listings are open listings?

Answer: Yes. He may terminate the agency at any time before performance on the part of any broker, without liability.

12. What is a Multiple Listing Agency Contract?

Answer: A device employed by brokers to obtain a wider market for the sale of property. It is usually of the Exclusive Authorization and Right to Sell type.

13. What is the net listing?

Answer: The net listing is usually an open listing in which the principal fixes a net price he will take for his property, the broker to retain as commission all above the net price he can obtain. Ordinarily, however, he must reveal the amount obtained by him for the property to his principal.

14. Must a contract for the employment of a broker to sell real property be in writing?

Answer: Not in all states. In some states statutes require such a contract to be in writing.

15. What is the purpose of executing a listing agreement?

Answer: To effect a binding and enforceable employment agreement between principal and broker, and to comply with the law in those states requiring such agreements to be in writing.

16. Under the usual printed form of listing agreement, may the broker execute a deed of conveyance on behalf of his principal?

Answer: No. The usual form does not confer a power on the broker to execute such a deed.

17. Could such a power be given the broker?

Answer: Yes. But the language conferring such a power would have to be explicit and leave no doubt that such a power was being conferred.

18. When has the broker performed under the usual listing contract?

Answer: When he has procured a purchaser who is ready, willing and able to purchase the property on the terms and conditions specified in the listing agreement.

19. If exact terms are not specified in the listing agreement, when has the broker performed?

Answer: When the purchaser is ready, willing and able to purchase the property upon such terms and conditions as shall be agreed upon between himself and the principal.

20. In such case, if the principal and the purchaser cannot agree upon terms, has the broker performed so as to be entitled to his commission?

Answer: Not ordinarily.

21. What language is usually employed to express the broker's position to become entitled to commission?

Answer: He must be "the efficient, procuring, proximate or inducing cause" of the sale of the property.

22. How may it be established that the purchaser is ready, willing and able to buy the property?

Answer: It is a general rule of law that when the principal accepts the offer of the prospective purchaser (usually by accepting the terms written into a Deposit Receipt) produced by the broker, he admits the readiness, willingness and ability of the purchaser to conclude the sale.

23. If the agency contract has no termination date how long does it continue?

Answer: Usually, for a reasonable time.

24. If there is no termination date in an agency contract, when may the principal revoke the authority without liability?

Answer: As a general rule, at any time before performance on the part of the broker.

25. What is meant by the expression "a limitation upon the authority of the broker"?

Answer: That the broker has a limited time within which he must perform.

26. What is meant by the expression "a limitation upon the power of the principal to revoke the agency"?

Answer: That the principal cannot revoke the agency before the expiration date specified therein.

27. What kind of power is conferred upon the broker in the ordinary listing agreement?

Answer: A "naked" power.

28. May a principal revoke a naked or bare power whether or not it is based upon a consideration?

Answer: Yes. What is being revoked is the power, or authority created by the agency status, and such status is never dependent upon consideration, but rather upon confidence and trust.

29. Is the power or authority given a broker in a listing agreement the same thing as the contractual rights established by the agreement?

Answer: No.

30. May a power coupled with an interest be revoked?

Answer: No.

31. Is it enough that such power be coupled with an interest in the exercise of the power?

Answer: No. The power must be coupled with an interest in the subject matter.

32. Does the revocation of a power affect the obligation of contract which may have been established between the parties?

    Answer: Revocation of the power does not relieve the party revoking from damages for breach of contract.

33. Actually, upon what does the liability of a principal for broker's commission largely depend?

    Answer: Upon whether a contract has been entered into by the parties supported by sufficient consideration.

34. May a partly performed unilateral contract be revoked, if performance is the only issue?

    Answer: The authorities are split on this question. Some allow it; some do not. If a bilateral contract can be shown, then the question takes on a different aspect.

35. Generally, in what instances will the courts favor the broker in part performance cases?

    Answer: Where bad faith is shown on the part of the principal to prevent or interfere with performance.

36. What is the usual safety provision in the ordinary listing agreement?

    Answer: A provision to the effect that the broker shall have additional time, usually three months, after the termination of the listing during which time the principal may not without liability to the broker for commission sell the property to any person with whom the broker was negotiating during the term of the listing, and whose name during that time was communicated to the principal.

37. In those listing agencies where the limitation is upon the broker's authority, is it necessary to give notice of revocation?

    Answer: Ordinarily it is not. Some jurisdictions, however, require notice prior to revocation in such cases.

38. When does revocation by operation of law occur? Name two instances.

    Answer: Insanity of one of the parties to the agency contract. Destruction of the property, the subject matter of the agency. Likewise, should the object of the contract become illegal.

39. May a broker accept a deposit on the sale of his principal's property?

    Answer: Yes, if he is so authorized.

40. The broker, being authorized by his principal to accept a deposit, accepts money on account of the purchase price. What must he do with it?

    Answer: As a fiduciary he must do what a trustee would do—deliver the money to his principal, deposit it in a trustee account, or place it in a neutral escrow impound.

41. Is the broker entitled to retain some portion of the deposited earnest money in the event of a failure or refusal of the purchaser to perform under the contract he has entered into with the principal?

Answer: Ordinarily provision is made in such contract for forfeiture of the earnest money in the event of breach of contract by the buyer; provision is also usually made for the broker to retain some portion, usually one-half, of such forfeited deposit, not to exceed his commission.

42. Name two ways in which an agency contract may come into being.

Answer: By precedent authority, or by subsequent ratification.

43. Briefly define a Land Contract.

Answer: The Land Contract is usually an executory installment agreement wherein one party agrees to convey title to real property to another party upon the satisfaction of specified conditions set forth therein.

44. In considering the use of a particular instrument to be used in the sale and purchase of real property, what major consideration should be kept in mind?

Answer: Among others, what effect such instrument has upon the title of the property, not only from a purely legal point of view, but from a tax point of view.

45. Under a Land Contract, who holds the title and what kind of title?

Answer: The seller holds the naked legal title in trust for the buyer.

46. What kind of title does the buyer have in such a land contract?

Answer: The buyer holds an equitable title, and is usually entitled to possession.

47. Is the Land Contract sometimes said to be a security instrument?

Answer: Yes. The seller retains the title as security for the payment of the purchase price.

48. How should the rents, issues and profits and growing crops be handled in a sales contract?

Answer: In the sales contract, or Land Contract, they should be disposed of between the parties by express agreement contained in the contract.

49. What is the rule with respect to the payment of taxes under a Land Contract?

Answer: It is sometimes said that taxes follow the title. However, it is the general rule that the party in possession at the time of the accrual of the tax, or when it becomes a lien, and before a conveyance, is bound to pay the taxes, as between buyer and seller; but it is customary to expressly provide for the payment of taxes in the agreement itself.

50. Have both buyer and seller an insurable interest in the property sold under a Land Contract?

Answer: Yes. Both buyer and seller have an insurable interest in the improvements.

51. What provision is there in the usual Land Contract for the payment of fire insurance?

Answer: It is usually expressly agreed that the buyer shall insure the improvements against fire and pay for the same.

52. Under the Uniform Vendor and Purchaser Risk Act, who bears the risk of loss?

Answer: The buyer in possession bears risk of loss of improvements, and loss of land by eminent domain.

53. Is delivery of the Land Contract necessary to its effectiveness?

Answer: Yes, either physically or constructively.

54. When, under the Vendor and Purchaser Risk Act, must the purchaser perform if all or a material part of the property is destroyed without the fault of the seller, or taken by eminent domain?

Answer: When either the legal title or the possession of the property has been transferred to the buyer.

55. Need the seller have title to the property sold under a Land Contract at the time he enters into such contract of sale?

Answer: No. But he must be able to deliver title at the time indicated in the contract.

56. What is a liquidated damage clause?

Answer: A clause to the effect that in the event of default on the part of the buyer, all payments on account of the purchase price may be retained by the seller, the seller thereafter being released from further performance.

57. Where "time is of the essence" of a Land Contract, what advantage is there to the seller?

Answer: The clause imposes a duty of strict compliance with performance provisions of the contract.

58. Is there some advantage taxwise in selling land under a Land Contract?

Answer: There can be. If the taxpayer is on the cash method of accounting he may adopt the Deferred Payment Method of reporting his income, and gain will be reported only after he has first recovered his cost basis and expenses of sale.

59. When is delivery of possession contemplated under the provisions of the usual Land Contract?

Answer: Ordinarily, at the close of the escrow or shortly thereafter.

60. Briefly define an Exchange Agreement.

Answer: The Exchange Agreement is an instrument by which the parties thereto exchange properties, agreeing upon an exchange price for each property, and balancing their respective equities by additional consideration from the party with the smaller equity.

61. How is the ordinary Exchange Agreement set up?

Answer: One party offers to exchange his property for the property of the other party, the latter accepting the offer. Both offer and acceptance are distinct in the printed form usually employed.

62. Is a lease for years a "freehold" or "less than freehold" estate?

Answer: Less than freehold.

63. When written and printed parts of an agreement are irreconcilable, what parts prevail?

Answer: The written parts.

64. What are the operative words in a lease?

Answer: "Demise," "let," "lease."

65. What privities are involved in a lease?

Answer: Privity of estate and privity of contract.

66. What two legal concepts does a lease combine?

Answer: A lease is both a contract and a conveyance; establishing rights based upon privity of contract and privity of estate.

67. What does the term "for years" mean when speaking of an estate, or lease "for years"?

Answer: It means any fixed period of time expressed in terms of the calendar, or otherwise.

68. Must a lease for one year to begin in the future be in writing?

Answer: Under the general rule, in order to satisfy the statute of frauds, it must in most jurisdictions.

69. Must a lease for one year be in writing?

Answer: Not ordinarily.

70. To become effective, must a lease be both executed and delivered?

Answer: Yes. This is the general rule to keep in mind. There are exceptional circumstances which enlarge the rule.

71. Is to "assign" a lease the same thing as to "sublet" the property?

Answer: No.

72. Does the usual printed lease give the lessor the right to re-enter the premises upon default of the lessee?

Answer: Yes.

73. May lessor terminate a lease for unlawful use of the premises?

Answer: No, not unless there is a covenant in the lease against such use. The lessor's remedy, in the absence of such a covenant, or statute, would be an action for damages, or an injunction.

74. May a tenant, while in possession under a lease, deny his landlord's title?

Answer: No.

75. What is the tenant bound to do upon termination of the tenancy?

Answer: Peaceably surrender the premisess to the landlord.

76. As between lessor and lessee, is a lease valid if not recorded?

Answer: Yes.

77. What is an "assignment" of a lease?

Answer: One assigns a lease when the balance of the entire term is transferred to the assignee, leaving no reversion or right of re-entry in the assignor.

78. What is a "subletting"?

    Answer: A subletting occurs when less than the entire balance of the term is transferred to the sublessee, leaving a reversion in the sublessor, or original lessee, subletting.

79. May the lessee ordinarily assign or sublet?

    Answer: Yes. Unless there is a provision in the lease against assigning or subletting.

80. Give one example of an assignment of a lease by operation of law.

    Answer: In case of the insolvency of the lessee resulting in bankruptcy, there is an assignment of the lease, by operation of law, to the trustee in bankruptcy.

81. What uses of the property are generally prohibited in the ordinary lease?

    Answer: Illegal uses and uses other than those for which the lease was given, the same being enumerated in the instrument.

82. What advantage is the covenant providing for re-entry upon breach of covenant or condition?

    Answer: It gives the lessor the right to re-enter the premises upon such breach and remove all persons therefrom.

83. What is a continuing covenant?

    Answer: It is one which binds the covenantor to the performance of like periodic acts.

84. What is a non-continuing covenant?

    Answer: It is one which binds the covenantor to perform a single act.

85. What is a dependent covenant?

    Answer: It is one arising when the performance of the covenant by one party is intended to depend upon the performance of another covenant whether made by the same or the other party.

86. What is an independent covenant?

    Answer: It is one the performance of which is not dependent upon the performance of another covenant by the same or the other party.

CHECKLIST

THE LISTING AGREEMENT

A. Advisably, for the ordinary transaction, use a standard printed form.

B. Determine if the contract of employment to sell real estate is required to be in writing in your state.

C. Determine what type of listing agreement is best suited to the transaction contemplated, i.e., exclusive right to sell, exclusive agency, open or net.

D. Be sure you understand what performance on your part is required before you will be entitled to a commission.

E. Be sure you understand the authority given you under the listing agreement (employment contract).

F. Make sure the terms and conditions upon which the property of your principal is to be sold or otherwise disposed of have been clearly, accurately and adequately set down in the listing agreement.

G. Determine if under the listing agreement you are obliged to do more than produce a buyer ready, willing and able to buy your principal's property upon the terms and conditions set forth in the listing agreement; and if so, just what you must do to earn a commission.

H. Determine if a bilateral contract comes into existence by the execution of the listing agreement.

I. If the listing has a termination date, determine if you have given a promise or any other consideration sufficient in your state to bind the principal not to revoke or withdraw the offer he has made in the listing agreement until the expiration of that termination date.

J. Be sure you understand the nature of the contract of employment (effected by the listing agreement) and the limitation of your authority thereunder.

K. Determine if you have the authority, under the listing agreement, to receive a deposit or any sum of money (as earnest money or otherwise) on behalf of your principal.

L. Make sure that all parties have signed the listing agreement whose signatures will be required, in your state, to convey title to the purchaser. See that all alterations, additions and deletions are properly initialed by all parties to the listing agreement before accepting that agreement.

THE DEPOSIT RECEIPT

A. Advisably, for the ordinary transaction, use a standard form as a market instrument.

B. Make sure the terms and conditions of the Deposit Receipt conform to the terms and conditions set forth in the listing agreement, unless you anticipate negotiation between the prospective purchaser and your principal; in which case be sure your principal will negotiate, or you may be wasting your time. If he will not negotiate, and the terms and conditions set down in the Deposit Receipt do not conform to those in the listing agreement, you have not produced a buyer ready, willing and able to buy on the terms your principal stipulated. In such case you would not be able to collect a commission were the matter to end there.

C. Determine if there is a provision for liquidated damages or forfeiture of deposit in the event of failure on the part of the purchaser to perform. In the standard printed form there will ordinarily be such a provision.

D. Determine if an auxiliary contract of sale is necessary in addition to the Deposit Receipt and Escrow Instructions. Such a contract is always desirable, but not always necessary.

E. Make sure the offer contained in the Deposit Receipt is a firm, unequivocal offer which may be accepted by your principal without further acts on his part. Such an offer should be accompanied by an earnest money deposit.

F. Make sure all alterations, additions and deletions are initialed by all the parties executing the Deposit Receipt.

THE LAND CONTRACT

A. Determine if this contract should be prepared by an attorney at law, or whether a standard printed form will be adequate.

B. Determine if all local laws applicable to this kind of contract, have been complied with.

C. Be sure all the necessary persons have been made parties to the contract, and have executed the same.

D. Be sure the property is properly described in the contract.

E. Be sure all the terms and conditions of sale and purchase are included in the contract, and that they are understood by all the parties, and clearly expressed.

F. Provide for liability, as between the parties, for destruction of the property, or loss by reason of eminent domain proceedings.

G. Provide for insurance of improvements.

H. If a liquidated damage clause is contemplated, check the laws of your state for anti-forfeiture legislation and determine the effect such legislation may have upon the efficacy of such a clause.

I. Determine if it is desirable to include a provision for a conveyance of the property before full payment, and conversion to a security transaction by the employment of a mortgage or deed of trust.

J. Advisably, make time of the essence of such a contract.

K. Be sure that all alterations, additions and deletions are initialed by all the parties.

THE EXCHANGE AGREEMENT

A. Advisably, use a standard printed form for the ordinary transaction.

B. Be sure the equities exchanged have been clearly indicated in this instrument.

C. Be sure that what each party is offering to exchange is clearly set out and understood by the other party.

D. Arrange for proration of fixed charges.

E. Be sure each party has authorized the broker to act on his behalf, and what commission each party is to pay him.

F. Be sure all alterations, additions or deletions have been initialed by all parties.

THE LEASE

A. Advisably, for the ordinary transaction, use a standard form.

B. Determine if all local laws have been complied with.

C. Make sure that there is a clear intention expressed to establish the relationship of lessor and lessee, or landlord or tenant.

D. Be sure the property is clearly and adequately described.

E. Be sure all the necessary names appear in the instrument.

F. Be sure the terms and conditions upon which the lease is given are understood and agreed to by all of the parties.

G. Be sure the rent is fixed.

H. Be sure the term is certain, or is capable of being made certain.

I. Be sure the length of the term for the character of the property leased is lawful in your state.

J. Determine if there is to be a provision against assignment or subletting.

K. Determine if it is desirable to provide for forfeiture in the event of assignment by operation of law, or in the case of insolvency.

L. Be sure there is a provision for maintenance and redelivery in good condition and repair.

M. Be sure there is a covenant against unlawful use and unauthorized use of the premises, and a provision for forfeiture for its breach.

N. Be sure there is a right of re-entry upon breach of covenant or condition.

O. Be sure there is a provision against vitiating the same or any other covenant in the event of waiver.

P. Be sure provision has been made for increased rent in the event of a holding over.

Q. Be sure all alterations, additions and deletions have been initialed by all the parties.

FOOTNOTES

1 See ante, where Agency by ratification is discussed.

2 Federal Income Tax Regulations January 15, 1963 §1.451–1-(a). Under the cash receipts and disbursements method of accounting such an amount is included in gross income when actually or constructively received.

3 See Federal Income Tax Reulations, supra, §1.453.

4 See Federal Income Tax Regulations, supra, §1.453.

5 See Federal Income Tax Regulations, supra, §1.453–4 (b) (2).

6 See Chapter 2, Real Property, 2, Real Estates.

7 This is the language of the ordinary lease. However, the term of a lease need not be expressed in terms of the calendar, however usual this custom may be; the term may be fixed reference to some collateral event which is bound to happen and will enable the duration of the term to be known at any time, such as a lease of the property to John Doe "during the minority of Richard Roe," an individual in existence whose age may be ascertained.

8 See Chapter 2, Real Property, 2 Real Estates.

6

The Patent and the Deed

1. The United States Patent

A patent may serve one of two purposes. It is a conveyance of land from the government to a person who has established a right to ownership of the land. It is also a document evidencing title to land already vested by legislative grant, where a Congressional Act is in words of present grant.

The general rule is that title passes only upon issuance of the patent. However, there are exceptions to this rule, one being when a federal statute has by its wording made an actual grant to take effect presently, needing only the performance of an act on the part of the grantee to enable the land to be identified. In such a case title passes by operation of law, by force and effect of the statute. A patent subsequently issued, even if it is conditioned upon the performance of specified acts of the grantee, is but evidence of title, the title already having vested in the grantee under the statute.

A patent is of the nature of a quitclaim deed, transferring only what interest the government has in the land. It passes no after-acquired title. Nevertheless, it is the highest evidence of title, and is conclusive as against the government and all claiming under junior patents or titles, until it is set aside or annulled by some judicial tribunal. Such action should be undertaken only upon the clearest proofs of fraud or mistake, or where it was not within the competence of the government to transfer the land. The Supreme Court of the United States has aptly said, in effect, that because of the immense importance and necessity of the stability of titles dependent upon these instruments, efforts to annul them, to set them aside or to correct mistakes in them should be successful only upon the most clear, unequivocal and convincing evidence recognized by the law as capable of effecting that result.

139

The decisions of the Bureau of Land Management, not induced by error in law, fraud or mistake, are conclusive as to the facts upon which a patent is issued. But there exists in courts of equity the jurisdiction and power to correct mistakes of law and fact, to relieve against fraud and imposition even though a patent must be annulled by reason thereof. A patent may be collaterally impeached when it can be shown that the government had no authority to dispose of the land.

A patent usually cites the Congressional Act under which the patent issues, and recites reservations and exceptions required by the law authorizing its issuance.

While it is not necessary to record a patent in the County Recorder's office where the land is located, it is good practice to do so, as it tends to show a marketable title.

A patent, to be valid, must be countersigned by the recorder in the Bureau of Land Management, although its validity does not depend upon its recordation.

To check title through a patent the following records should be examined.

Records of the local Land Office
Records of the Bureau of Land Management in Washington, D.C.
Records of the County Recorder's Office where the land is located.

2. The Deed

Estates in land are usually transferred *inter vivos* (between living persons) by deed and by lease. The lease has been discussed in Chapter 5. Here the deed will be considered.

A deed is a writing by which title to real property is conveyed from one legally existing person to another. While there are various kinds of deeds used

in the establishment or perfection of real property rights in land, three principal forms are usually employed in the transfer of interests in real estate transactions. These are the grant, bargain and sale deed, the warranty deed and the quitclaim deed. A simple grant deed is used in some states.

A distinction is made between the indenture and the deed poll. The indenture is executed by both grantor and grantee. Each party's signature to the deed binds him to perform the covenants on his part to be performed.

The deed poll is executed only by the grantor. Nevertheless, the acceptance by the grantee of delivery of the deed, in most jurisdictions, binds him to the performance of the covenants written into the instrument on the theory of an implied promise to perform them evidenced by acceptance of the deed.

In most American jurisdictions neither a seal nor attesting witnesses are required to give a deed validity. In some states, however, both a seal and an attesting witness or witnesses are requisites.[1] In other states a seal is required, but witnesses are dispensed with,[2] while in others no seal is necessary, but attesting witnesses are demanded.[3] In some of these states attesting witnesses are not required if the deed is acknowledged.

Certain matters of form and substance ought to be considered in appraising the validity and effectiveness of a deed. The deed should be a writing containing effective words of conveyance indicating the intention of the grantor to pass title to the grantee. The grantor should be capable in law of conveying real property, that is to say, he must not be a minor, an insane person or any other person under the law incapable of transferring real property. Both the grantor and the grantee should be identified in the deed, and neither of them may be a fictitious person. The grantee must be a legal person in existence and capable in law of accepting delivery of the instrument, and of taking title. The property to be transferred must be identified in the deed. The deed must effect a present transfer of the title, although the interest conveyed may be a future interest postponing the right to possession and enjoyment of the estate by the grantee.

The instrument must be signed (if a deed poll, by the grantor; if an indenture, by both grantor and grantee), sealed (in those states where a seal is required), attested by witnesses (where required), acknowledged (where required), delivered to the grantee and accepted by him.

A deed takes effect upon delivery. There is a rebuttable presumption that it was delivered upon its date. The date does not affect the deed's validity.

A deed does not, in the absence of statute, require a consideration to give it validity. But covenants in a deed may need a consideration to support them, and its absence may well prevent their enforceability. Where creditors of the grantor are concerned lack of consideration may prove fatal as when such creditors (under the Uniform Fraudulent Conveyance Act) have an equity superior to the transferee, and a right to prevent the grantor from making a voluntary conveyance of his property, or one without adequate consideration.

When a deed is said to be "executed" it is meant that it has been signed by the parties, and, where such acts are required, sealed, attested and acknowledged. It also implies its delivery by the grantor and acceptance by the grantee. However, the term is frequently used only to include the signing, and where necessary the sealing, attesting and acknowledging formalities.

A deed may contain EXCEPTIONS and RESERVATIONS. An exception in a deed excepts out of the grant a part of the property or thing granted, which then remains in the grantor.

> *EXAMPLE:*   John Doe grants to Richard Roe that certain parcel of land located in White County, State of Y, particularly described as the Northwest Quarter of the Northwest Quarter of Section 20, Township 18 North, Range 10 West, M.D.B. & M., excepting therefrom that certain piece or parcel of land heretofore and on or about the tenth day of August,

1965, conveyed by John Doe to Allen Poe and consisting of two acres, more or less, deed recorded August 11, 1965, in Book 121 of Official Records at page 100, of White County Records, State of Y.

THE RESERVATION

A reservation in a deed creates a right for the benefit of the grantor in the property granted which did not exist prior to the reservation as a separate and distinct right.

> *EXAMPLE:* John Doe grants to Richard Roe that certain parcel of land located in White County, State of Y, particularly described as the Northwest Quarter of the Northwest Quarter of Section 20, Township 18 North, Range 10 West, M.D.B. & M., reserving to the grantor, his heirs and assigns forever an easement for a road and right of way twenty feet in width along the west line of said parcel of land and for its full length.

DELIVERY ACTUAL, CONSTRUCTIVE

Title passes upon delivery of the deed. Delivery may be actual or constructive. It is actual when there has been a physical delivery of the instrument to the grantee by the grantor with intent to pass title. In the absence of physical delivery, there may be constructive delivery if it is evident that the grantor by his words and conduct intends to relinquish all control and ownership of the deed (even though it is still in his possession) and has no right to retain it, intending title to pass to the grantee.

RECORDING NOT DELIVERY

Recording a deed by the grantor raises only a presumption of delivery. It is not delivery in law. Subsequent acceptance of the deed by the grantee would ordinarily, effect legal delivery.

REDELIVERY OR CANCELLATION OF DEED DOES NOT RETRANSFER TITLE

When a grantor has delivered a deed with intent to transfer title and the grantee has accepted delivery, title is vested in the grantee and a mere redelivery or cancellation of the deed does not have the effect in law of restoring the property to the grantor.

Any interest in real property may be conveyed, whether present or future, vested or contingent; also an equitable interest.

PROPERTY DESCRIPTION MUST IDENTIFY THE LAND

The purpose of describing property in a deed is, of course, to identify the land to be conveyed. And while the courts have exercised much patience in the matter of passing upon the adequacy of descriptions, it is the prudent thing to exercise reasonable care in preparing descriptive material for inclusion in conveyances. LEGAL description should be employed whenever possible, with resort to popular description only when none other is available under the pressure of circumstances. Great care should then be exercised to identify with certainty the property to be transferred.

DEED MUST BE DELIVERED UNCONDITIONALLY

The general rule is that a deed cannot be delivered conditionally to the grantee. It may, however, be deposited in escrow or "delivered" to a third person to be held pending the happening of a certain event, upon the happening of which it is to be delivered unconditionally to the grantee. In such case the instrument becomes effective as a conveyance upon the "second delivery," when title passes, unless the doctrine of relation back is applied, in which case, the rights of creditors not intervening, title would be deemed as having passed upon the first delivery.

An exception to the general rule is where the grantor delivers his deed to a third person, or into escrow, intending an immediate transfer of title to the grantee named in the deed, but postponing possession and enjoyment of the estate to a future time, usually to the death of the grantor. The condition of the escrow is that the deed is to be delivered unconditionally to the grantee upon the death of the grantor. See Chapter 10 for further discussion of this exception to the general rule.

EXCEPTION

Generally, delivery is not effective to transfer title without acceptance by the grantee. But acceptance will be presumed under some circumstances, and by the doctrine of relation back title will be deemed to have passed at the time of conditional delivery, unless the equities of third persons entitled to protection, have intervened.

DELIVERY MUST BE ACCEPTED

In the absence of statute the signatures of the parties to a deed need not be in ink. Pencil will suffice. A signature may be by mark if properly authenticated and attested to; or in the handwriting of another if lawfully authorized, either by prior authority or by adoption and ratification; or when subscribed to the instrument at the request and in the presence of the party whose signature is required.

SIGNATURES HOW SUBSCRIBED

In both the warranty and the grant, bargain and sale deed, when the grant is not limited to a particular estate, the instrument carries all the interest the grantor has in the land conveyed, which in the ordinary real estate transaction is a fee simple. The grant also passes any after-acquired title to property the grantor had intended or purported to convey in his warranty or grant deed.

WARRANTY AND GRANT DEEDS CARRY ENTIRE INTEREST OF GRANTOR UNLESS ESTATE GRANTED IS LIMITED: ALSO AFTER-ACQUIRED TITLE

A mere quitclaim deed (which carries only the right, title and interest of the grantor in the land at the time of the execution of the deed) does not pass to the grantee any title or interest subsequently acquired by the grantor. To understand what this means, the true character of a quitclaim deed must be understood. Such a deed, properly speaking, does not convey the land itself; it releases or quit-claims to the grantee whatever interest or title the grantor may have in the land. If such a deed does more than this, and actually conveys the land, the fee simple estate in the land, it is something more than a simple quitclaim deed of release. The question is one of intention of the parties, and becomes important when the grantor's after-acquired title is claimed by the grantee. If the deed is a mere quitclaim it does not carry such after-acquired title to the grantee. If however, the language of the deed indicates the unimpeached intention of the grantor to convey the land itself, then, notwithstanding words of quitclaim may have been used in the deed, the instrument will ordinarily pass after-acquired title to the grantee.[4]

QUITCLAIM DEED NATURE: DOES NOT PASS AFTER-ACQUIRED TITLE

Upon delivery of the deed by the grantor and acceptance by the grantee title passes and the deed ceases to be an operative instrument. Henceforth, in law, it is merely evidence of title. Its loss, destruction, assignment, re-delivery to the grantor, or other disposition can ordinarily, in law, have no effect upon title and ownership of the land conveyed. However, there are certain equitable remedies open to the parties not available to them in a court of law in those cases where justice and good conscience dictate relief, which may very definitely affect the title and ownership of property previously conveyed. But these remedies are not within the scope of this book.

QUESTIONS AND ANSWERS

1. What, briefly, is a patent?

   Answer: A government conveyance of public land.

2. What two functions may a patent serve?

   Answer: It vests title. In some cases it is merely evidence of title.

3. What is the nature of a patent?

   Answer: It is in the nature of a quitclaim deed, but it is the highest evidence of title.

4. Briefly define a deed.

   Answer: It is a writing by which title to real property is conveyed from one legally existing person to another.

5. Name two kinds of deeds used in real estate transactions.

   Answer: Grant, bargain and sale deed. Warranty deed.

6. What is a quitclaim deed?

   Answer: A quitclaim deed transfers all the right, title and interest a person has in property.

7. Distinguish between a deed poll and an indenture.

   Answer: Briefly, a deed poll is executed only by the grantor. An indenture is executed by both grantor and grantee.

8. Does the acceptance of a deed poll by the grantee bind him to the performance of the covenants on his part to be performed in the deed?

   Answer: Yes, ordinarily.

9. Is a seal required in most states to make a deed valid?

   Answer: No.

10. Are attesting witnesses required in most states?

    Answer: No. However, seals and attesting witnesses are required in a number of the states.

11. Name some essentials of a valid deed.

    Answer: It must be in writing. The grantor and grantee must be identified. Grantor must be capable in law of conveying property. The parties cannot be fictitious persons. Grantee must be a legal person in existence and capable in law of accepting delivery of the instrument and taking title. Property must be identified and described. The deed must effect a present transfer of title, although possession or enjoyment of the estate may be deferred or postponed.

12. When does a deed take effect?

    Answer: Upon delivery to the grantee and acceptance by him.

13. Does a deed need consideration to support it?

   Answer: Not ordinarily.

14. What is an exception?

   Answer: That property or thing excepted out of the grant and retained by the grantor or his prior grantee.

15. What is a reservation?

   Answer: It is a right created by the deed for the benefit of the grantor in the property granted which did not exist prior to the reservation; as for instance, the creation of an easement by reservation.

16. Does the recording of a deed effect a delivery?

   Answer: No. It merely raises a presumption of delivery.

17. After delivery and acceptance of a deed, will a re-delivery of the deed to the grantor re-convey the estate to him?

   Answer: No. But there may be some equitable remedy here depending upon the circumstances.

18. In the absence of statute, must the signatures of the parties to a deed be in ink?

   Answer: No. Pencil will suffice.

19. Does a mere quitclaim deed, as distinguished from one sometimes referred to as a quitclaim but actually conveying the land itself, pass after-acquired title?

   Answer: No, unless more than the mere release of an interest in land is involved.

20. When does the deed cease to be an operative instrument?

   Answer: Upon delivery by the grantor to the grantee and the latter's acceptance, title passes, the function of the deed is completed, it ceases to be operative, and is thereafter only evidence of title.

CHECKLIST

A. If a United States patent is involved, determine if the patent was a conveyance, or a document evidencing title vested by prior legislative grant or operation of law.

B. Determine what reservations, if any, the patent contains.

C. Determine what warranties are desirable in the transaction you are handling, and tailor the deed to include the warranties desired, whether implied or expressed.

D. Determine if title insurance will be demanded.

E. Determine if transaction requires that the deed contain specific exceptions or reservations, and if so, be sure such are properly handled.

F. Determine the need for restrictive covenants in the deed.

G. Determine the need for conditions in the deed, and provide accordingly. If limitation of future estates is involved, consult an attorney.

H. Determine if a seal is required to make deed a valid instrument.

I. Determine if an attesting witness or witnesses are required to make deed a valid instrument.

J. Determine the essential requirements of a deed in your state.

K. Determine if the grantee is a legal person capable of accepting a grant.

L. Determine if deed has been properly executed.

FOOTNOTES

1 Check Connecticut, Delaware, Maine, Maryland, New Hampshire, North Carolina, South
  Carolina, Vermont, Wisconsin.

2 Check District of Columbia, Illinois, Massachusetts, New Jersey.

3 Check Alabama, Alaska, Arkansas, Florida, Georgia, Michigan, Minnesota, Missouri, New
  York, Ohio, South Dakota, Tennessee.

4 The statutes and case law of the several states should be examined for more comprehensive
  treatment.

7

The Mortgage and the
Deed of Trust

1. The Mortgage

A. Introduction

The early common law mortgage was a conveyance defeasible upon a condition subsequent, the condition being the payment of the mortgage debt when it became due. Title to the property passed to the creditor, the debtor regaining ownership when he paid the debt. This is what we speak of today as the TITLE[1] THEORY of mortgage as contrasted with the LIEN THEORY.

Courts of equity early recognized the need for the debtor to pay his debt and do it within a resonable time if he would recover his land freed from the obligation of the debt. Equity therefore developed the doctrine of the equity of redemption (the right to redeem). This equitable relief permitted the debtor to recover ownership of his property upon payment of the debt within a time after it became due fixed by a proceeding to foreclose the equity of redemption. If this equity was foreclosed by failure of the debtor to pay the debt within the time fixed, the effect was to vest an indefeasible title to the land in the mortgagee. The procedure later became known as a strict foreclosure, and is allowed in a number of states[2] recognizing the title theory of mortgage. Mortgages in one or two of the title theory states are also foreclosed by peaceable entry[3] of the mortgagee, or under a WRIT OF ENTRY,[4] or by a WRIT OF SCIRE FACIAS.[5]

The development of the method of foreclosure is away from the practices just mentioned. The modern tendency in the majority of the states, whether recognizing the title or the lien theory, is to break away from the old common law doctrine and to adopt procedures, usually statutory, which in effect enforce a special lien against the property to secure payment of the debt. And to realize such payment, the levy and execution of a deficiency judgment is allowed in

CONVEYANCE DE-
FEASIBLE UPON A
CONDITION
SUBSEQUENT

TITLE THEORY

EQUITY OF
REDEMPTION

STRICT FORECLO-
SURE

PEACEABLE ENTRY

WRIT OF ENTRY

WRIT OF SCIRE
FACIAS

SUIT IN EQUITY
AND SALE OF
PROPERTY

151

most of the states in the event the proceeds of the sale do not satisfy the mortgage debt. The statutes of a particular state should be examined to determine the nature of this kind of judgment and its qualifications.

B. The Lien Theory of Mortgage

THE LIEN THEORY OF MORTGAGE

For all practical purposes, except in a few states which have adopted strict foreclosure, or its equivalent, the foreclosure of mortgages is effected as though they were special liens on the mortgagor's property (whether or not the instrument takes the form of a grant) to be enforced by a suit in equity, or a similar proceeding, followed by a sale of the mortgaged property to satisfy the mortgage debt. This is the usual practice in those states recognizing the lien[6] theory. In the lien theory states title does not pass to the mortgagee. The title remains in the mortgagor, the mortgagee having a mortgage lien on the property to secure the payment of the debt.

Very often in the lien theory states an absolute conveyance is made to secure an obligation. In these states such a conveyance can be proved, by evidence outside of the instrument itself, to be a mortgage, and will then be treated as a lien on the property of the mortgagor (grantor) and disposed of as a conventional mortgage. Such a conveyance does not transfer title to the grantee (mortgagee) as against the grantor (mortgagor); but a bona fide purchaser for value without notice of the character of the instrument will be protected.

C. The Form of the Mortgage

FORM OF THE MORTGAGE

In some states the form of mortgage to be used is prescribed by statute. In others, no form is prescribed. Nevertheless, in all of the states it will be found that statute, court decision and custom have all contributed to fix the form of mortgage generally employed in a particular jurisdiction. Unless the reader is familiar with the commonly acceptable form recognized in the state in which he wishes to do business, he would be well advised to make proper inquiry. But here, again, he must be cautioned not to assume the responsibilities or the functions of an attorney at law.

D. The Right to Possession of the Mortgaged Land

RIGHT TO POSSESSION

Broadly stated, it may be said that the mortgagee's position with respect to title and the right to possession of the mortgaged land runs, in the several states, all the way from no title and no right to possession,[7] through both title and the right to possession upon default of the mortgagor,[8] to the right to possession and title, the estate being defeasible upon a condition subsequent.[9] Of course, the parties may agree between themselves as to whom possession may be given.

MORTGAGEE IN POSSESSION

By taking possession of the mortgaged property as a mortgagee in possession, in those states which permit this to be done, the mortgagee acquires no additional right to enforce the mortgage debt, but he cannot ordinarily be ejected by the mortgagor so long as the mortgage debt is unpaid. On the other hand, the mortgagee assumes the burden of accounting to the mortgagor for the rents, issues and profits from the operation of the property, and must conduct himself as a reasonably prudent man would be expected to manage his own affairs.

Whether possession should or should not be taken will depend largely upon the character of the property and the moral and financial integrity of the mortgagor-debtor. An unscrupulous mortgagor in possession under a purchase money mortgage, for instance, could very well destroy the value of a good piece of property in a short time. In such case it might be well for the mortgagee to go into possession not only to increase his security, but to preserve the property from destruction should he be obliged to repossess it. The mortgage ought to provide for the right to such possession in the event of breach or default on the part of the mortgagor, or for an obvious physical impairment of the mortgage security.

E. The Obligation Secured

Generally speaking, a mortgage is given to secure a debt or obligation, past, present or future. While the ordinary obligation is usually evidenced by a promissory note, it need not be. The mortgage secures the obligation itself, not the evidence of the obligation. Therefore, the general rule is that even though an action to enforce payment of the note were to be outlawed by a statute of limitation, this fact would not affect the validity of the obligation and the mortgage securing it, although by statute an action may not lie for the collection of the note, nor a remedy be available to foreclose the mortgage. However, an obligation is not destroyed by lapse of time, and therefore equity will not permit a mortgagee lawfully in possession to be ejected until the mortgage obligation is paid.

ORDINARY OBLIGATION EVIDENCED BY NOTE

RIGHTS OF MORTGAGEE IN POSSESSION

The mortgagor is not necessarily personally liable for the mortgage debt. The mortgage may be given to secure an obligation and a provision written therein exempting the mortgagor from personal liability. In some states, by statute, the creation of a lien does not imply that any person is bound to perform the act for which the lien is a security; nor does a mortgage bind the mortgagor personally to perform the act for the performance of which it is a security, unless there is an express covenant therein to that effect. This has sometimes been called a "dry" mortgage. In such cases payment would be limited to the proceeds from the sale of the mortgaged premises, no deficiency judgment being available to the mortgagee. Often this exemption is effected by statute, as in the case of a purchase-money mortgage, the foreclosure of which in a number of the states does not permit a deficiency judgment over against the mortgagor, should the sale price of the property fall short of the amount due on the note or mortgage. In some states, even in the case of the ordinary mortgage, the amount which may be recovered by a deficiency judgment is limited in such a way that the full dollar benefit-of-bargain acquired by the

THE "DRY" MORTGAGE

WHEN MORTGAGOR NOT PERSONALLY LIABLE

MORTGAGEE MAY
BE DENIED HIS
BENEFIT OF BAR-
GAIN

mortgagee in his negotiations with the purchaser-mortgagor, may be substantially minimized, if not completely lost. This may occur where a statute
provides that the court shall render a deficiency judgment against the mortgagor for the amount by which the indebtedness exceeds the fair value of the
property at the time of its sale.[10]

HOW PERSONAL
LIABILITY IS AS-
SUMED

To the extent that the mortgagor is required by the laws of the several
states to meet his obligation, he may become personally liable for the mortgage
debt in any number of ways by which a man may lawfully contract to pay an
obligation. However, the usual manner of binding himself personally is to
accompany the mortgage with his personal note, or to write a covenant in
the mortgage instrument to pay the debt secured. In some states a bond accompanies or is combined with the mortgage, forming the basis for personal
liability of the mortgagor.

OTHER COVE-
NANTS, AND AC-
CELERATION
CLAUSE

A mortgage may be security for the performance of an act, or it may indem-
nify against loss. Frequently the mortgagor covenants to perform certain acts,
such as to pay current taxes assessed against the property, to provide adequate
fire insurance coverage, to maintain the premises in good condition and repair,
and not to commit waste. These covenants are usually followed by an acceleration clause making all sums secured by the mortgage immediately due and
payable upon breach of any covenant or condition in the instrument. Inasmuch as the principal sum is likewise secured by the mortgage, a breach of
any such covenant permits remedy by foreclosure if the principal obligation
is not then promptly paid. State law will, of course, regulate the procedure
required successfully to foreclose the mortgage.

F. Assignment of the Mortgage Debt

ASSIGNMENT OF
MORTGAGE DEBT

The general rule is that an assignment of the debt carries with it the mortgage security. But an assignment of the mortgage itself will not ordinarily carry
the debt unless the intention of the parties can be made out to that effect.

G. Change in the Form of the Evidence of the Mortgage Debt
Does Not Discharge the Mortgage

NOVATION

Should there be an effective novation, as where a new note and mortgage
was substituted for the old note and mortgage, or where the new note was
intended to pay off the original obligation, thereby extinguishing the old
mortgage debt, such a novation, or new note, will usually have the effect of

DEBT SUBSTAN-
TIALLY THE SAME

CHANGE IN THE
FORM OF THE
EVIDENCE

discharging the mortgage. But if the principal obligation remains substantially
the same and not entirely paid, a change in the manner of payment, or in the
form of the evidence of the obligation will not discharge the mortgage security,
unless it is so intended by the parties. While it would seem that to change the
interest rate, or the manner of making payments, or the due date of a note,
would be in effect to substitute a quite different obligation for the one recognized at the time the mortgage was written, yet, except in the case where a
mortgage is given by a surety to secure the debt of a third person, or suretyship

is otherwise involved, the general rule supports the equitable doctrine that the original debt remains the same for the purpose of keeping the mortgage alive. Only the manner of payment of the obligation, or the evidence of its existence, is deemed changed.

The broker, or other person interested in the real estate business, is cautioned, however, not to change or alter the evidence of indebtedness secured by a mortgage without first consulting a lawyer.

WARNING

H. Sale of Mortgaged Property

The mortgagor has a right to sell the mortgaged property. He may pay off the mortgage debt and sell it discharged of the mortgage lien, or he may sell it subject to the mortgage, or, he may require the purchaser to *assume* the mortgage and pay the debt.

SALE OF MORT-GAGED PROPERTY

• PURCHASER TAKING SUBJECT TO THE MORTGAGE

Where the purchaser takes subject to the mortgage, the following relationships are here considered: Mortgagor-mortgagee; mortgagor-purchaser; mortgagee-purchaser.

The purchaser taking subject to the mortgage is, ordinarily, not personally liable to the mortgagee for the mortgage debt, whatever his liability might be to the mortgagor, his transferor, on the theory of implied convenant. The land is primarily liable for the debt secured, and must be sold to satisfy that debt or so much of it as the proceeds from the sale might satisfy, if the debtor defaults. Any deficiency remaining after the sale is ordinarily charged to the mortgagor. The law may, however, disallow or qualify the deficiency remaining according to the particular circumstances surrounding the transaction involved, or in conformance with area-developed considerations of expediency or justice.

MORTGAGOR'S GRANTEE TAKING SUBJECT TO THE MORTGAGE

Ordinarily, in a case where the grantee [purchaser] of the mortgagor takes the property subject to the mortgage, the liabilities, as between the mortgagor, the purchaser and the mortgagee, unless altered by statute, are usually as follows: 1—the land is primarily liable for the debt; 2—the mortgagor is personally liable to the mortgagee for any deficiency; 3—the purchaser is not personally liable for a deficiency, but if he wishes to hold possession and obtain clear title he must pay the amount due on the debt; 4—the mortgagee may foreclose the mortgage and obtain a deficiency judgment against the mortgagor.

LIABILITIES OF THE PARTIES WHEN PURCHASER TAKES SUBJECT TO THE MORTGAGE

• PURCHASER ASSUMING THE MORTGAGE DEBT

When there has been an assumption of the mortgage debt by the mortgagor's grantee [purchaser], the law applicable to the liabilities of the parties will vary somewhat in the several states. The relationships here considered are: Mortgagor-mortgagee; mortgagee-purchaser; mortgagee-second purchaser (from first purchaser).

The assumption of the mortgage debt and agreement to pay it is ordinarily

MORTGAGOR'S GRANTEE ASSUM-ING THE MORT-GAGE

effected by express language contained in the deed of conveyance, or in a supplemental agreement between the mortgagor and his grantee (purchaser).

LIABILITY OF MORTGAGOR TO MORTGAGEE

The broad, general principle underlying the liability of the mortgagor to the mortgagee is that, ordinarily, this liability is not altered by a transfer of the property to a purchaser.

LIABILITY OF MORTGAGOR'S GRANTEE WHO ASSUMES THE MORTGAGE

A purchaser from the mortgagor who assumes the mortgage ordinarily becomes personally liable to the mortgagee for the mortgage debt. Likewise, such a purchaser's grantee who assumes the mortgage would become liable to the mortgagee. But, had the first purchaser not assumed the mortgage debt, the second purchaser would not, in some jurisdictions, be held liable to the mortgagee notwithstanding he had assumed the mortgage. This result fol-

LIABILITY OF GRANTEE'S PUR-CHASER

lows from the nature of the assumption agreement, or covenant, whereby the purchaser agrees to assume the mortgage debt owing by his grantor. If his grantor has never assumed and agreed to pay the debt, there is nothing his grantee (second purchaser) can assume; and unless a contract for the special benefit of the mortgagee can be made out, the second purchaser cannot be held liable. However, in some states the second purchaser in such a situation is held liable to the mortgagee for the mortgage debt notwithstanding that his grantor did not assume the mortgage obligation. Statutes in a number of states have fixed the rule of law with respect to the liabilities of purchasers of the equity of redemption. These statutes should be consulted.

I. The Purchase-Money Mortgage

THE PURCHASE MONEY MORT-GAGE

A purchase-money mortgage is one usually given by the purchaser to the vendor simultaneously with the delivery of the vendor's deed. It is given to secure payment of the purchase price of the land conveyed. The mortgage need not be given to the vendor to make it a purchase-money mortgage; it may, by statute, be given to anyone who advances the purchase money.

PRIORITY OF PUR-CHASE MONEY MORTGAGE

The purchase-money mortgage ordinarily has priority over all liens with which the purchaser might have attempted to encumber the property before he acquired title, or such general liens as would have attached to the property upon delivery of the deed to him. The delivery of the vendor's deed and the taking back of the purchase-money mortgage is deemed but one, single transaction in which there is no room for a lien to attach.

In some states no deficiency judgment is permitted after foreclosure of a purchase money mortgage.[11]

J. The Power of Sale

POWER OF SALE

Mortgages containing a power of sale are generally recognized throughout the United States, a few states, however, requiring foreclosure by judicial proceeding. In other states the validity of such a power is recognized, but the power is strictly regulated by statute. The power of sale tied into its natural vehicle, the Deed of Trust, is finding much favor in the law of real property, and is receiving increasing support in the several jurisdictions.

2. The Deed of Trust

A. The Deed of Trust a Security Instrument

The deed of trust is a security instrument (executed by the trustor, the trustee and the beneficiary) which transfers title of the property securing the debt to the trustee named therein. The trustee is obligated to hold the title in trust for the purpose of securing payment of the indebtedness. This is usually evidenced by a promissory note of even date with the deed of trust and identified by it. Additional sums which may thereafter be loaned to the trustor or his successors or assigns by the beneficiary are usually covered by the instrument. The deed also secures performance of each promise of the trustor contained in it.

THE DEED OF TRUST

B. Covenants of Trustor for Protection of the Security

The trustor ordinarily agrees to keep the property in good condition and repair; not to remove or destroy any building, and to restore in good, workmanlike manner any building damaged or destroyed, and to complete any structure commenced on the property. The trustor also covenants to provide and maintain fire insurance satisfactory to, and with the loss payable to, the beneficiary; to pay before delinquent all taxes which might become a lien on the property.

COVENANTS OF TRUSTOR FOR PROTECTION OF THE SECURITY

The trustor covenants that should he fail to make any payment or to do any act as required in the instrument to preserve and protect the security of the deed of trust, then in such event, the trustee or the beneficiary, but without obligation so to do, may make or do the same and enter upon the property for that purpose; that the cost and expense of such work may be charged to the trustor, who agrees to pay, immediately and without demand, all such sums expended by the trustee or beneficiary.

C. Mutual Covenants

The deed of trust also ordinarily provides for the allocation of proceeds in the case of condemnation proceedings. The right of the beneficiary to go into possession upon default of the trustor and apply the rents, issues and profits of the property to payment of the secured debt is likewise agreed between the parties.

MUTUAL COVENANTS

D. The Default Clause

A default clause provides that upon default by the trustor in payment of any indebtedness secured by the instrument, or in performance of any agreement thereunder, all sums secured by the deed of trust shall immediately become due and payable at the option of the beneficiary. Upon demand of beneficiary, and in accordance with the law, the trustee is obliged to cause the property to be sold under the power of sale contained in the deed of trust, and apply the proceeds of the sale, after deducting proper costs, to the parties

DEFAULT CLAUSE

legally entitled thereto. The trustee must deliver his trustee's deed to the purchaser of the property at the sale.

OTHER PROVISIONS

Provision is made for a substitution of trustees by the beneficiary, in accordance with law.

The parties agree that the deed of trust applies to, inures to the benefit of, and binds all parties thereto, their heirs, legatees, devisees, administrators, executors, successors and assigns. The term "beneficiary" as used in the instrument is defined as signifying the holder and owner of the note secured by the deed, or, if the note has been pledged, the pledgee thereof.

A provision is often incorporated to the effect that the trustee accepts the trust set forth in the instrument when the deed of trust, duly executed and acknowledged, shall have been made a public record as provided by law.

There is not yet a complete uniformity in the use of deeds of trust in the several states. The practice in a particular state should be enquired into before choosing the security instrument best suited to the transaction in hand.

QUESTIONS AND ANSWERS

1. What is the title theory of mortgages?

   Answer: Title to the property mortgaged is transferred to the mortgagee.

2. What is the lien theory of mortgages?

   Answer: The mortgagor retains title to his property, the mortgage being but a lien, or charge against the property.

3. In the lien theory states, may an absolute deed be shown to be a mortgage?

   Answer: Yes.

4. What advantage has a mortgagee in possession?

   Answer: He ordinarily cannot be ejected until the mortgage debt is paid.

5. Does a mortgage ordinarily secure a promissory note?

   Answer: Strictly speaking, it secures the obligation, not the evidence of the obligation.

6. May a mortgage become the security for an act other than the payment of a debt?

   Answer: Yes.

7. When the mortgage debt is assigned, what is the effect upon the mortgage?

   Answer: The mortgage accompanies the debt.

8. Will a change in the manner of payment (i.e., changing the manner of making payments, the form of the note, etc.) ordinarily discharge the mortgage security?

   Answer: Not ordinarily, so long as the original obligation remains.

9. May the mortgagor sell the mortgaged property?

   Answer: Yes.

10. Ordinarily, when a purchaser from the mortgagor takes subject to the mortgage, is he personally liable to the mortgagee for the mortgage debt?

    Answer: No. The mortgagee could not have a deficiency judgment over for the balance of the debt.

11. What is always primarily liable for the debt?

    Answer: The land mortgaged.

12. Is the mortgagor's vendee, who assumes the mortgage, personally liable to the mortgagee for the mortgage debt?

    Answer: Yes.

13. Is the vendee of the mortgagor's vendee (who assumes the mortgage) personally liable to the mortgagee for the mortgage debt, where the mortgagor's vendee took only subject to the mortgage?

    Answer: In some states he is not liable. In others he is.

14. Does a purchase-money mortgage have priority over a judgment lien against the purchaser before purchasing the property, or charged against the property by the purchaser before he acquires title to the property?

Answer: Yes, in both instances.

15. May a deficiency judgment be obtained after foreclosure of a purchase-money mortgage?

Answer: The general rule is, no.

16. Is a power of sale in a mortgage generally recognized throughout the United States?

Answer: Yes. A few states require foreclosure by judicial procedure; in others the power is strictly regulated.

17. Is the deed of trust recognized generally in the several states?

Answer: Yes, it is receiving increasing support.

18. Does employment of the deed of trust as a security instrument expedite enforcement of the secured obligation, and settlement of the title to the property?

Answer: Ordinarily it does. There is no equity of redemption, nor statutory redemption after sale under the power in a deed of trust; nor, ordinarily, other delays incident to foreclosure by judicial proceedings.

CHECKLIST

A. If your principal is not assuming the mortgage debt, be sure the proper language is used in the deed or other instrument employed.

B. Check your state law to determine what liability to the mortgagee is imposed by operation of law upon a grantee taking subject to the mortgage.

C. Check your state law to learn in what circumstances a deficiency judgment may be taken against your principal (this will depend upon his position in the transaction) in the event of a default in the payment of the mortgage debt. Good business practice suggests you know this.

D. Determine if your state is a *title* theory or a *lien* theory state.

E. If your principal is the creditor, consider the desirability of a deed of trust over a mortgage as a security instrument in your state.

FOOTNOTES

1 The title theory is recognized in Alabama, Arkansas, Conecticut, Illinois, Maine, Maryland, Massachusetts, Mississippi, New Hampshire, New Jersey, North Carolina, Ohio, Pennsylvania, Rhode Island, Tennessee, Vermont, Virginia, West Virginia.

2 Connecticut, Vermont, Illinois.

3 Maine, Massachusetts, New Hampshire and Rhode Island.

4 Maine, Massachusetts, New Hampshire.

5 Delaware, Pennsylvania.

6 The lien theory is recognized in Alaska, Arizona, California, Colorado, Delaware, Florida, Georgia, Hawaii, Idaho, Indiana, Iowa, Kansas, Kentucky, Louisiana, Michigan, Minnesota, Missouri, Montana, Nebraska, Nevada, New Mexico, New York, North Dakota, Oklahoma, Oregon, Puerto Rico, South Carolina, South Dakota, Texas, Utah, Virgin Islands, Washington, Wisconsin, Wyoming.

7 This is the usual situation in a majority of the states recognizing the lien theory.

8 This is, in effect, a compromise between the title and lien theories effected to better carry out the concept of justice in security matters in the particular jurisdiction adopting this intermediary procedure.

9 This is generally true in those states which recognize the title theory of mortgage.

10 California Code of Civil Procedure §726

11 California Code of Civil Procedure §580b

8

The Mechanic's Lien

1. The Lien

A. The Nature of the Lien

The mechanic's lien is a particular lien as distinguished from a general lien. It is purely statutory, being unknown to the common law and to equity. Its purpose is to secure payment of labor performed on, and materials going into a work of improvement on real property.

A PARTICULAR LIEN SECURES PAY-MENT FOR LABOR AND MATERIALS

Practically every state has enacted mechanic's lien laws. Inasmuch as the lien, its status and enforcement, is controlled by statutes which in some degree differ in the several states, discussion will be limited to general principles of law recognized in many jurisdictions.

2. The Contract

A. Need for a Contract

A written contract is not essential in all jurisdictions to establish a foundation for the lien. Nevertheless, improvements are usually undertaken by written contract between the party initiating the work of improvement and either a general contractor, or a number of separate contractors. The labor performed or the materials furnished must be performed or furnished under a valid, enforceable agreement made with the owner of the improvement or his authorized agent, before a mechanic's lien can be asserted. The owner in such case is either the owner of the fee, or the owner of a lesser estate or equitable interest in the land. This is not to say that a mechanic's lien will not attach to the property of a noncontracting owner if he has knowledge of the work of improvement and fails to file and post a Notice of Non-Responsibility within the time allowed by law. In some states the owner will not be held liable even though he has knowledge of the work of improvement.

USUALLY A WRITTEN CONTRACT

The statutes in the several jurisdictions establish the mechanic's lien laws of each jurisdiction. These statutes are interpreted by the courts of the state in which they are found in harmony with the theory of lien law developed in that jurisdiction. Therefore, the statutes and decided cases of the state in which the law is to be applied should be carefully read and understood.

3. Property Which May Be Liened and Its Owners

A. Common Situations

In determining to what property the mechanic's lien will attach it is essential to understand the relationship the land, as distinguished from the improvement, bears to the party contracting for the labor and materials. It is also important to know the character of the estate held by the contracting party. These factors give rise to a number of relevant situations. The usual situations are:

> The fee owner contracting with the contractor.
> The lessee contracting with the contractor.
> The vendee in possession under an executory contract of sale contracting with the contractor.
> The vendor under an executory contract of sale contracting with the contractor.
> The landlord owning the fee contracting with the contractor.

There are other situations, but these are the common ones.

• THE FEE OWNER CONTRACTING WITH THE CONTRACTOR SITUATION

This situation imports no other property interest or persons, the fee owner simply contracting for the erection of the structure or improvement for his own use and benefit. The property involved is the fee simple to which the "owner" has title, and the work of improvement. And the question is—to what does the lien attach?

LIEN ATTACHES TO
LAND AND IM-
PROVEMENT

WHEN IMPROVE-
MENT IS DE-
STROYED: TWO
LINES OF DE-
CISIONS
The general rule is that the lien will attach to both the land and the improvement. When, however, the improvement has been involuntarily destroyed, whether or not the lien continues to attach to the land depends upon the wording of the statute in the particular jurisdiction. If the statute creates an unqualified lien upon both land and improvements, the destruction of the improvement will not ordinarily discharge the lien on the land. But, if the statute makes the lien attach primarily to the improvement or structure, and only secondarily or incidentally to the land, then it is likely to be held that the lien will be lost with the destruction of the improvement. Where the destruction has occurred by reason of the fault of the owner, the land has been held subject to the mechanic's lien.

• THE LESSEE CONTRACTING WITH THE CONTRACTOR SITUATION

To simplify the situation, we are assuming the lessor is a fee owner of the land leased. Frequently the lessee makes the improvement under the terms and conditions of the lease contract. At other times, the lessee constructs the improvement without first consulting the lessor.

The general rule is that ordinarily an owner's land cannot be liened for improvements placed thereon by a lessee, unless it can be said that the owner has "ratified" the contract of the lessee with the builder, either actually or by his conduct. Sometimes it is said merely that he "consents" to, or authorizes the construction of the improvement by failing to file a Notice of Non-Responsibility.

ORDINARILY OWNER'S LAND NOT LIENABLE FOR LESSEE'S WORK OF IMPROVEMENT

If the owner-lessor has no knowledge, either actual or constructive, of the lessee's work of improvement, under the general rule a lien will not attach to his land. But when the lease contract provides that the lessee shall make certain improvements, the courts generally hold that the land of the lessor-owner may be liened inasmuch as the lessor has under such provisions in the lease appointed the lessee his agent to contract for the labor and materials required for the improvement. This is not generally the rule, however, if the language of the lease is permissive rather than mandatory, the lessor-owner in such case being usually able to protect his land by posting and recording a Notice of Non-Responsibility.

FAILURE OF OWNER TO POST AND RECORD NOTICE OF NON-RESPONSIBILITY

LESSOR WITHOUT KNOWLEDGE OF IMPROVEMENT

LEASE REQUIRES LESSEE TO IM-PROVE, OR MERELY PERMITS LESSEE TO IM-PROVE

If the lessor-owner has protected his land against the lien by posting and recording a Notice of Non-Responsibility, the lien would, ordinarily, be enforceable against the building or structure and the lessee's interest in the land, which would, of course, be his leasehold estate.

LIEN ATTACHES TO IMPROVEMENT AND LESSEE'S INTEREST IN LAND

- *THE VENDEE IN POSSESSION UNDER AN EXECUTORY CONTRACT OF SALE, CONTRACTING WITH THE CONTRACTOR SITUATION*

The general rule is that for the purpose of the mechanics' lien law the vendee in possession under an executory contract of sale is the "owner" contracting with the builder. Therefore, the fact that the vendee has erected a building on the land does not, of itself, make the interest of the vendor liable to a mechanic's lien. When and under what circumstances then, may the vendor's interest be liened? And here the language of the several state statutes, as interpreted by the appellate courts in the particular jurisdiction, will control.

VENDEE IN POS-SESSION DEEMED OWNER

STATUTES AND INTERPRETATION BY APPELLATE COURTS DECIDE RULE OF LAW APPLICABLE

Some courts have held that the interest of the vendor cannot be made liable to the lien even though he has knowledge that the labor and materials are being furnished the vendee. On the other hand, it has been held that to protect his interest the vendor, if he has knowledge of the work of improvement, must post and record a Notice of Non-Responsibility, in which case the mechanic's lien extends only to the improvement.

If it can be said that the improvement was made with the consent and permission of the vendor, or that the vendor authorized the construction of the improvement, as where the executory contract of sale expressly provides that the vendee shall erect certain improvements, then the lien will attach to the vendor's interest under some statutes. And where the contract obligates the vendee to build, it is sometimes said that the vendee is made the agent of the vendor, and where statutes permit a lien to attach for work done at the

VENDEE AGENT OF VENDOR

request of the owner or his agent, the lien will attach to the vendor's interest in the land. But in other jurisdictions the vendor's property may escape the lien by the timely posting and recording of a Notice of Non-responsibility.

• THE VENDOR UNDER AN EXECUTORY CONTRACT OF SALE CONTRACTING WITH THE CONTRACTOR SITUATION

VENDOR CON-TRACTING

The land cannot escape mechanic's liens where the owner-vendor of record has contracted for a work of improvement thereon, although previously having secretly conveyed such land to another. The contractor would, ordinarily, be entitled to enforce his lien for materials and labor furnished before he knew that such a conveyance existed. Likewise, the lien would follow the property into the ownership of a conditional vendee, with knowledge of work performed, who had acquired title after the lien had attached to the property, for labor and material furnished the conditional vendor.

• THE LANDLORD OWNING THE FEE CONTRACTING WITH THE CONTRACTOR SITUATION

LANDLORD CON-TRACTING

If the landlord contracts for the construction of the improvement on land he has leased, either under a provision in the lease contract or where the tenant has acted as his agent in the premises, ordinarily the lien will attach to both the land and the improvement.

4. The Notice of Non-Responsibility and Persons Entitled to Lien

As we have seen, an owner's land, or the estate or interest he has in it, is generally liable to be liened by persons performing labor or supplying materials used in the construction of a work of improvement thereon, if the owner can, in any manner indicated by the several mechanic's lien law statutes, be said to be responsible for or consent to such improvement.

PURPOSE OF NOTICE OF NON-RESPONSIBILITY

The Notice of Non-Responsibility is an instrument intended to prevent a mechanic's lien from attaching to an owner's estate or interest in land when he is not responsible for, or has no knowledge of a structure or building erected thereon. After acquiring knowledge of the work of improvement, he has a statutory period of time within which to file such a notice. He must, however, have neither actual nor constructive knowledge of such improvement for a longer time than the statute allows in order to avail himself of the protection of the notice. And even though a lien may have been filed before the owner has knowledge of the work being done, it will be made ineffective upon his posting and recording a Notice of Non-Responsibility within the statutory time allowed after acquiring knowledge.

Generally speaking, owners in fee simple, lessors and vendors may avail themselves of the advantage offered by posting and recording, in the manner provided by statute, the Notice of Non-Responsibility in those states in which such instrument is recognized.

Among those who may acquire a mechanic's lien upon property upon which they have bestowed labor and furnished materials or appliances, are mechanics, materialmen, contractors, subcontractors, artisans, architects, registered engineers, licensed land surveyors, machinists, builders, teamsters and generally all persons and laborers of every class. It is against the lien claims of such persons that the Notice of Non-Responsibility is used to protect the owner of property having no knowledge of the labor or materials being performed or furnished for a work of improvement on land in which he has an interest. If, upon becoming aware of such improvement, and not otherwise prevented by law from so acting, he act diligently and within the time allowed by statute and in accordance with the requirements of the law regulating the posting and recording of such notice, he will be protected in those states where the notice is effective; otherwise he may find his property liable to the attachment of a mechanic's lien.

5. The Enforcement of the Lien

Ordinarily the lien claimant is required to give the owner a written notice stating generally the kind of labor and materials furnished by him, its value and the person to whom they were furnished or the improvement benefited thereby. Because the lien law is strictly statutory, compliance with the particular statutes of the jurisdiction is essential.

To enable the lien claimant to enforce his lien, it is generally required that he file for record a verified statement setting forth his claim. If the statement is not filed for record as provided by statute, the lien is lost. The several state statutes prescribe the filing for record of the statement by reference to the completion of the contract, or other events such as cessation of labor, or by reference to permissive acts of the contractor, or to the furnishing of materials.

Ordinarily no lien can be enforced until the lien claim or statement is properly and timely filed. The filing amounts to constructive notice that the claimant is demanding payment which the lien is intended to secure.

When neither the contract nor a bond to assure payment of liens has been filed, as between the contractor and the owner, the contract will nevertheless limit the contractor's right to a lien to the contract price. However, subcontractors, laborers and materialmen who have no actual knowledge of the provisions of the contract are not limited in the amount of their liens to material or labor called for by contract. Filing of the contract, without bond, can only limit the lien claims of laborers and materialmen to those items covered by the contract; it does not limit the amount of claims to the contract price.

If the original contract is filed and a statutory bond of the contractor is recorded in the office of the county recorder before the work is commenced,

---

Margin notes:

THOSE WHO MAY ACQUIRE A MECHANIC'S LIEN

OWNER MAY POST AND RECORD NOTICE OF NON-RESPONSIBILITY

NOTICE TO OWNER

FILING OF LIEN STATEMENT

FILING CONSTRUCTIVE NOTICE OF DEMAND FOR PAYMENT

WHEN NEITHER CONTRACT NOR BOND IS FILED

CONTRACT FILED EFFECT

CONTRACT AND BOND FILED EFFECT

the liens of all persons performing labor or furnishing materials to be used in the work of improvement are restricted to an aggregate amount found due from the owner to the contractor.

The right to a mechanic's lien is purely statutory, as we have seen. It may be waived by the lien claimant, it having been said that such waiver is not against public policy. Such liens may be extinguished by the act or the agreement of the parties, as well as by operation of law.

Remember, mechanic's Lien law is Statutory law. See the statutes of your state.

QUESTIONS AND ANSWERS

1. What is the purpose of a mechanic's lien?

    Answer: To secure the payment of labor and materials going into a work of improvement on land.

2. Is it a general or a special lien?

    Answer: It is a special lien.

3. Name a few structures to which the term "work of improvement" has been applied?

    Answer: A building, wharf, bridge, well, fence, machinery.

4. If the person who caused work to be done on a building is the owner in fee simple, to what does the lien attach?

    Answer: Ordinarily to the building and the land.

5. If the person mentioned in the previous question owned only an estate for years, to what would the lien attach?

    Answer: Only to his interest in the property; except in some circumstances the fee owner's land may also be liened.

6. Ordinarily, can land be liened if there is no structure on it for which labor has been performed or materials furnished?

    Answer: No, not ordinarily.

7. Name instances when a lien will attach both to the improvement placed on the land by another and to the land of an owner in fee.

    Answer: When a lessee, for example, constructs a building, the owner of the fee authorizing the construction, or having knowledge of it, does not record and post a Notice of Non-Responsibility.

8. Can you think of an instance in which the posting and recording of a Notice of Non-responsibility will avail the owner in fee nothing?

    Answer: Where a lessee is in possession and the terms of the lease obligate him to make improvements.

9. How much can the lien claimant demand?

    Answer: When the contract is not recorded, nor a bond filed, in the case of the contractor, ordinarily not to exceed the contract price; in the case of others entitled to lien the property, the amount of the liens need not be limited to the contract price, nor need such liens be for labor or materials covered by the contract; provided, however these others have no actual knowledge of the provisions of the contract.

10. What effect has filing the contract of record, no bond being filed?

    Answer: Ordinarily, the only effect is to limit the lien claims of laborers and materialmen to those items covered by the contract; it does not limit the amount of claims to the contract price.

11. Has the lien claimant constructive notice of the contents of the original contract?

Answer: If the original contract is filed for record, before the commencement of the work, in the Recorder's office in the county in which the improvement is located, the lien claimant has such constructive notice.

12. Must, if requested by the owner, the lien claimant, before filing a lien claim, give the owner and the original contractor any notice of his demand?

Answer: Some state statutes provide for such a notice. It is some times referred to as a "stop notice."

13. Need there be a contract to support a mechanic's lien?

Answer: Yes. Ordinarily such a contract is in writing, but in some jurisdictions this is not necessary.

14. Who are the parties to such a contract?

Answer: The contractor and the owner.

15. To whom does the term "owner" usually apply?

Answer: To the owner in fee, or to any person having a lesser estate, or an equity or interest in the land, which the lien statutes recognize.

16. Can the lien attach to the property of a non-contracting owner?

Answer: Yes, if he has authorized the improvement, or has knowledge of it and fails to file a Notice of Non-Responsibility, or take other steps to prevent the lien from attaching to his property.

17. In the fee owner contracting with the contractor situation, to what will the lien ordinarily attach?

Answer: To both the improvement and the land.

18. In the same situation as in the foregoing, does the lien attach to the land if the structure or improvement is destroyed?

Answer: If the statute in the particular jurisdiction is so worded as to create an unqualified lien upon both land and improvements, the destruction of the improvement will not ordinarily discharge the lien on the land. If the statute makes the lien attach primarily to the improvement and only incidentally to the land, then it is likely to be held that the lien will be lost with the destruction of the improvement.

19. May lessor's land ordinarily be liened for improvements placed thereon by a lessee?

Answer: Ordinarily, it may not.

20. When may the lien attach to the lessor's land in such a case?

Answer: If the lessor can be said to have authorized or ratified the construction of the improvement, or in some jurisdictions if he had knowledge of the construction and did nothing about it, or if it can be said he "consents" to the construction of the improvement.

21. When the terms of the lease provide for the construction by the lessee of certain improvements, the lessor's land will ordinarily be liable to the lien. On what theory is this said to be based?

Answer: It is said that in such case the lessor impliedly appoints the lessee his agent to enter into a contract for the improvement.

22. If the language of the lease is permissive rather than mandatory with respect to the construction of a certain improvement, or improvements, by the lessee, will the lien ordinarily attach to the lessor's land?

Answer: No, not when the language is permissive.

23. In this latter case, how may the lessor protect his land from the attachment of the lien?

Answer: By timely posting and recording a Notice of Non-Responsibility as provided by law.

24. If the lessor posts and records such a notice in the foregoing case, to what would the lien ordinarily attach?

Answer: To the improvement and the estate of the lessee.

25. Ordinarily, does the construction of an improvement by the vendee in possession under an executory contract of sale make the vendor's interest liable to a mechanic's lien?

Answer: No.

26. Under what circumstances, in the foregoing situation, may the vendor's interest be liened?

Answer: Some courts have held that the vendor's interest cannot be liened by his mere knowledge of the construction of the improvement. But other courts hold that if the vendor has knowledge of the improvement he must timely file a Notice of Non-Responsibility, in which case the lien extends only to the improvement.

27. If the vendor gives his consent or permission to build the improvement, will the lien attach to his interest?

Answer: In such case some courts hold that the lien will attach.

28. If the contract call for the construction of improvements by the conditional vendee, does the lien attach to the vendor's interest?

Answer: Under some statutes the lien will so attach.

29. If the sales contract obligates the vendee to build in the foregoing situation, will the lien attach to the vendor's interest?

Answer: Ordinarily, if the vendee is obligated to build by the contract, it is said the vendor has appointed the vendee his agent to build, and the lien will attach to the vendor's interest.

30. If a builder contracts with the vendor who has executed an executory contract with another person, to build an improvement, will the lien attach to the vendor's land?

Answer: It has been so held, on the ground that the contractor is not to be charged with notice of a secret conveyance of the land to another, so as to defeat a mechanic's lien attached to the land.

31. If the landlord contracts for construction of an improvement on land he has leased, either under a provision in the lease contract, or where the tenant has acted as his agent in the premises, to what will the lien attach?

    Answer: It has been held to attach to both land and improvement.

32. What is the purpose of the Notice of Non-Responsibility?

    Answer: To prevent a mechanic's lien from attaching to an owner's estate or interest in land when he is not responsible for, or has no knowledge of a work of improvement being made on the land.

33. How does such an owner protect himself?

    Answer: By posting a Notice of Non-Responsibility on the property where the improvement is being constructed, and recording such notice in the county Recorder's office in the county where the land is located; and otherwise complying with all statutes in the premises.

34. Is the Notice of Non-Responsibility known in all of the states?

    Answer: Not in all of the states.

35. Is the waiver of a lien against public policy?

    Answer: It has been held that such waiver is not against public policy.

CHECKLIST

A. Keep in mind that the mechanic's lien is purely statutory.

B. Check to determine:
    [1] if the lien has been of record for more than the statutory period (fixed by law within which the lien may bind the property to which it is attached) or, for more than the statutory time allowed since the extended date of the lien, or credit given, as indicated by a recorded notice;
    [2] if no action is pending to foreclose the lien;
    [3] if the foreclosure period has not been tolled by the bankruptcy of the owner or by the fact that either the owner or the claimant was in the military service during the first-mentioned statutory period;
    [4] If your client is a bona fide purchaser acquiring his interest in the property subsequent to the expiration of the aforesaid statutory period.

C. If a mechanic's lien is shown as a title insurance policy exception, advise your principal to consult an attorney.

9

Bills and Notes

1. Negotiable Instruments

A. Introduction

Today the law of "bills and notes," a part of the law merchant,[1] is an extensive branch of private jurisprudence. It covers a number of commercial instruments. Emphasis in the HANDBOOK is placed upon two of these instruments in common daily use—the negotiable promissory note and the bank check.

THE PROMISSORY NOTE AND THE BANK CHECK

B. The Uniform Commercial Code

A Uniform Commercial Code has been adopted in most of the states, succeeding the older negotiable instruments law of the particular state.[2] There has been effort by the several legislatures to resolve conflicts in the old law and to bring into statutory form the developed case law. While the material has been reorganized and amplified by adoption of a Uniform Commercial Code, basically the law of negotiable instruments remains much the same as it was before the revision. Wherever there may appear to be some divergence in the law of the several states, the HANDBOOK will follow the rule expressed in the uniform code.

THE UNIFORM CODE

One of the commendable aspects of the new code is its conversion into statutory law of much of the generally acceptable case law which had developed through the interpretation and construction of the negotiable instruments law and related statutes and court decisions in the several states. The language of the uniform code is less labored and more informative than that of many of the older statutory provisions. It is more nearly self-assertive and closer to the mark than many of the clumsily expressed ideas wrapped up in the diction of a past era.

LANGUAGE EXPRESSIVE

C. Distinction Between Negotiable and
Non-Negotiable Instruments

The difference between a negotiable and a non-negotiable instrument lies, principally, in the current transferability of the paper discharged of all prior defenses, except certain so-called "real" defenses.

A non-negotiable instrument ordinarily carries with it all the defenses and the equities the maker may have had at the time of the indorsement. Such an instrument, being a written contract for the payment of money or personal property, may be transferred by indorsement in like manner as a negotiable instrument. But such an indorsement, unlike the indorsement of a negotiable instrument, will transfer the rights of the assignor under the instrument to the assignee subject to all equities and defenses existing in favor of the maker at the time of the indorsement, or arising in his favor before notice of the assignment or indorsement.

A negotiable instrument in the hands of a holder in due course is, unlike a non-negotiable instrument, taken by such holder free from all claims to it on the part of any person. It is also taken free of all defenses of any party to the instrument with whom the holder has not dealt, except those REAL defenses recognized by the law. These real defenses are set forth in a subsequent paragraph.

D. Definition of a Negotiable Instrument

A negotiable instrument is not distinguishable from a non-negotiable instrument by any naturally basic characteristic of its obligation. The distinction rests largely upon expedient rules of statutory law and judicial precedent growing out of a long history of commercial transactions stemming from the old *lex mercatoria*. These rules and precedents have been qualified and augmented by modern uniform practices and codes of law. As a result certain forms of commercial paper pass freely in an exchange of credit, unchallenged by undisclosed equities and unrestricted defenses. Such commercial paper is capable of assuring unimpeded currency in the prosecution of commercial enterprise. This is negotiable paper, the negotiable instrument.

Any writing, to be a negotiable instrument, must be signed by the maker or drawer. It must contain an unconditional promise or order to pay a sum certain in money. It must contain no other promise, order, obligation or power given by the maker or drawer except as authorized by the negotiable instrument law. It must be payable on demand or at a definite time, and payable to order or to bearer. A writing which complies with these requirements is: a DRAFT, or BILL OF EXCHANGE if it is an order; a CHECK if it is a draft drawn on a bank and payable on demand; a CERTIFICATE OF DEPOSIT if it is an acknowledgement by a bank of receipt of money with an engagement to repay it; a NOTE if it is a promise other than a certificate of deposit.

The terms draft, check, certificate of deposit and note may refer to instruments which are not negotiable, as well as to instruments which are negotiable.

2. Essentials of Negotiable Instrument

A. The Unconditional Promise

The promise or order to pay a sum of money must be unconditional if the instrument is to be negotiable. However, a number of statements may be included in the note or instrument without destroying its negotiability. Among such are those of "consideration" for the note, reference to the transaction out of which the note arose, or that the instrument will mature in accordance with, or "as per" such transaction. Prepayment rights, or an acceleration clause, will not destroy negotiability; neither will the fact that the note is secured, or that it indicates a particular account to be debited, or any other fund or source from which reimbursement is expected. It may be limited to payment out of the entire assets of a partnership, unincorporated association, trust or estate by or on behalf of which the instrument is issued. If the instrument is issued by a government or governmental agency or unit, it may state that it is limited to payment out of a particular fund or proceeds of a particular source. However, the promise to pay contained in the instrument is not unconditional, and its negotiability will be destroyed if it is to be paid only out of a particular fund or source other than in the two previously mentioned cases. Nor can it state that it is subject to or governed by any other agreement.

B. The Sum Certain

A negotiable instrument must promise to pay a sum certain. A sum is certain even though it is to be paid with stated interest or by stated installments, or with stated different rates of interest before and after a specified date. A stated discount or addition if paid before or after the date fixed for payment does not destroy the certainty of the sum to be paid. Nor does payment with or less exchange, whether at a fixed rate or at the current rate. And the instrument may contain provision for costs of collection or an attorney's fee. The sum certain will not be made uncertain thereby. The instrument will still retain its negotiability.

C. Time of Payment

Negotiable instruments are payable on demand, at a definite time, and by stated installments.

Instruments payable on demand include those payable at sight or on presentation and those in which no time for payment is stated. An instrument is payable at a definite time if by its terms it is payable on or before a stated date or at a fixed period after a stated date; or at a fixed period after sight, or at a definite time subject to any acceleration; or at a definite time subject to extension at the option of the holder, or to extension to a further definite time at the option of the maker or acceptor or automatically upon or after a specified act or event.

TIME UNCERTAIN

An instrument which by its terms is payable only upon an act or event uncertain as to time of occurrence is not payable at a definite time, even though the act or event has occurred.

An acceleration clause will not destroy the negotiability of the instrument.

EXTENSION AT ELECTION OF HOLDER WITHOUT TIME LIMIT

EXCEPTION

DOESN'T APPLY TO MAKER OR ACCEPTOR

The holder may extend the time of payment without a definite time limit, except that he may not exercise his option to extend an instrument over the objection of a maker or acceptor or other party who tenders full payment when the instrument is due.

The maker or acceptor may not extend without time limit, for this would destroy the negotiability of the instrument by making the promise to pay indefinite.

• DEMAND PAPER

DEMAND PAPER

Instruments payable on demand include those payable at sight or on presentation and those in which no time for payment is stated. It has been held that where no maturity date was shown in the note, or where the blank for the insertion of a date was left unfilled, the instrument was a demand note.

• ORDER PAPER

ORDER PAPER

An instrument is payable to order when it is payable to the order or assigns of any person specified with reasonable certainty in the instrument, or to a named person or his order. It may be payable to the order of the maker or the drawer or the drawee. It may be made to the order of a payee who is not the maker or drawer or drawee. It may likewise be made to the order of two or more payees together, or in the alternative. And it may be payable to the order of an estate, trust or fund, an office, or an officer by his title, or to a partnership or unincorporated association.

• BEARER PAPER

BEARER PAPER

An instrument is payable to bearer when it is payable to bearer, or to the order of bearer, or to a specified person or bearer. It is likewise bearer paper if it is payable to "cash" or to the order of "cash." In fact, it may be made payable to any other designation which does not purport to identify a specific payee.

3. Negotiation is Transfer by Indorsement

NEGOTIATION

THREE KINDS OF INDORSEMENT

Negotiation of bearer paper is made by mere delivery. If the instrument is order paper, negotiation is effected by indorsement and delivery.

The uniform act provides for three kinds of indorsement—special, blank and restrictive. A special indorsement specifies the person to whom or to whose order the instrument is payable, as

SPECIAL

> "Pay to John Doe
> (signed)Richard Roe" or
> "Pay to order of John Doe
> (signed) Richard Roe."

An indorsement in blank specifies no particular indorsee and may consist of a mere signature, as

BLANK

> "Richard Roe."

The three common restrictive indorsements are "for collection," "for deposit" or "pay any bank."

RESTRICTIVE

4. The Holder in Due Course

A holder in due course is a holder who takes the instrument for value, in good faith and without notice that it is overdue, or has been dishonored. He must take it without notice or knowledge of any defense against it or claim to it on the part of any person. A payee may be a holder in due course. But a holder does not become a holder in due course by purchase at judicial sale, or taking the instrument under legal process. Nor does he achieve that status by acquiring it in taking over an estate, or by purchasing it as part of a bulk transaction not in the regular course of business of the transferor.

THE HOLDER IN DUE COURSE

Unless he has the rights of a holder in due course any person takes the instrument subject to all valid claims to it on the part of any person. He takes it subject to all defenses of any party which would be available in an action on a simple contract. He takes it subject to the defenses of want or failure of consideration, nonperformance of any condition precedent, nondelivery, or delivery for a special purpose. He also takes it subject to the defense that he or a person through whom he holds the instrument acquired it by theft, or that payment or satisfaction to such holder would be inconsistent with the terms of a restrictive indorsement.

ONE NOT A HOLDER IN DUE COURSE TAKES SUBJECT TO VALID CLAIMS AND DEFENSES

5. Guaranties and Warranties

The GUARANTY is the engagement or undertaking of the maker or indorser; that is to say, what he promises to do. The WARRANTY is the assurance the maker or indorser gives, or that is implied in law, over and above his engagement or undertaking, with respect to certain legal and factual matters connected with the instrument, and his relationship to it.

GUARANTIES AND WARRANTIES

A. The Maker

The maker admits, as against all subsequent parties, the existence of the payee and his then capacity to indorse. He engages or undertakes to pay the

THE MAKER'S UNDERTAKING

instrument according to its tenor at the time of his engagement, or, if it be an incomplete instrument, as completed, pursuant to the provisions of the uniform act.

B. The Indorser

The indorser ordinarily engages to pay the instrument, according to its tenor at the time of his indorsement, upon dishonor and any necessary notice of dishonor and protest, to the holder or to any subsequent indorser who takes up the instrument. This is the indorser's guaranty.

In addition to this guaranty, the indorser, when presenting the instrument for acceptance, or for payment, warrants:

> that he has a good title to the instrument or is authorized to obtain payment or acceptance on behalf of one who has a good title;
>
> that he has no knowledge that the signature of the maker or drawer is unauthorized, except that this warranty is not given by a holder in due course acting in good faith
>
>> to a maker with respect to the maker's own signature, or
>>
>> to a drawer with respect to the drawer's own signature, whether or not the drawer is also the drawee, or
>>
>> to an acceptor of a draft if the holder in due course took the draft after the acceptance or obtained the acceptance without knowledge that the drawer's signature was unauthorized;
>
> that the instrument has not been materially altered, except that this warranty is not given by a holder in due course acting in good faith
>
>> to the maker of a note, or
>>
>> to the drawer of a draft whether or not the drawer is also the drawee, or
>>
>> to the acceptor of a draft with respect to an alteration made prior to the acceptance if the holder in due course took the draft after the acceptance, even though the acceptance provided "payable as originally drawn" or equivalent terms, or
>>
>> to the acceptor of a draft with respect to an alteration made after the acceptance.

When the indorser negotiates the instrument by indorsement he warrants to his indorsee and any subsequent holder who takes the instrument in good faith that

he has a good title to the instrument or is authorized to obtain payment or acceptance on behalf
of one who has a good title and the transfer is
otherwise rightful; and that

all signatures are genuine or authorized; and that
the instrument has not been materially altered;
and that

no defense of any party is good against him; and
that he has no knowledge of any insolvency proceeding instituted with respect to the maker or
acceptor or drawer of an unaccepted instrument.

Incidentally, it should be here said that any person who transfers an instrument and receives consideration warrants to his transferee the foregoing facts.
By transferring WITHOUT RECOURSE the transferor limits the warranty "that no
defense of any kind is good against him" to a warranty that he has no knowledge of such a defense.

A selling agent or broker dealing with negotiable instruments who does not
disclose the fact that he is acting only as an agent or broker gives the warranties above set forth, but if he makes such disclosure warrants only his good
faith and authority.

6. "Payment Guaranteed": "Collection Guaranteed"

"Payment guaranteed" or equivalent words added to a signature mean that
the signer engages that if the instrument is not paid when due he will pay it
according to its tenor without resort by the holder to any other party. In
effect, the guarantor is a co-maker.

"Collection guaranteed" or equivalent words added to a signature mean
that the signer engages that if the instrument is not paid when due he will pay
it according to its tenor, but only after the holder has reduced his claim against
the maker or acceptor to judgment and execution has been returned unsatisfied,
or after the maker or acceptor has become insolvent or it is otherwise apparent
that it is useless to proceed against him.

In neither of these cases where words of guaranty are used is presentment,
notice of dishonor and protest necessary.

When words of guaranty do not specify what is guaranteed, payment is
guaranteed.

7. "Without Recourse"

The indorser "without recourse" makes no promise to pay; makes no engagement. However, he does not relieve himself of certain warranties. He warrants that he has good title, that all signatures are genuine or authorized, that
the instrument has not been materially altered, and that he does not have

knowledge of any defense by any party good against him and that he has no knowledge of any insolvency proceeding instituted with respect to the maker or acceptor or drawer of an unaccepted instrument.

8. Disclaimer of Warranties

DISCLAIMER OF
WARRANTIES

It is a general rule, in the sale of goods, that warranties may be disclaimed, both express and implied. The Uniform Commercial Code seems to intend [§3417] the disclaimer of warranties in connection with negotiable paper inasmuch as its language is phrased in general terms applicable to warranty law. It would seem then, that the disclaiming indorser may rid himself of all warranties, express and implied, if he make the proper endorsement. The indorsement, to be effective, should be broad enough to encompass all warranties, express or implied, whether statutory, by operation of law, or otherwise, and if he employ the words "without recourse" he may also be relieved of any further engagement.

9. Charging the Parties with Liability

CHARGING THE
PARTIES WITH
LIABILITY

The maker of a note or the acceptor of a draft is primarily liable on its obligation. Unless excused, the holder of a note or draft must present it for payment to the maker or acceptor if he wishes to charge an indorser with liability.

PARTIES SECOND-
ARILY LIABLE ON
NEGOTIABLE
PAPER

Should the note be dishonored, resort must be had to parties secondarily liable, which ordinarily are the indorsers. If, upon presentment for payment, the maker or acceptor should fail or delay to pay the note or draft, it being then due, the holder may, by giving the proper notice of dishonor, charge any indorser, unless his indorsement relieved him from liability. Both presentment for payment and notice of dishonor, unless excused, are necessary to charge any indorser.

10. "Real" Defenses, or Defenses Good Against a Holder in Due Course

To the extent that a holder is a holder in due course he takes the instrument free from all claims to it on the part of any person. He likewise takes it free from all defenses of any party to the instrument with whom he, the holder, has not dealt, except that the following defenses are good against him:

REAL DEFENSES

Infancy, to the extent that it is a defense to a simple contract;

Such other incapacity, or duress, or illegality of the transaction, as renders the obligation of the party a nullity;

Such misrepresentation as has induced the party to sign the instrument with neither knowledge nor

reasonable opportunity to obtain knowledge of its
character or its essential terms;
Discharge in insolvency proceedings;
Any other discharge of which the holder has notice
when he takes the instrument.

11. The Check

A negotiable instrument, if it is a draft drawn on a bank and payable on demand, is a check.

THE CHECK

Deposits in a bank may be "special" or "general." Special deposits may be distinguished by two classes, (1) a trust fund held by the bank wherein the identical coins, or other articles, are held in trust for the depositor, and (2) where money is deposited with the bank under an agreement that it shall be used in a particular manner, or to pay some specified claim. In either case the ownership of the money remains in the depositor. But in the latter case it is not necessary that the identical coins be retained; it is sufficient that the bank keep on hand at all times cash equal to the deposit. The amount of cash constitues a fund which the bank is not authorized to use in its general banking operations.

THE SPECIAL DEPOSIT

A general deposit is, in effect, a loan to the bank, the money upon deposit becoming the property of the bank, a part of its general assets which may be used in its general banking operations.

THE GENERAL DEPOSIT

12. The Checking and Savings Accounts

Deposit of money in either a checking or a savings account in a bank effects a debtor-creditor relationship, the bank being the debtor and the depositor the creditor. There is an implied obligation of the bank to repay the loan at any time and in the amounts of checks drawn against the deposit by the customer, or depositor.

CHECKING AND SAVINGS AC-COUNTS

If the bank wrongfully dishonors a check drawn against it by its customer it is liable in damages proximately caused by the wrongful dishonor. However, if the dishonor occur through mistake, liability is usually limited to actual damages proved, that is to say, where mere mistake is involved punitive damages will not be allowed.

LIABILITY OF BANK

A bank is liable to its customer for the actual loss incurred by him resulting from the payment of a check contrary to a binding stop-payment order, not exceeding the amount of the item, unless the bank is guilty of negligence. The burden of establishing the fact and amount of loss resulting from the payment of a check contrary to a binding stop-payment order is on the customer.

A customer, and in some states, any person authorized to sign checks or make withdrawals may stop payment of checks drawn on the customer's account. The stop-payment order must be in writing, however, signed by the

THE STOP-PAY-MENT ORDER

customer or authorized person, and must describe with certainty the check on which payment is to be stopped. The official version of the Uniform Commercial Code does not require a written stop order, but in some jurisdictions it is necessary. Furthermore, it must be received by the bank in such time and in such manner as to afford the bank a reasonable opportunity to protect itself in the matter.

A written stop-payment order may be disregarded by the bank six months after receipt, unless it is renewed in writing.

A bank is under no obligation to a customer having a checking account to pay a check, other than a certified check, which is presented more than six months after its date, but it may charge its customer's account for a payment made thereafter.

13. Forged and Altered Checks

FORGED CHECK LIABILITY OF BANK

A bank in receiving ordinary deposits becomes the debtor of the depositor. An implied contract arises to discharge this indebtedness by honoring the depositor's checks. The bank is charged with knowledge of its depositor's signature. It pays a forged check at its peril, and in such case payment in legal contemplation will be deemed to have been made from the bank's own funds, so that it has no right to charge the depositor's account with the amount disbursed contrary to his genuine order. It will be liable to him for so doing.

DEFENSE BY BANK

While no degree of care on the part of the bank will excuse it from liability, it may justify the payment of a forged check on principles of estoppel, or on the basis of negligent or misleading conduct of the depositor which directly or proximately caused the bank to pay. However, the bank must show due diligence before it can assert such defenses.

14. Bank Statement and Checks

DEPOSITOR MUST EXAMINE BANK STATEMENT AND RETURNED CHECKS FOR FORGERIES AND IRREGULARITIES

A depositor has the responsibility of examining his bank statements and returned checks for forgeries and alterations. He must exercise reasonable care and promptness, and must promptly notify the bank upon discovery of any such irregularity.

Without regard to care or lack of care of either the customer or the bank, a customer who does not within one year from the time the statement and items are made available to him discover and report his unauthorized signature or any alteration on the face or back of the item or does not within three years from that time discover and report any unauthorized endorsement, is precluded from asserting against the bank such unauthorized signature or indorsement or such alteration. In some jurisdictions the one year period likewise covers an unauthorized endorsement.

15. Holder in Due Course: Payment to, on Forged Check

With some exception, payment or acceptance of any instrument is final in favor of a holder in due course, or a person who has in good faith changed his position in reliance on the payment. The payor bank may not, therefore, recover back money paid the holder in due course on a forged check. The rule of finality applied here prevents the unsettling of a series of business transactions upon the discovery of a forgery, and protects a bona fide purchaser for value.

RULE PREVENTS UNSETTLING OF SERIES OF BUSINESS TRANSACTIONS

16. Payment on Forged Indorsement is Conversion

The uniform act makes a bank liable to the payee for payment of a check upon a forged indorsement. An instrument is deemed converted when it is paid on a forged indorsement.

BANK LIABLE TO PAYEE ON FORGED INDORSEMENT

QUESTIONS AND ANSWERS

1. How many states have adopted the Uniform Commercial Code or some part of it?

   Answer: Forty-seven states, the District of Columbia and the Virgin Islands.

2. Has the law of negotiable instruments been materially changed by the UCC?

   Answer: The law of negotiable instruments remains much the same as it was before the revision.

3. Name one distinction between a negotiable and a non-negotiable instrument.

   Answer: A non-negotiable instrument carries with it all the defenses and equities the maker may have had at the time of its transfer. A negotiable instrument, however, in the hands of a holder in due course, is discharged of all defenses and equities which may exist between all prior parties, except such "real" defenses as are defined in the act.

4. May a non-negotiable instrument be transferred by indorsement?

   Answer: Yes.

5. What does the indorsement of a non-negotiable instrument transfer?

   Answer: It transfers all the rights of the assignor under the instrument to the assignee, subject to all equities and defenses existing in favor of the maker at the time of the transfer.

6. Must the promise or order to pay be unconditional in a negotiable instrument?

   Answer: Yes.

7. Will the following, included in a note, destroy its negotiability?

   A statement of the "consideration" for the note.
   Reference to the transaction out of which the note arose.
   That the instrument will mature in accordance with, or "as per" such transaction.
   Prepayment rights
   That the note is secured
   A particular account to be debited
   Any fund or source from which reimbursement is expected
   That it is limited to payment out of the entire assets of a partnership, unincorporated association, trustee or estate by or on behalf of which the instrument is issued.
   If issued by a government or governmental agency, it is limited to payment out of a particular fund, or proceeds from a particular source.

   Answer: No. None of these provisions will destroy its negotiability. But the promise to pay is not unconditional and negotiability will be destroyed if the note is to be paid only out of a particular fund or source (except as indicated when it is a government issue); nor can it state that it is subject to or governed by any other agreement.

8. Must the promise to pay a sum of money be a "sum certain"?

Answer: Yes.

9. When are negotiable instruments payable?

Answer: 1) On demand, 2) at a definite time, and 3) by stated installments.

10. May the maker or accepter extend the time for payment?

Answer: No.

11. What paper is demand paper?

Answer: When it is payable
  - on demand
  - at sight
  - upon presentation
  - when time for payment is not stated

12. To make the instrument negotiable how must it be payable?

Answer: To order or to bearer.

13. How is negotiation of bearer paper effected?

Answer: By delivery.

14. How is negotiation of order paper effected?

Answer: By indorsement and delivery.

15. How many kinds of indorsements does the UCC provide for?

Answer: Special, blank and restrictive.

16. Who is a holder in due course?

Answer: One who takes the instrument for value, in good faith and without notice that it is overdue, or has been dishonored, and without knowledge of any defenses against it or claim to it on the part of any person.

17. What is the guaranty involved in negotiable paper?

Answer: The guaranty is the engagement or undertaking of the maker or endorser, i.e., what he promises to do.

18. What are the warranties involved in negotiable paper?

Answer: The warranties are the assurances the maker or indorser gives, or that are implied in law, over and above his engagement or undertaking, with respect to certain legal and factual matters connected with the instrument and his relationship to it.

19. May warranties be disclaimed?

Answer: Yes, by the proper indorsement.

20. Who are primarily liable on negotiable paper?

Answer: The maker of a note, and the acceptor of a draft.

21. Who are secondarily liable?

Answer: Usually the indorsers.

22. How is an indorser charged with liability to pay the note?

   Answer: Should a note be dishonored the holder may, by giving the proper notice of dishonor, charge any indorser, unless his indorsement relieved him from liability.

23. What is a check?

   Answer: A negotiable instrument, if it is a draft drawn on a bank and payable on demand, is a check.

24. What is a "special" deposit in a bank?

   Answer: In such a deposit the ownership of money remains in the depositor, the bank holding it in trust for the depositor, or to be paid out according to his directions.

25. What is a "general" deposit?

   Answer: A "general" deposit is, in effect, a loan to the bank, the money becoming the property of the bank, a part of its general assets, to be repaid to the depositor upon demand.

26. Is a bank under any obligation to pay a check drawn on it six months before it is presented for payment?

   Answer: No, not ordinarily. But it may, nevertheless, do so and charge the depositor's account therewith.

27. Is a bank liable to the customer for the payment of a forged check?

   Answer: Ordinarily, a bank pays a forged check at its peril.

28. May negligence of depositor estop him from asserting lack of authority of bank to pay forged check?

   Answer: Yes, but the bank must first show due diligence.

29. May the bank recover back money paid a holder in due course on a forged check?

   Answer: No. Payment or acceptance of any instrument is final in favor of a holder in due course.

30. Is the bank liable to the payee for the payment of a check upon a forged indorsement?

   Answer: Yes.

CHECKLIST

A. Remember, although the Uniform Commercial Code has been adopted by practically all of the states, there will have been omissions, alterations, deletions and additions to the official code in the statutory systems of the several states. Be alert to such changes in your state.

B. Check the instrument you are dealing with to ascertain if it meets the requirements of a negotiable instrument before accepting it as such.

C. Be sure the promise to pay is unconditional.

D. Be sure it is a promise to pay a sum certain.

E. Be sure the time of payment is definite.

F. Determine if the instrument is demand, order or bearer paper.

G. Determine if for negotiation purposes the instrument requires indorsement and delivery, or only delivery.

H. Determine if the indorsement is special, blank or restrictive.

I. Be sure you do not have notice that the paper is overdue if you wish to stand as a holder in due course.

J. Determine if you take the instrument as a holder in due course.

K. Determine what are the warranties and what the undertaking.

L. Determine if what you want is the indorsement "collection guaranteed" or "payment guaranteed."

M. Determine if you wish to disclaim all warranties; and if so, use adequate language to effect this result.

N. Be sure your "stop-payment order" has been timely and properly presented to your bank. Check the statutes of your state.

O. Be sure to examine the checks returned with your bank statement regularly for forgeries and alterations.

FOOTNOTES

1 Thomas Atkins Street, The Foundations of Legal Liability (Northport, Long Island, N.Y., Edward Thompson Company 1906) Vol. II, p. 334.

2 Forty-seven states, the District of Columbia and the Virgin Islands have adopted the Uniform Commercial Code, or parts thereof. These states are: Alabama, Alaska, Arkansas, California, Colorado, Connecticut, Delaware, Florida, Georgia, Hawaii, Illinois, Indiana, Iowa, Kansas, Kentucky, Maine, Maryland, Massachusetts, Michigan, Minnesota, Mississippi, Missouri, Montana, Nebraska, Nevada, New Hampshire, New Jersey, New Mexico, New York, North Carolina, North Dakota, Ohio, Oklahoma, Oregon, Pennsylvania, Rhode Island, South Carolina, South Dakota, Tennessee, Texas, Utah, Vermont, Virginia, Washington, West Virginia, Wisconsin, Wyoming.

10

The Escrow—the Parties
and Transactions

1. The Escrow

A. Defined

An ESCROW has been referred to as a transaction, and also as a grant or instrument. It is both of these. It is the thing held upon condition, or escrowed, and the transaction involved in holding it as an escrow. When one speaks of an escrow in the real estate business both meanings of the word are usually intended. It is a transaction wherein any written instrument, money or other thing of value is delivered to a third-party depositary under a valid contract to be held until the happening of a specified event or the performance of a prescribed condition, when it is then to be delivered out of escrow to a specified person discharged of the condition upon which it was held. While it is in the possession of the depositary it is called an "escrow."

ESCROW BOTH A THING AND A TRANSACTION

In the real estate business the usual escrow is created when an executed deed is deposited with an "escrow holder," usually a title company, to be delivered out of escrow and unconditionally, upon the happening of a specified event arising out of contract. When an executed deed is escrowed to be delivered upon the death of the grantor, no contract is needed to support the escrow.

The details involved today in the sale or exchange of real estate have created a need for a neutral agency by which papers and instruments, as well as money, may be conditionally held pending performance on the part of each party to the transaction of those acts and things agreed to be done and performed by each in accordance with an agreement or contract between them. The seller of property cannot justifiably deliver his deed until payment, or an acceptable obligation to pay for the property, is received by him. The buyer cannot risk payment until he receives the deed to the property, or some acceptable

DETAILS OF THE ESCROW TRANS-ACTION

obligation to deliver it. The buyer must have proper evidence of merchantable title, or title insurance. Liens, encumbrances and all charges against the property must be settled as agreed by the parties. Prorations of rent, taxes, assessments, insurance premiums and interest charges must be made. Instruments must be drawn and executed by the parties. All these things take time, and executed instruments cannot safely be delivered before correlative instruments or performances are delivered or performed. In short, the transaction on both sides should be consummated at the same moment in order to be of the greatest protection to both parties; that is to say, the escrow should reveal the true status of all relevant facts at the moment it is closed and the deed recorded. At this time there should be no room for dispute between the parties, nor for third-party equities to inject themselves.

THE ESCROW HOLDER

THE AUXILIARY CONTRACT

THE ESCROW AGREEMENT, OR INSTRUCTIONS

What has just been said ought to suggest to the reader at least three things. It is apparent that there must be an "escrow holder" or agency through which, or by which, these details may be worked out. There must also be an agreement, or contract between the parties, i.e., the seller and the buyer, definitely fixing their respective rights and obligations. This is often referred to as the "auxiliary contract." There must likewise be an escrow agreement, or what are usually called "escrow instructions," agreed to by the principal parties and the escrow holder, and directed to the latter, instructing him exactly what he is expected to do in the premises. In the ordinary residential sale the Deposit Receipt and the escrow instructions together are usually enough to bind the parties in an effective escrow, the auxiliary contract being dispensed with.

B. The Valid Escrow

INSTRUMENT MUST BE BEYOND THE CONTROL OR RECALL OF THE PARTY DEPOSITING IT

It is generally held that to effect a valid escrow there must be an enforceable contract between the parties. The instrument, and if it be a deed, the deed, delivered into escrow must be beyond the control or recall of the grantor under a binding contract, for so long a time as it is to remain in escrow. A Deposit Receipt and escrow instructions, if signed by all of the parties and containing all the elements of a binding contract, may be sufficient to place such a deed beyond recall. The instrument is not withdrawable, nor can the escrow be revoked by either party absent the approval of the other. However, where there has been a failure of performance on the part of the other party, the instrument may be withdrawn by the party depositing it in escrow.

WHERE THERE IS FAILURE OF PERFORMANCE

AN OPTION SUPPORTED BY CONSIDERATION

An option supported by a sufficient consideration will sustain a valid escrow. An option unsupported by consideration may be revoked at any time before it is exercised, and consequently is not capable of sustaining a valid escrow.

PSEUDO-ESCROWS

Many so-called "escrows" are not escrows at all. They are sometimes called "pseudoescrows" and are common in real estate sales not involving complicated transactions or those not of any considerable magnitude. In these so-called "escrows" auxiliary contracts are not employed, complete written instructions are lacking, and very often deeds are not delivered to the escrow holder. That they succeed is due very largely to the fact that such sales go through without mishap or controversy. But should a situation arise where it became necessary to test the validity of such an escrow, some damaging effects might well be expected to result to one or the other of the parties. Suppose, for example, John Doe executes a deed to Richard Roe and deposits it in escrow intending it to be delivered out of escrow and unconditionally to Richard Roe when he, the grantee, shall have paid into escrow within ninety days the sum of $10,000. There is no auxiliary contract. There is no Deposit Receipt, nor have effective escrow instructions been signed by either of the parties. Richard Roe does however, intend to buy the property. John Doe dies before Richard Roe puts up the money. It was held in a leading case that in a similar situation there was a mere offer not accepted before the grantor's death, which could have been revoked by him at any time before acceptance; that without an auxiliary contract binding the grantor and the grantee there could be no true escrow, and therefore the so-called "escrow holder" was no more than an agent authorized to deliver the deed upon the payment of the purchase price; that under well-established principles of agency, by the death of the principal (in this case the grantor) the authority of the agent, (the so-called escrow holder) was terminated and he had, therefore, no authority to make delivery of the deed upon tender of the purchase price in "escrow."

A MERE OFFER REVOCABLE AT ANY TIME BEFORE ACCEPTANCE

GRANTOR'S DEATH REVOKED AGENT'S AUTHOR-ITY TO DELIVER DEED

Had there been, in such a situation, a binding and enforceable auxiliary contract between the grantor and the grantee, then a true escrow would have been established. In that event Richard Roe could have accepted the offer by paying into escrow the $10,000 after the grantor's death, and demanded the deed be delivered to him, which the escrow holder would have been bound to do.

It may be laid down as a general rule of law that when a true, or valid escrow has been established by a binding and enforceable auxiliary contract deposited with the escrow holder along with a fully executed deed, the death or incapacity of one of the parties to the escrow will not have the effect of terminating the escrow during the time fixed for performance. If the party entitled to accept performs within that time, he is entitled to have the escrow concluded according to the terms of the auxiliary contract.

Another example of where the grantee might suffer considerable inconvenience is presented in a second case worth considering. Grantor and grantee signed separate instructions addressed to the escrow holder, which together constituted a binding and enforceable contract, the grantor stating in his instructions that he "will hand the escrow holder the deed called for." It was held that a valid escrow had been established, and that the grantee could demand specific performance. But if, in such a case, the grantor were to die before the escrow was closed, how would the grantee get his deed? The answer probably is that if he performs under the contract, he must obtain a deed from the executor or administrator of the grantor's estate, made pursuant to the order of the probate court. If the deed had been delivered into escrow along with the aforesaid binding instructions, the escrow holder would have been authorized to deliver it to the grantee, notwithstanding

WHEN BINDING CONTRACT AND EXECUTED DEED ARE DELIVERED IN ESCROW, DEATH OF ONE OF THE PARTIES WILL NOT TERMINATE ES-CROW

VALID CONTRACT BETWEEN PARTIES, BUT NO DEED DELIVERED IN ESCROW the grantor's death. This would assume, of course, full performance by the grantee under the terms of the contract as established by the instructions. In such case the grantee would not be obliged to go into the probate court to get the deed delivered to him.

FIRST AND SEC-OND DELIVERY

It is sometimes said that there is a first and second delivery of a deed which has passed through an escrow; first, the delivery into escrow, and secondly, the delivery out of escrow to the grantee. Ordinarily, as we have seen, title will not pass until there has been an effectual delivery to the grantee. However, in these escrow transactions, for the purpose of doing equity and justice, and preventing hardship, and likewise to carry out the intentions of the parties, the courts have developed the doctrine of RELATION BACK. If the escrow transaction is consummated, title will relate back to the time of the delivery of the deed into escrow. The relation back rule will not be applied, however, if injustice may result by reason of its application.

THE DOCTRINE OF RELATION BACK

Where one of the parties to an escrow has died before the escrow is closed, the effective delivery of the deed out of escrow and unconditionally may depend upon whether such an instrument has actually been delivered into escrow, or whether a valid, enforceable contract existed between the parties; in other words, whether or not there was a true and valid escrow in existence.

In the cases previously mentioned the death of either party has not been made the condition upon which the deed shall pass to a grantee as an effective instrument. The condition is not the death of a party, but some other contingency, or performance.

DEED TO BE DELIVERED OUT OF ESCROW AND TO GRANTEE UPON DEATH OF GRANTOR

A fairly well-established exception to the general rule of law which fixes the validity of an escrow and separates it from the so-called pseudo-escrow permits a valid escrow to be created by the delivery into escrow of a deed with instructions not to deliver it to the grantee until after the grantor's death. In such case the grantor can reserve no right to recall the deed, or otherwise control its disposition. He must intend it to be a gift of the property conveyed. There must likewise be no intent on his part to make a testamentary disposition of the property.

In such case it is held that title passes immediately to the grantee, the grantor reserving a life estate in the property. The rule is justified upon the theory that a gift being intended, and not a sale of the property, and the death of the grantor being certain to occur, the "escrow" is a limitation upon the general rule requiring a binding and enforceable auxiliary contract to support it. The exception will not be allowed if it can be shown that a testamentary disposition was intended.

2. The Escrow Holder

STATUS OF ESCROW HOLDER

The status of the escrow holder partakes of the nature of both an agent of limited powers and a trustee. Before the close of the escrow his office is no more than that of a mere depository for the property of both parties to the escrow.

He is not a general agent, being invested with a peculiar status in the law. He must observe a strict compliance with the terms of his instructions. After the performance of the condition, or at the close of the escrow, he holds instruments and funds as trustee of the party to whom they are to be delivered.

Until the performance of the condition, the escrow holder is the agent of all of the parties, but may have different responsibilities of disclosure to different parties because of the limited character of this special agency. After the performance of the condition, or at the close of the escrow, the character of the agency changes. The agent-principal relationship at once springs into existence between the escrow holder and each party to the escrow with respect to escrowed property to which each such party is, under the escrow instructions, then entitled to possess, or have properly disposed.

NATURE OF AGENCY BEFORE AND AFTER PERFORMANCE OF CONDITION

In modern practice escrow holders are usually corporate organizations authorized under the law to handle escrows. And it is this type of escrow holder with whom the reader will ordinarily deal. Such holders should be well informed of their duties and responsibility. Co-operation with them will be helpful in successfully initiating and concluding an escrow transaction.

MODERN ESCROW AGENTS

3. The Escrow Instructions

Instructions in escrow are confidential. As between the parties to whom the instructions relate, each party has the right to see the instructions of the other party. When an escrow is actually two escrows in one, the escrow instructions of each separate group are private to that group, and cannot be inspected by the other group.

ESCROW INSTRUCTIONS

Although there is some variation in the practice of preparing escrow instructions, it is probably better practice to prepare formal instructions addressed to the escrow holder, not inconsistent with the terms of the auxiliary contract. These could take the form of instructions prepared to cover the entire transaction and signed by each of the parties. Or, they could be composed of two sets of instructions, one set prepared by and signed by the buyer, and the other prepared by and signed by the seller. Such instructions signed by, or approved by each of the parties, are better qualified to fix the responsibilities and limitations of the escrow holder's agency in the premises. They have a decided tendency to keep the transaction shaped to the form intended by the parties. However, printed instructions supplied by title companies handling escrows serve a useful purpose, and are particularly desirable in small transactions, or in those cases where the parties are largely relying upon such companies to work out the details of the negotiation.

TYPES OF INSTRUCTIONS

If the escrow holder agrees to act under the instructions presented, he is bound by them. Escrow instructions should be adequate to achieve what the parties intend so far as the "escrow" is concerned. Too much emphasis cannot be placed upon the need to have clear and adequate instructions on file with the escrow holder.

ESCROW HOLDER BOUND BY INSTRUCTIONS ACCEPTED BY HIM

The parties should be able to rely upon the assistance of present-day licensed escrow agents to give them proper advice in the matter of opening an escrow. However, need for preparing instructions in more detail might suggest the advisability of consulting an attorney. Inasmuch as no escrow agent, as such, ought to give legal advice, it would be good practice for a party to let his attorney look over any proposed instructions, especially if the transaction is substantial.

In fact, whenever any question of law presents itself to the mind of a party to the escrow, an attorney should be consulted. If a real estate broker is involved he should not put himself in a position where, if things turn out badly for the principal, he could be charged with the unlawful practice of the law in those jurisdictions in which rigid statutes and administrative regulations impose severe penalties upon brokers and laymen engaged in what is deemed the unlawful practice of the law.

**THE EARNEST
MONEY DEPOSIT**

It is customary for brokers to take earnest money deposits when negotiating a sale of property. Conservative escrow agents usually refuse to handle escrows calling for forfeiture of a purchase money deposit, requiring such deposits to be paid outside of the escrow. The balance of the purchase price will be deposited in escrow without provision for forfeiture. Considering the present attitude of the law favoring the purchaser, there is every reason why these escrow agents should proceed with caution in this area.

Should controversy arise between the parties to an escrow, the escrow holder is not obliged to decide such matters. He may bring an action in interpleader to settle the controversy.

4. The Closing Statement

**THE CLOSING
STATEMENT**

In preparing a closing statement it is well to keep in mind three classes of items to be entered, to wit:

**THREE CLASSES
OF ITEMS IN
CLOSING STATE-
MENT**

> One: Items which involve the actual sales trans-
> action between the seller and the buyer.
> Two: Items the payment of which is to be divided
> by seller and buyer, or prorated between them.
> Three: Items of expense which one of the parties
> has agreed to assume, or which by custom in the
> area he is usually called upon to pay, or which
> he has contracted to pay to third parties,
> the money for the payment of which has been
> placed in escrow, or is to be accounted for in
> an adjusted balance.

Classes Two and Three do not represent sums of money directly and primarily involved in the sale and purchase of the property. They are only indirectly and secondarily involved—Class Two as an adjustment of obligations and property interests between the parties, or that proportion of a particular expense each party has agreed to pay; and Class Three as those obligations chargeable to each party in full by reason of custom, or for services rendered to one party which he is passing on to the other, or because one party has agreed to assume and pay the full amount of a particular cost or expense, or for impounded sums assigned to the other party.

Items included under Class One are directly related to the principal transaction and the sales price, i.e., the sale and purchase of the property, and are such as purchase price, deed of trust, mortgage, etc. The purchase price being paid by the buyer to the seller is charged, or "debited," to the buyer, and "credited" to the seller because it represents an amount of money which will reduce what the buyer will receive, and increase what the seller will receive at the close of the escrow.

CLASS ONE— PURCHASE PRICE

Suppose the case where the buyer takes subject to a deed of trust, or assumes and agrees to pay the debt secured by it. How are these items entered in the Closing Statement? Obviously, the buyer will be credited with the deed of trust because it will decrease what he must pay at the close of the escrow, and the seller will be debited with the deed of trust because it will decrease what he will receive at the close of the escrow.

CLASS ONE—ASSUMED EXISTING DEED OF TRUST

Again, let us suppose the buyer pays the seller cash, and refinances, there being a first deed of trust against the property. How would these entries be handled? The new deed of trust the buyer would obtain by refinancing would be credited to him because it will decrease what he has to pay at the close of the escrow. The old first deed of trust will be debited to the seller because it will decrease what the seller will receive at the close of the escrow.

CLASS ONE—REFINANCING ENTRIES

Interest is adjusted between the parties with respect to the time each party owns the property to be conveyed. Title passes, ordinarily, at the close of the escrow when deed is recorded. All prorates are made as of that date.

CLASS TWO— INTEREST

EXAMPLE: Seller pays $300 interest quarterly on a note secured by a deed of trust buyer will assume, or take subject to. $300 interest payment falls due August 31. Escrow closes July 31. Buyer will have owned the property only one month at that time. Entries in seller's and buyer's closing accounts will be; credit buyer with $200, debit seller with $200.

In the example interest was not payable until a time after the closing date of the escrow; hence the buyer is credited and the seller is debited with the interest charge while he was owner of the property. Insurance premiums, however, have been paid in advance by seller at a time before the closing date of the escrow. The following example indicates how they will be prorated.

EXAMPLE: Seller pays for three years' insurance one year before the closing date of the escrow, paying in advance the sum of $300. Buyer then has the advantage of two years of insurance for which the

seller has already paid $200. The entries in seller's
and buyer's closing accounts will be; credit seller
with $200; debit buyer with $200.

**CLASS TWO—
OTHER PRORATES**

**CLASS THREE—
ITEMS**

All other prorates will be adjusted in like manner according to on which side of the closing date of the escrow they fall.

Items in Class Three are those obligations which one or the other of the parties have assumed by agreement, or in some manner obligated themsleves to pay, or have paid, third parties. Such an item may be a broker's commission for selling the property. This is usually paid by the seller and debited to the seller's account; no entry in the buyer's account. Another such item may be a loan charge, which could be points charged to the seller against a loan for the buyer. It would be debited to the seller; no entry in the buyer's account.

Escrow charges may be paid by the seller, or paid in proportion as agreed upon by the parties. They are often divided equally between the principals. Debit the party, or parties, to be charged. Impound accounts connected with government loans grow out of impounded monies set up in a trust account to be accumulated for the purpose of paying, usually, insurance and taxes. When a property, against which there is an existing loan, is sold "subject to" such loan, or taken by the buyer who assumes the existing loan, the buyer is usually assigned the impound account. This will ultimately benefit the buyer, so he is debited with the impound, and the seller is credited with it.

The seller will usually be required to pay for the preparation, acknowledgment and recording of all documents he is required to deliver to the buyer at the close of the escrow. Likewise will the buyer be charged with the preparation, acknowledgment and recordation of those documents he must deliver to the seller at the close of the escrow.

QUESTIONS AND ANSWERS

1. What is an escrow?

    Answer: It is a transaction wherein any written instrument, money or other thing of value is delivered to a third-party depositary under a valid contract to be held until the happening of a specified event or the performance of a prescribed condition, when it is then to be delivered out of escrow to a specified person discharged of the condition upon which it was held.

2. Is a contract necessary to a valid escrow?

    Answer: Ordinarily there must be a binding and enforceable contract.

3. How is this contract usually referred to in an escrow transaction?

    Answer: It is sometimes referred to as an auxiliary contract.

4. Must that which is deposited in an escrow be beyond the control or recall of the party depositing it to create a valid escrow?

    Answer: Yes.

5. Does a properly executed deposit receipt fulfill the requirements of an auxiliary contract?

    Answer: Yes.

6. Would escrow instructions meet the requirements of an auxiliary contract?

    Answer: Yes, if they contain the elements of a binding and enforceable contract between the parties.

7. Can an option unsupported by consideration form the basis for a valid escrow?

    Answer: No. It may be revoked at any time and therefore is not beyond the control of the party depositing it. But an option supported by consideration would suffice.

8. If there be a failure of performance within the time required under the terms of the escrow, may the other party withdraw his instruments from the escrow?

    Answer: Yes.

9. What are the elements ordinarily lacking in a pseudo-escrow?

    Answer: No auxiliary contract; faulty instructions which do not amount to a binding contract between the parties; failure to deposit an executed deed in escrow, etc.

10. Is there a well-settled exception to the rule that title does not pass upon the first delivery?

    Answer: Yes. This is in the case where a deed is to be delivered out of escrow and unconditionally upon the death of the grantor who deposits such deed in escrow. In such case a gift is intended. Title passes upon the first delivery, the grantee taking the fee, the grantor reserving a life estate.

11. Why is the transaction not a testamentary disposition of the property?

Answer: Because the conveyance is *inter vivos*, the grantor intending an immediate grant of the property. If transfer of title were to be conditional upon his death, then there might well be an attempted testamentary disposition.

12. What is the status of the escrow holder before the performance of the conditions upon which the escrow rests?

Answer: He is an agent of both parties to the escrow, although he may have different responsibilities of disclosure.

13. What is his status after performance of the conditions?

Answer: The dual character of his agency changes to a several principal-agent responsibility, the escrow holder becoming the agent of each of the parties for certain purposes. He is a kind of trustee at this point for the purpose of disposing of the instruments and funds in the escrow to the proper parties, or their nominees.

14. Is the escrow holder obliged to decide controversial matters between the parties?

Answer: No. He may bring an action in interpleader to settle the controversy.

15. If a transaction is a complicated one, how should escrow instructions be handled?

Answer: Good practice would suggest the advice of an attorney at law in the premises.

16. For what items does the seller ordinarily pay?

Answer: The seller will usually be required to pay for the preparation, acknowledgment and recording of all documents he is required to deliver to the buyer at the close of the escrow.

17. For what items does the buyer ordinarily pay?

Answer: The buyer will usually be required to pay for the preparation, acknowledgment and recording of all documents he is required to deliver to the seller at the close of the escrow.

18. Does the death or incapacity of one of the parties to a valid escrow terminate it?

Answer: No, not if the escrow is a true escrow valid in every respect.

19. Why is the doctrine of "relation back" employed by the courts in escrow transactions?

Answer: Usually to avoid injustice or hardship, or to effect the intention of the parties.

CHECKLIST

A. Determine if escrow holders are regulated or controlled in your state by statutory or administrative law.

B. Determine who may act as escrow agents in your state.

C. Determine if the proposed escrow holder (in the transaction you are handling) qualifies under the law, and otherwise, in your state.

D. Determine if the escrow you have opened contains the elements of a valid escrow.

E. Check the auxiliary contract for errors or ommissions.

F. Check the escrow instructions to determine if they have been carefully and adequately prepared. If printed forms, determine if they cover all contingencies and conditions.

G. Determine if an executed deed has been deposited in escrow.

H. Determine if all the necessary and proper instruments and documents have been deposited in escrow by all of the parties.

I. Determine if all required sums of money have been timely deposited in escrow.

J. Determine if arrangement has been made for the preparation and disposition of all instruments, documents and monies necessary to the effective closing of the escrow.

K. Determine if the closing date of the escrow has been fixed or indicated with certainty, and if possession of the property has been arranged for.

L. If you are ready to close, determine if all conditions have been complied with on both sides.

M. Determine if you have handled earnest money deposits in a manner agreeable to the escrow holder.

N. Determine if all prorations have been arranged for, title insurance provided for, and the division of costs and charges adjusted to the satisfaction of the parties.

O. Check the closing statement delivered by the escrow holder for accuracy.

11

The Appraisal

1. The Value Judgment

The market value of real estate is affected by social standards, economic factors, political theories, and government encroachment upon private rights, as well as by the wear and tear of physical forces in time.

APPRAISAL—A
VALUE JUDGMENT

A real estate appraisal is a value judgment. It is an estimate, an expert opinion. Its efficacy depends largely upon the intelligence, the integrity, the qualifications and the experience of the appraiser.

AN EDUCATED
ESTIMATE

A person dealing in real estate is frequently called upon to give his opinion of the value of a parcel of real property. It is perfectly proper that he should do so. But here, as in other areas of special professional skills, the ethical and serious-minded person will exercise every precaution not to exceed his competence or experience in estimating the value of property. If he be an expert himself in the particular area in which the appraisal falls, he will not hesitate to undertake the appraisal himself. But should there be any doubt in his mind as to his qualification to make the appraisal, he should recommend a professional appraiser. Mistakes have a way of plaguing a man's life and destroying his reputation.

However, to be totally ignorant of what is involved in an appraisal is entirely inexcusable in one practicing the real estate business. The purpose, therefore, of what follows is to set down some fundamental concepts and rules with which every real estate broker and every individual dealing in real property should be familiar.

2. Value

A. The Concept of Value and Influencing Factors

In the appraisal of real estate the important value is market value. Market value is the price for a piece of property which a seller and buyer would, respectively, take and give in an open market, each reasonably familiar with all of the uses to which it may be put, and neither acting under a compelling necessity to enter into the transaction or to deal in less than a reasonable time, and both willing to negotiate a transfer of the property.

BASIC FACTORS INFLUENCING VALUE

In real estate valuation value is the legal tender equivalent of the estimated worth of property. Basic factors which operate to qualify value are utility, supply and demand, financial capability of the prospective purchaser and both the legal and actual transferability of the thing sought to be acquired.

• UTILITY

UTILITY

The capacity to satisfy subjective attitudes of human wants is called utility. A thing has utility when after it is possessed it satisfies the desire to possess and use it.

• SHORT SUPPLY

SHORT SUPPLY

A thing is in short supply when it is scarce in the market. It may have utility, be in short supply, and yet have little demand. In other words, it may be capable of inducing an inclination to buy, have the power to satisfy that inclination, be in short supply and yet, because of some restraining influence or financial inability of people to buy it, be in little demand. The willingness or ability to buy is influenced by a number of economic, social and psychological factors.

• DEMAND

DEMAND

Demand may be thought of as emerging from a degree of desire to acquire a thing. In the economic sense it is restricted to the inclination of people to purchase those desirable things in the market for which they have the financial ability to pay. This financial ability to pay, coupled with the inclination to buy, materially affects the stability of market value.

• TRANSFERABILITY

TRANSFERABILITY

Is the property readily transferable in law? Or, is it encumbered or burdened, and if so, to what extent? The legal status of the property will affect its exchange or sale value.

B. Other Determinative Facts Underlying Value

• HIGHEST AND BEST USE

HIGHEST AND BEST USE

The use [not unlawful] which at the date of the appraisal is determined to be that use capable of producing the greatest net return to the land and improvements within a limited time is recognized as the highest and best use to which the property may be put.

CHANGE

Economic, social and physical forces constantly operate upon urban, suburban and rural communities, influencing the value of properties in these areas.

From the appraiser's point of view it is important to know what aspect of the life span of the property the appraisal covers; i.e., is the neighborhood in a process of growth, or is it in balance where there is no great change one way or the other; or has disintegration set in? The appraiser must attempt to measure the strength of these aspects to estimate their duration and effect upon value.

• CONFORMITY

Conformity asserts that maximum value is realized when the qualities of a property bear a reasonable likeness to the qualities of other properties in an area which has achieved a reasonably certain degree of socially, economically and morally acceptable standards of living; or uniformity of design in commercial or industrial districts.

The application of the concept of conformity is responsible for zoning ordinances, restrictive covenants in deeds, and equitable servitudes by which property, and its uses, are conformed to area standards. Such regulatory devices are calculated to maintain the highest excellence in the area of property utility, and consequently tend to support maximum values.

The application is somewhat modified, however, by the principles of REGESSION and PROGRESSION. Regression asserts that of properties of the same type the value of the better property, located among cheaper properties, will be affected adversely. Progression asserts that the value of a property of less worth, located among more valuable properties of the same type, is enhanced by such association.

One of the reasons for the these two tendencies in residential neighborhoods is that people financially able to buy only in the cheaper neighborhood cannot afford to pay the price of the more expensive house; while people with limited financial means, accustomed to a better neighborhood will not buy in the cheaper neighborhood, but will buy a cheaper house, paying a little more for it than its real worth, in the better neighborhood.

CONFORMITY

• COMPETITION

Profit develops competition. Reasonable and fair competition can be a stimulant to increased land value. But excess profits can bring about unhealthy competition, which in turn, by reducing net income to land, may depress its value.

COMPETITION

• SUBSTITUTION

Briefly, the principle of substitution affirms that a property is generally no more valuable than what people will pay for a substitute like property of equal quality and utility in the area. Or, put another way, the lowest-priced of a number of like properties with equal quality and utility in an area will tend, within limits, to fix the value of other properties in the same area.

SUBSTITUTION

3. The Appraisal Report

PURPOSE OF THE APPRAISAL

Should a broker or other person have occasion to examine an appraisal report on a piece of property he may become interested in offering for sale, or in purchasing, he should determine the purpose and function the report was intended to serve at the time it was made.

The date it was prepared is also important. Change affecting the value of property is constant, and time alters attitudes toward old patterns of utility. Social and economic obsolescence must be taken into consideration.

If such person learns the purpose of the appraisal, he should be able to follow the method employed by the appraiser in arriving at his evaluation of the property, and thus have a better understanding of the factors which were responsible for the appraised value. He will be in a far better position to discuss value intelligently with a prospective buyer if he can assign a reason for value factors indicated in the report than he would be if he were not able to follow the analysis of the appraiser. He might, too, be more persuasive with an owner who may be holding out for an unrealistic selling price.

4. Valuation Approaches

A. The Three Major Approaches

VALUATION AP-PROACHES

When the appraiser is told the function of the appraisal, the date to which it is to apply, the particular purpose for which value is to be estimated (as, for example, value for sale of the property in the current market, value for condemnation proceedings, for tax purposes, etc.) and after he has made a preliminary survey to determine the scope and breadth of the appraisal, he is in a position to begin the accumulation of data required to appraise the property.

THREE MAJOR APPROACHES

There are three major valuation approaches to be considered, and some variations in these. The major approaches are market data, capitalization of net income, and replacement new, less depreciation. These methods are commonly referred to as the "market data," "income" and "cost" approaches.

If the property is income property, the appraiser will use all three approaches, checking one against the others. But his judgment will usually suggest the greater efficacy of one over the other two in the appraisal of the particular property in hand. He will obviously, therefore, emphasize that approach which in his opinion has the greatest significance in pointing up value for the purpose desired.

B. Market Data and the Depreciation Concept

THE MARKET DATA APPROACH

Before a value can be arrived at by the use of one or more of these approaches, the appraiser must ordinarilly make a field survey of the socio-economic factors present. The survey may reach beyond the neighborhood in which the property is located.

Economic trends in the national economy, population growth and the general level of purchasing power are pervading influences in neighborhood and regional economies. So is the extent of the impingement of government control and regulation upon private enterprise in the area of activity examined. High local taxes will often shift building activity to suburban areas, changing the pattern of neighborhood autonomy, structure and development. The social characteristics of the people living in a residential neighborhood will influence its property values. Social and cultural conflicts depress values.

If the site and improvements to be appraised are for business purposes and are in a commercial district, the surrounding neighborhood conditions are important, as the character of this neighborhood may largely determine the quality and quantity of purchasing power that may be drawn upon.

When the appraiser has collected and collated the data he requires, he is ready to appraise the property. The purpose for which the appraisal is to be made will, as has been pointed out, suggest some selection in the acceptance and accumulation of data, to the end that those data are selected which, in the judgment of the appraiser, have the greatest significance in pointing up the value desired.

In the process of valuation he will ordinarily reach the actual estimate of value by the application of the market data, income and cost approaches in a setting developed by the general economic, social and political factors he has uncovered in the area.

In estimating the value of real property, depreciation plays a most important role. It is therefore necessary to have at least an elementary understanding of the depreciation concept. **THE DEPRECIATION CONCEPT**

Generally speaking, depreciation is the decline or loss in value of an asset due to deterioration and obsolescence.

Accrued depreciation is actual loss already effected from all causes of depreciation existing in a property up to a specified date, usually the date of the appraisal. It accounts for not only the loss of capital already invested, but that also which has been recaptured. It includes physical deterioration (both curable and incurable), functional obsolescence (curable and incurable), economic and social obsolescence, which is seldom curable. **ACCRUED DEPRECIATION**

It is an estimated gross-sum factor employed in the cost approach to appraisal. **DEPRECIATION APPLIED IN COST APPROACH TO APPRAISAL**

Accrued depreciation must be distinguished from accruals for future depreciation, the latter, generally speaking, being estimated amounts chargeable to the recapture of economically acceptable capital investment in the improvements affixed to the land. These accruals represent the annual recurring amount in dollars and cents allocated to recapture of the value of a wasting asset (the improvements) spread over the economic life of the property. It is set up as a rate, or percentage of value lost annually, and is deducted from income over a period of time within which the property should be amortized. It is used when appraisal is reached by the income approach, and is commonly measured by the straight-line or the sinking fund methods. **ACCRUALS TO RECAPTURE INVESTMENT** **AN ANNUAL PERCENTAGE OF LOST VALUE** **USED IN INCOME APPROACH OR SINKING FUND METHODS**

C. Straight-line Capitalization

STRAIGHT-LINE CAPITALIZATION

Straight-line capitalization is an income approach to value. It contemplates declining income, the recapture in equal installments of capital investment in improvements, and interest on investment in land and improvements outstanding and not recaptured. Most income properties respond to the requirements of the straight-line method.

An example will make the method clear.

Assume a net annual return before depreciation of $12,000 on land and improvements; 7 per cent acceptable investor interest rate; capital investment in improvements to be recaptured in 25 years, the economic life of the improvements (making the recapture rate 4 per cent); land value $20,000.

What is the value of the whole property?

SOLUTION:

Net before recapture	$ 12,000.00
Income on land .07 × $20,000	1,400.00
Net before recapture, improvements	$ 10,600.00

Overall rate 11% (7% interest rate plus 4% recapture rate)

11% =	$10,600.00
1% =	963.64
7% =	6,745.48
4% =	3,854.56

Capitalize improvements at 11%

$$\frac{\$10,600}{.11} = \$96,363.64$$

Value of improvements	$ 96,363.64
Add value of land	20,000.00
Appraised value of whole property	$116,363.64

Or, briefly set up as:

Net before recapture	$ 12,000.00
Imputable to land	1,400.00
Net imputable to improvements	10,600.00
Capitalize improvements at 11%	96,363.64
Add land value (market data)	20,000.00
Appraised value	$116,363.64

ANNUAL INTEREST RETURN ON LAND AND IMPROVEMENTS

The following will indicate net annual interest return on land and improvements, recapture sum to recover investment in improvements within 25 years, declining investment and interest return. The figures will indicate a 7 per cent return on capital for 25 years and recapture of improvements within that time. The value of the land is not affected by the computation.

In these figures the interest income is figured on the investment in both land and improvements, the investor being entitled to have a reasonable return on capital invested in both these commodities.

The total of interest return and recapture money is the least net income the investor can receive if he has paid the right price for the land and improvements. The appraised value of the whole property is rested on this assumption.

Investment in land and improvements		$116,363.64
(at beginning of first year)		
Value of land (market data)		20,000.00
Value of improvements		$ 96,363.64
Investment in land and improvements		$116,363.64
Int. at 7% on land and improvements		
(.07 × $116,363.64)	$ 8,145.45	
Recapture of improvements		
(.04 × $96,363.64)	3,854.52	−3,854.52
Net income end of first year	$11,999.97	
Remaining investment at end of first year		$112,509.11
Int. at 7% on land and improvements		
(.07 × $112,509.11)	$ 7,875.64	
Recapture of improvements		
(.04 × $96,363.64)	3,854.52	−3,854.52
Net income end second year	$11,730.16	
Remaining investment at end of second year		$108,654.59
Int. at 7% on land and improvements		
(.07 × $108,654.59)	$ 7,605.82	
Recapture of improvements		
(a constant)	3,854.52	−3,854.52
Net income end of third year	$11,460.34	
Remaining investment at end of third year		$104,800.07

This process would continue until full recapture of investment in improvements, i.e., $96,636.64.

An examination of the declining capital balance will indicate that the decline is equal annually, in the amount of $3,854.52, the recapture figure.

It will also be seen that income on land and improvements likewise declines equally annually, in the amount of $269.80+, as follows:

$8,145.45
− 7,875.64
$ 269.81

$7,875.64
− 7,605.82
$ 269.82

D. Direct Capitalization Method

A much simpler method of estimating value is the direct capitalization method. By this approach an overall rate is established by which the whole property is capitalized. This rate is determined by market data, the appraiser going into the field and developing by the inspection and analysis of a number of like properties the annual net income before depreciation of each, and its selling price. To get the overall rate the appraiser divides the income of each property by its selling price, which gives him a separate rate for each property. With this kind of information he is in a position to select a rate which he believes to be an appropriate overall rate to apply to the particular property he is appraising.

This direct method does not take into consideration the relative values of land and improvements, which can make a considerable difference in the rate to be applied. And too, it can only be implied that the overall rate adequately covers recapture money due to the very considerable variation in the ratio in value of the improvements to the land.

However, if well-informed investors in the several properties examined by the appraiser have been satisfied with the overall rates of return on properties held by them, and developed by the appraiser in his field work, it is reasonable to believe that an overall rate approximating these will fairly develop the value of the property being appraised.

Suppose the overall rate established by the appraiser was 10%, and the net annual income from the property before depreciation was $10,000, and that this income might reasonably be expected for the economic life of the improvements—then

$$\frac{\$10,000}{.10} = \$100,000 \text{ appraised value.}$$

From the foregoing discussion of the capitalization method of estimating value it will be noticed that we started with net income before depreciation. The following problem will indicate how this starting point of "net income" is arrived at.

PROBLEM: Using the capitalization method, determine the appraised value of the following property from the facts given:

The property is a two-story building having four apartments on the second floor, and three stores on the sidewalk level. Two of the apartments rent for $125 a month each; two rent for $100 a month each. The stores rent for $300 a month each.

The appraiser is given the following list of "expenses," which he finds to be correct: $750 monthly payment on note secured by first deed of trust; property taxes $1,700; insurance $600; management expense $50 a month; maintenance and janitor $50 a month; annual accruals for depreciation $2,000; annual reserve for replacement of furniture and fixtures $1,500; water monthly, $25; lights monthly, $10; heating, monthly, $75.

The appraiser sets up the above data as follows:

Gross income

Two apartments	$125 × 2, or $250 × 12	$ 3,000
Two apartments	$100 × 2, or $200 × 12	2,400
Three stores	$300 × 3, or $900 × 12	10,800
Total gross income		$15,400

Vacancy factor and collection losses, annual (.10 × $15,400)	1,540
Adjusted gross annual income	$13,860

Operating charges

Property tax, annual		$1,700
Insurance, annual		600
Management, monthly	$50 × 12	600
Maintenance and janitor, monthly	50 × 12	600
Water, monthly	25 × 12	300
Lights, monthly	10 × 12	120
Heating, monthly	75 × 12	900
Annual reserve to replace furniture and fixtures		1,500
Annual accruals for depreciation		2,000

Total operating charges	8,320
Net annual income	$ 5,540
Net income capitalized at 11% overall ($5540/.11 = $50,363.64, or $50,364)	
Appraised value	$50,000

It should be noticed that the item of $750 monthly payment against the note secured by a first deed of trust on the property as part of the purchase price was not allowed as an annual operating charge. It is not an operating expense to be deducted from gross income when the capitalization method is employed to estimate value. The charge would be a proper one, however, in determining net capital investment return.

E. Building Residual and Land Residual Methods

BUILDING RESIDUAL

If the value of land is known and the total net annual return from land and building, the value of the building may be obtained by the building residual method.

PROBLEM: Given: $20,000 value of land
5,000 net annual income from property
7% interest rate
2% recapture rate

From these data determine the value of the build-ing. What is the value of the real estate?

SOLUTION: .07 × $20,000 = $1,400 annual return on land

$5,000 net annual return on land and building
−1,400 return attributed to land
$3,600 net annual return attributed to building

Capitalize income from building so as to return
7% plus 2% recapture rate

$$\frac{\$3,600}{.09} = \$40,000$$

$40,000 value of building
 20,000 value of land
$60,000 value of real estate

LAND RESIDUAL   The land residual technique would start with the value of the building, let us say $40,000, the income from which must reflect return of investment as well as interest on investment. Using the same figures as in the foregoing example (.09 × $40,000), the net income of the building amounts to $3,600. This income figure subtracted from the given $5,000 leaves $1,400 of total income allocated to the land, which, capitalized at 7 per cent, gives the land a residual value of $20,000.

F. Replacement New, Less Accrued Depreciation

REPLACEMENT NEW, LESS AC-CRUED DEPRECIATION   The cost approach to appraisal contemplates the estimated present value of of the land plus the cost of replacing the improvements new, less accrued depreciation.

The normal estimate of land value is reached through the market data approach.

The building cost, while it involves both direct and indirect costs, may be reasonably arrived at, under ordinary conditions, by using square foot cost data obtained in the area.

While in the capitalization approach to appraisal only straight-line depreciation, or physical deterioration, was allowed, in the replacement new method a deduction of all factors of depreciation is permissible; that is to say, physical deterioration, functional and economic obsolescence. A refinement would break the physical deterioration into curable and incurable deterioration, and the functional obsolescence likewise into curable and incurable. Economic obsolescence is rarely curable, and is therefore generally treated as incurable.

Deferred maintenance must be added to physical deterioration, functional and economic obsolescence.

EXAMPLE :   Eight-year-old dwelling house with life expectancy of 50 years.

4,200 sq.ft. living space
   $20 per square foot observed area cost to build
   160 sq.ft. of covered porches
   $8 per square foot observed area cost to build
   75′ × 100′ landscaping
   $.50 per sq.ft. observed area cost
   2.5′ × 100′ sidewalks
   $.50 per sq.ft. observed area cost

        5% functional obsolescence factor
      $1,000 deferred maintenance
      $10,000 value of land, market data

QUESTION: What is present value?

SOLUTION:

4,200 sq.ft. × $20 =		$84,000
160 sq.ft. × $ 8 =		1,280
Cost to replace, new		$85,280
Less depreciation		
Straight-line		
$\dfrac{\$85,280 \times 8}{50} =$	$13,645	
Functional obsolescence		
$85,280 × .05	4,264	
Deferred maintenance	1,000	
Total depreciation	$18,909	18,909
Replacement new, less depreciation		$66,371
Add landscaping		
[75′ × 100′] × .50		3,750
Add sidewalks		
[2.5′ × 100′] × .50		125
Add land		10,000
Appraised value		$80,246

The replacement cost, new, approach assumes the upper limit of value. To offset the advantages of new construction the cost must be adjusted by accrued depreciation of every character. This should approximate the present value.

However, it must always be remembered that any of these appraisal techniques are but tools and guides to value. The intelligence, experience and common sense of the appraiser will very largely determine the validity of the appraisal estimate. He will be greatly assisted by a knowledgeable employment of the approaches suggested here. But they must be employed with more than casual understanding of their function in approximating value.

5. Gross Multipliers

Gross multipliers are quick rule-of-thumb approaches to value. They may be used for annual or monthly gross income. Operating expenses are not considered. Only gross income is the measure. Net income, or what the property will actually return on an investment, can only be inferred from the relation of gross income to value established in connection with like properties in the area. These multipliers are limited in use, but can roughly approximate value when rental units in a property are related to sales price.

**THE GROSS
MULTIPLIER**

6. Economic Rent

ECONOMIC RENT

Economic rent is a theoretical figure. It is, generally speaking, what the appraiser, by market analysis and sound economic theory, has determined the space should rent for in the open market at the time of the appraisal, if it were available.

ACTUAL RENT

Actually, the space in the building being appraised may rent for more or for less than the economic rent. The rent actually received is actual rent.

CONTRACT RENT

Economic rent must therefore be distinguished from actual rent. It should also be distinguished from contract rent, which is rent fixed by contract, such as a lease. Economic rent may vary from year to year depending upon economic conditions. But contract rent is fixed for the rental term, or is adjustable by a measure determined by the terms of the rental agreement.

GROUND RENT

Economic rent is sometimes defined in the same terms as ground rent, but modern usage has enlarged the boundaries of economic rent.

7. The Operating Statement

THE OPERATING STATEMENT

If an income property is being offered for sale, the prospective purchaser is entitled to have, and will most likely demand, an Operating Statement. This statement is prepared to show the net income before depreciation, and can be the source of reliable information to the purchaser. It can also be an incompetent, or even fraudulent, instrument.

Particular care should be taken to see that the data supplied by an Operating Statement are accurate factually, and sound economically. Too often an Operating Statement is allowed to indicate a profitable operation in cases where a more scrupulous attention to cost items would suggest caution. This is particularly so when the prospective buyer is not entirely familiar with the operation of a property similar to the one offered for sale.

CAPITAL INVESTMENT RETURN AND NET SPENDABLE INCOME

The Operating Statement will show the net income, before depreciation, which may be expected from the operation of the property. The purchaser-investor may very well want to know what his capital investment return will be should he buy the property, and what net spendable income he may expect.

In such case all annual charges not set forth in the Operating Statement, will be determined, including a depreciation reserve, interest and principal on a mortgage or trust deed against the property, business license fees, income taxes, etc. When the investor's net spendable income is thus established, his capital investment return may be determined by dividing net spendable income by his cash down payment on the property.

Operating Statement	
Gross income estimate—rent	$15,400
Vacancy factor and loss of rent (10%)	1,540
Effective gross rental	$13,860

Expenses

   Fixed expenses

      Taxes $1,700

      Insurance   600

                                   $2,300

   Operating expense

      Management   600

      Maintenance and janitor   600

      Water   300

      Light   120

      Heat   900

      Annual reserves to
replace furniture and
fixtures   1,500

                                   4,020

  Total expense   6,320

  Net income before depreciation $ 7,540

There are other items of operating expense which might legitimately be included in the operating statement. Their inclusion will depend upon the operation.

QUESTIONS AND ANSWERS

1. Name several things which affect value.

   Answer: Social standards, economic factors, political theories, government impingement upon private rights, the wear and tear of physical forces and time.

2. What is a real estate appraisal?

   Answer: It is a value judgment.

3. What is market value?

   Answer: It is the price for a piece of property which a seller and buyer would,
   respectively, take and give in an open market, each reasonably familiar
   with all of the uses to which it may be put, neither acting under a compelling necessity to enter into the transaction, or to deal in less than a
   reasonable time, and both willing to negotiate a transfer of the property,
   and both having the ability to do so.

4. What, briefly, is "utility"?

   Answer: The power to satisfy a human want.

5. When is a thing in "short supply"?

   Answer: When it is scarce in the market.

6. What is "demand"?

   Answer: It may be thought of as aroused desire to acquire a thing.

7. What, generally, is transferability?

   Answer: A thing has transferability if it may be readily transferable in law.

8. What is the highest and best use?

   Answer: That use [not unlawful] which at the date of the appraisal is determined
   to be the use capable of producing the greatest net return to the land
   and improvements over an estimated period of time.

9. What is the principle of "conformity"?

   Answer: This principle holds the maximum of value to be realized when the
   qualities of a property bear a reasonable likeness to the qualities of other
   units in the area.

10. What is the principle of "substitution"?

    Answer: This principle affirms that a property is generally no more valuable than
    what people will pay for a substitute like property of equal quality and
    utility in the area.

11. What are the three major approaches to value used by the appraiser?

    Answer: Market data; capitalization; and replacement new, less depreciation.

12. Briefly, what is depreciation?

Answer: It is the loss from the upper limit of value due to deterioration and obsolescence.

13. Briefly, what is accrued depreciation?

Answer: It is actual loss from all causes of depreciation existing in a property at a specified time.

14. In what approach is accrued depreciation used?

Answer: In the cost approach to value.

15. Briefly, say what straight-line capitalization is in the appraisal of property.

Answer: It is an income approach to value.

16. What does straight-line capitalization contemplate?

Answer: Declining income, the recapture in equal installments of capital investment in improvements, and interest on investment in land and improvements outstanding and not recaptured.

17. Comment on the building residual method of estimating value.

Answer: If the value of the land is known and the total net annual return from land and building, the value of the building may be obtained by the building residual method.

18. How about the land residual method?

Answer: Likewise, the residual value of the land could be determined if the value of the building is known and the net annual return from the building and land.

19. What does the replacement new, less depreciation method of estimating value contemplate?

Answer: The estimated present value of the land, plus the cost of replacing the improvements new, less accrued depreciation.

20. What is an Operating Statement?

Answer: A statement intended to show the net annual income of a property before depreciation.

CHECKLIST

A. Check to determine the purpose of the appraisal before selecting the method of appraisal to be emphasized in estimating the value of the property to be appraised.

B. Select the method of appraisal best suited, in your judgment, to value the property for the purpose intended, and emphasize this approach to value.

C. Check the accuracy and soundness of collected and collated market data, to the end that they are basically factual and bear a reasonable relevancy to the property being appraised.

D. Check to determine the present highest and best use to which the property can be put.

E. Check the property's conformity to other like units in the area.

F. Check the value of substitute properties in the area of equal quality and utility.

G. If the property to be appraised is income property, check the sources of data available to all three approaches to value; i.e., "market data," "income" and "cost."

H. Check carefully for deferred maintenance.

I. When using either the "land residual" or the "building residual" approach, be sure to check the accuracy of all necessary market data employed.

J. Check the breadth and base of all "gross multipliers" when these form any part of the estimate of value.

K. If gross income is based upon economic rent, check this figure against contract or actual rent, and justify the differential, if any.

L. Check the accuracy of the Operating Statement, and be sure it is supported by actual facts and sound estimates.

M. When using the capitalization approach to value, check the reliability of the "interest" and "recapture" rates employed.

N. When using the replacement new, approach to value, check to be sure all factors of depreciation have been allowed.

Pitfalls to Avoid

Pitfalls ordinarily resolve themselves into ignorance, negligence and bad judgment. They appear to be objective when, in fact they are products of the mind. We fancy we see pitfalls because we approach apprehensively, or foolishly, the solution of our problems.

A few suggestions might help to establish a better approach to the business in hand, and thus do much to clear away some pitfalls that ought to be avoided. We should observe three cardinal rules at the very outset:

1. Never assume that to be the law which you do not know, with reasonable certainty, to be the law. If there is doubt, and the matter is important, consult a lawyer.
2. Acknowledge to yourself that the other fellow just might know as much, if not more, than you yourself know about the law and the facts with which you are dealing, and proceed cautiously from that point of view.
3. Don't try to monopolize all of the advantages the situation offers; there is more than one party to a transaction.

Contracts

Don't fall into the error of providing an "insufficient" consideration to support a promise you intend to be enforced.

Be sure the "object" of the contract is not against public policy, or otherwise unlawful in your state.

Don't overlook the formalities in your state necessary to give validity to the particular kind of contract you are dealing with.

Don't write contracts with minors which cannot be enforced.

Don't write contracts with persons who you have reason to believe may be mentally incompetent to enter into the contractual relationship.

Don't fall into the error of dealing with "names." Deal with real people, or legal entities capable of contracting.

Don't fall into the common error of making the contract too "skimpy." Get the real understanding of the parties into the language of the agreement. Leave nothing to the secret intentions of the parties.

Don't fall into the error of believing that a continuing offer, or option, remains open indefinitely.

Don't overlook the fact that the law changes, and that it might be something quite different than it was when you last had a transaction similar to the one presently engaging your attention.

Be constantly alert to any signs of duress, undue influence or fraud, from whatever source.

Avoid too much reliance upon oral promises and representations. If a man intends to keep his promises, or stand behind his representations, he should have no objection to setting them down in black and white.

Real Property

Don't fail to distinguish between the several kinds of estates. Statutory requirements must be observed.

Don't fall into the error of confusing a tenancy at will with a periodic tenancy, or with a tenancy at sufferance. Each requires different treatment in many respects.

Don't fail to determine how the property is held [i.e., in sole ownership or in co-tenancy] and arrange to have all signatures required in the instrument involved.

In those states in which dower and curtesy are recognized, check the law to learn what the rights of the parties are with respect to the acquisition and sale of real estate.

In the community property states and those where estates by the entireties are recognized, check the law to determine what the rights of the parties are with respect to the acquisition and sale of real property.

Don't fail to determine what estate will be vested in the co-tenants as the deed is presently drawn; if you are purchasing the property decide if that kind of estate is desired, otherwise redraft the deed to effect the desired tenancy.

Don't fall into the error of assuming that every chattel may be removed by the vendor of a building or residence.

Don't fall into the error of believing every chattel attached to the building is a fixture and cannot be removed.

Don't guess what is, or is not, a fixture, removable or not removable from the real estate.

Don't fail to take into consideration [when chattels affixed to the property are concerned] the relationship of the interested parties with respect to their possession or ownership of the estate, the character of the chattels, themselves, and how they are annexed to the building or ground, as well as the intent of the parties at the time of annexation.

Don't overlook, when dealing with industrial properties, the constructive annexation of industrial fixtures.

Don't fall into the error of assuming an asserted easement is appurtenant to the estate. Determine its origin before representing that it passes with the land. If an easement is one that is implied in grant or reservation, in the nature of a way of necessity, or grows out of pre-existing quasi-easements, do not fail to determine the basis in fact for such easement, before representing that it exists.

When dealing with titles acquired by adverse possession, it is well to obtain, or suggest, the advice of an attorney at law.

When an incorporeal hereditament acquired by prescription is involved, it is likewise advisable to obtain competent legal advice.

Don't fall into the error of assuming that a particular covenant in a precedent deed of conveyance runs with the land. The law in this area is highly technical.

If restrictive covenants are involved, a careful research is required to determine their validity. The doctrine of equitable servitudes may be of primary interest in the solution of your problem.

If homestead exemptions are claimed, seek competent legal advice.

Recording and Title Insurance

In this area the important practical thing would be to inspect the property for occupation and claim of title, and examine into any facts available outside of the public records which might be the basis of a legal contest. Ordinary title insurance will usually take care of the record title.

The Subdivision

Don't underestimate the strength of the police power of the state.

Many pitfalls can develop in the area of the subdivision. The subdivision laws of the state in which the subdivision is located, or in which it is to be sold, should be thoroughly studied and understood by all persons interested in the promotion of subdivision properties.

The text, Chapter 4, outlines generally the subdivision requirements in a state where legislation in this field of the law is somewhat extensive.

Real Estate Forms

Don't fall into the error of making the Listing Agreement, or employment contract, too brief. The terms and conditions upon which the property is being offered for sale, or other disposition, should be complete.

The terms and conditions contained in the Deposit Receipt, which is a form of "acceptance," should conform strictly to those set forth in the Listing Agreement. If these terms do not meet the terms and conditions as written in the offer [Listing Agreement], the broker has not earned his commission if the principal refuses to conclude the transaction. While the Deposit Receipt is written as an "offer" and must be "accepted" by the principal, it is an "acceptance," as suggested, in the sense that what the prospective purchaser is actually doing is "accepting" the principal's offer to sell his property on the terms and conditions contained in the Listing Agreement given the broker. The prospective purchaser very well could, of course, be offering to buy the property on quite different terms than those indicated by the principal. However, from the broker's point of view, if the transaction were to stop right there, he would not be entitled to his commission. This pitfall should be avoided as far as possible by getting the prospective purchaser and the principal agreed upon terms and conditions before the Deposit Receipt is written.

The broker should not fall into the error of believing the owner of the property listed cannot sell it himself without liability to the broker for commission if he, the broker, does not have an *exclusive authorization and right to sell* employment contract.

The distinction between the several types of agency contract of employment should be understood by the broker, and the rights of the parties under each contract kept clearly in mind.

Don't fall into the error of confusing a "power" with the "obligation of contract."

Don't confuse a "naked" power with a power "coupled with an interest."

Don't fall into the error of believing a "bare power" cannot be revoked by your principal at any time. But don't confuse this with his obligation of contract to perform, if performance is due.

Don't fail to comply with the law of your state with respect to the deposit, or other disposition, of money entrusted to your care, such as a deposit on account of the purchase price.

Don't fail to prepare and keep the proper book accounts of such funds, if required by the laws of your state.

Don't fail to determine early in the negotiations whether the land contract or some other form of security instrument is best suited to the transaction you are handling.

Don't overlook the possible advisability of a clause in the land contract converting the transaction from one of an executory contract of sale to one of a conveyance of title with a security instrument back, to become effective upon stipulated conditions.

In the Exchange Agreement, inflated equities should be reduced as nearly as possible to actual market values.

The broker should not fall into the error of accepting commission from both seller and purchaser without the consent of both.

In the area of leases, don't fail to understand that the lease partakes of the nature of both a contract and a conveyance. There are continuing contractual obligations.

Don't overlook statutory limitations on the terms of various types of leases.

Don't fall into the error of confusing an assignment of a lease with a subletting.

Be sure the lease is for a lawful purpose.

If you are a real estate broker, determine if statutes in your state regulate dealing in "hard money" loans, particularly with respect to commissions and costs.

Deeds and Patents

Don't fall into the error of believing that any form of deed is satisfactory. Use the form best suited to the purpose in mind—warranty, bargain and sale or quitclaim.

When a deed, or any other instrument, is required to be acknowledged, don't let the parties whose signatures are required get away before their acknowledgments are taken. It may be very difficult to get them before a notary later.

Don't fail to describe properly the property to be conveyed.

Don't fall into the error of believing that "redelivery" or "cancellation" or "destruction" of a deed has the effect of reconveying the estate or reinvesting it in the grantor.

Don't fall into the error of attempting to deliver a deed with the intention of title passing to the grantee named therein after the grantor's death.

Don't fall into the error of believing a deed is not effective unless the grantor's signature is in "ink."

Don't fail to see to it that the deed is fully "executed." This includes delivery to the grantee, either physically or constructively, and acceptance by him.

Bear in mind that while a deed cannot be delivered conditionally; it may be delivered "constructively."

Don't fall into the error of believing that merely recording a deed amounts to its delivery as an effective conveyance.

If you are dealing with a United States patent, do not fail to determine what reservations, if any, are recited.

Mortgages and Deeds of Trust

Don't fall into the error of confusing the liabilities of the parties when a purchaser of real property takes the property *subject to the mortgage* [being a present lien on the property] and when he *assumes the mortgage*, and agrees to pay the mortgage debt.

If your buyer is to assume a mortgage, be sure you know what his liability will be to the mortgagee; and if you are the mortgagee, or represent him, be sure you know whether such purchaser will be obligated to pay the mortgage debt should the original or any subsequent purchaser be unable to do so. This will involve a number of factors, primarily, whether the assuming purchaser's grantor had assumed to pay the mortgage debt, the amount of the debt remaining unpaid, and the market value of the security.

Be cautious of purchase-money mortgages; the pitfall there is connected with the character and financial integrity of the purchaser-mortgagor.

Don't fall into the error of believing that in most jurisdictions the assignment of a mortgage carries the note with it.

Before you decide to use a mortgage with a power of sale, see how your state law regulates such mortgages.

If your state recognizes the Deed of Trust, determine who may act as trustee, and what his qualifications must be.

The Mechanic's Lien

In this area there are too many pitfalls to attempt a solution to a problem of any consequence. It is better to seek the advice of some competent person.

Negotiable Instruments

If you are interested in negotiable paper, don't assume the paper you hold, or are handling, is negotiable. Know that it is by checking a few simple rules, and putting yourself in possession of some pertinent facts.

If you intend depositing negotiable checks in a bank, make the restrictive endorsement "for deposit only." It may save you money.

If you wish to put yourself in the position of a "holder in due course," do not accept paper that you know to be overdue, or which you know to have been dishonored.

Don't fall into the error of believing that when you indorse "without recourse" you relieve yourself of all obligation on the paper. You are still liable on certain warranties.

Don't fall into the error of believing that you cannot by proper indorsement relieve yourself of all undertakings and warranties. You can.

Don't assume that a bank cannot successfully defend against payment of a forged or altered check. It can.

The Escrow

Don't fall into the error of believing that the mere opening of an "escrow" with an escrow holder will create a valid and binding escrow.

Don't fail to get some binding agreement between the parties into the escrow, together with an executed deed, if the transaction is a conveyance of real property.

Don't fail to get adequate escrow instructions on file with the escrow holder so that he may know exactly what he is supposed to do, and become liable for under the escrow.

Don't overlook the fact that unless a valid escrow has been established, the grantor's death may vitiate the entire transaction.

If you are a real estate broker, don't fall into the error of giving legal advice in connection with matters you are handling. Some dissatisfied principal might bring charges against you before a disciplinary tribunal regulating brokerage in your state.

Don't fall into the error of accepting deposit money, or any other funds on behalf of your principal, unless you are properly authorized so to do.

Appraisal

Don't assume to know too much about appraising real estate unless you have seriously studied appraisal methods and techniques.

Don't discount the value of a good appraisal report, even if it seems to disagree with some of your own ideas. You may be unconsciously prejudiced.

If you are going to make the appraisal report yourself, give serious consideration to the methods of approach you ought to emphasize.

Don't rely upon what appears to be uninformed sources of information in your field survey. Look for expert comment if it is available.

If you use the land residual or the building residual techniques, be sure your basic building or land values are sound.

Don't get out of perspective with gross multipliers.

If you are a real estate broker, exercise the greatest integrity in preparing an Operating Statement. Better to lose a sale than to be charged with misrepresentation.

Glossary of Legal Terms

[The meanings found in this section are not intended to be scholarly definitions. The object is to convey only a general and easily understandable idea of their logical intension in the context in which they are used in the HANDBOOK.]

Ab initio: A Latin phrase meaning "from the beginning."

Absolute ownership: Occurs when a single person has absolute dominion over a thing, as compared with a limited or qualified ownership, when ownership is shared with others.

Abstract, the: A summary, in brief form, of all recorded evidence of title to land, containing all instruments and records of judicial proceedings touching and concerning title.

Acceptance of an offer: An act, verbal or physical, which the law recognizes as capable of binding the offeror to the promise contained in his offer.

Accrued depreciation: Loss already effected from all causes of depreciation.

Adverse possession: The possession of land against the will of the owner for a longer period of time than within which the prevailing statute of limitation permits an action to be maintained for its recovery, with intent to own it. A corporeal hereditament is involved.

Affirmative easement: The right of the owner to perform an act on the servient tenement or on his own land which affects the servient tenement, which he could not do absent the affirmative easement. See *Negative easement* this glossary.

After-acquired title: Title acquired by the grantor of property after the property has been conveyed to the grantee.

After possibility of issue extinct: An estate tail after possibility of issue extinct was a common law estate by which the tenant in special tail succeeded to the estate when the person from whose body the issue is to spring dies without issue, or having issue, the issue becomes extinct. Estates tail have been abolished in most states.

Allodial: As applied to land, land held in absolute ownership as opposed to feudal tenures.

Ancillary easement: A use necessary for the full enjoyment of a *profit a prendre* or some other use in the land of another.

Appraisal: An expert opinion, or estimate of value.

Appurtenant: That which is annexed to or belongs to another thing.

Assignable: That which may be lawfully assigned.

Assignee: One to whom an assignment is made.

Assignment: The act of assigning, or transferring a thing, or the ownership of a thing.

Assignor: One who assigns a right, an obligation or an instrument, or ownership of a thing capable of being assigned.

Assign: To transfer or set over. A lease is assigned when the entire interest in the leasehold is transferred or set over to a third person.

Assume the mortgage: One who assumes a mortgage, or more nearly correct, who takes the property subject to the mortgage and assumes and promises to pay the mortgage debt, is personally liable to the mortgagee for the mortgage debt.

Attesting witness: A witness to the signing of a deed or other instrument.

Authority or power: As used in the text, the liberty or authority of the broker to perform under the listing agreement. The authority or power so to act is created by the agency status between principal and broker based upon trust and confidence.

Auxiliary contract: A contract between parties to an escrow fixing their respective rights and obligations in a real estate transaction.

Bare power: See *Naked power.*

Benefit: In the law of contracts concerning "consideration," benefit is any advantage, gain or profit to the promissor.

Benefit of bargain: The advantage a vendor of land may have as measured by the profit he makes in the sale of his land.

Bilateral contract: A contract in which there are mutual promises.

Blanket encumbrance: Usually refers to an encumbrance placed on an entire tract of land which is thereafter carved into separate parcels for sale. A partial release clause is sometimes employed to permit separate parcels to be released from the lien of the blanket encumbrance so as to enable these parcels to be sold and clear title to be given to the purchasers of them.

Broker's loan statement: A disclosure statement required by statute for brokers dealing in *hard money* loans.

Certificate of title: A certification that the record title to property is in a certain person, subject to named exceptions. The certification is based upon the examination of the relevant public records.

Change: Contemplates all factors involved in growth, equilibrium, decline and decay. A term used in an appraisal.

Chattel: Personal property.

Chattel real: An estate for years is known as a chattel real.

Collateral heir: An heir not in the direct line from a common ancestor, as contrasted with a lineal heir.

Collateral impeachment: As used in the text, an attack upon a patent not made in a direct action against the government to annul it, or modify it.

Collection guaranteed: The indorser by so indorsing engages that if the instrument is not paid he will pay it, but only after the holder has reduced his claim to judgment and execution has been returned unsatisfied; or after insolvency of the maker or acceptor; or if it is otherwise useless to proceed against him.

Community interest: An interest of husband and wife recognized in community property states.

Condition subsequent: The happening of an event which may terminate an estate in real property if the grantor exercises his right of re-entry.

Conformity: Principal of conformity says that the greatest value is realized when qualities of a property bear a reasonable likeness to others of like quality in the neighborhood.

Consensual contract: A contract enforceable because of the mutual consent of the parties.

Consideration: Any detriment suffered by the promisee, or a benefit received by the promisor as determined by the act or the promises of the contracting parties.

Contingent: See *Vested.*

Continuing covenant: One that binds the covenantor to the performance of a series of like acts.

Continuing offer: See *Option,* this glossary. If a continuing offer is not supported by a consideration, it ordinarily may be withdrawn at any time. If not withdrawn it continues for a reasonable time, if there is no fixed termination date.

Contract rent: Rent arrived at by bargaining.

Contract, where made: A contract is generally considered made at the place the last essential act is performed necessary to make it an effective and binding agreement.

Conventional estates: See *Legal estates.*

Coparcenary: A tenancy partaking somewhat of the nature of both joint tenancy and tenancy in common. It has been resolved into tenancy in common under modern doctrine.

Corporeal hereditament: Briefly, land. See *Incorporeal hereditament.*

Co-tenancy: A joint or shared ownership.

Court decision: The judgment of a court in a matter before it.

Court opinion: The reasons of a court by which it arrived at its decision.

Covenantee: One for whose benefit a covenant is made, or to whom a promise is given.

Covenantor: One who obligates himself by covenant.

Covenant running with the land: A covenant is said to run with the land when its legal effect is binding upon subsequent transferees of the estate conveyed or leased, notwithstanding such persons have not contractually assumed any responsibility for its performance.

Coverture: The status of a married woman.

Curtesy: Curtesy is the life interest acquired, in some states, by the husband in his deceased wife's real estate, children having been born of the marriage.

Deed: As used in this text, an instrument conveying real property or some interest therein.

Deed of Trust: A security instrument by which property is conveyed to a trustee by the trustor [the owner of the property transferred] to be held by such trustee to secure payment of a debt owing the beneficiary named in the trust deed, by the trustor, subject to foreclosure by the beneficiary upon default of the trustor. Foreclosure is made by sale of the property under a power of sale contained in the deed.

Deed poll: A deed executed only by the grantor. Compare *Indenture.*

Defeasible fee: A fee which may terminate by special limitation, condition subsequent or by an executory limitation.

Demand: Demand emerges from a degree of desire to acquire a thing—as used in appraisal of real estate.

Dependent covenant: Such a covenant arises when the performance of the covenant of one party is intended to depend upon the performance of another covenant whether made by the same or the other party.

Deposit receipt: A form of contract [offer and acceptance] employed by real estate brokers in initiating the purchase and sale of real estate. It is called a deposit receipt because in practice it takes the form of a firm offer made by the prospective buyer to the principal for the purchase of his property, accompanied by an earnest money deposit.

Depreciation: The decline or loss in value of an asset due to deterioration and obsolescence.

Descendible freehold: The heirs of a deceased tenant holding an estate *pur autre vie* inherit a "descendible" freehold.

Descent: Succession to property upon the death intestate of an ancestor.

Design: In a subdivision; usually refers to street alignment, grades and widths, alignment and widths of easements and rights of way for drainage and sanitary sewers; and minimum lot area and width.

Detriment: A detriment in the law of contracts concerning "consideration" is a prejudice suffered by the promisee, or any act or forbearance on his part.

Dominant tenement: The tenement which enjoys an easement appurtenant thereto laid upon the servient tenement.

Dower: Dower is the life interest acquired, in some states, by a married woman in her deceased husband's real estate.

Duress: Any unlawful threat or act which overcomes the will of a party and induces or compels him to do an act or consent to a proposal which he is not bound by law to do or to consent to, and would not, but for such threat or act, have done or consented to.

Earnest money deposit: Money paid on account of the purchase price of real property, to indicate the bona fide character of the offer of the prospective purchaser. An earnest money deposit usually accompanies the Deposit Receipt in a real estate transaction.

Easement appurtenant: The right to a limited use of another's land [called the servient tenement], the right being attached to, or appurtenant to the dominant tenement.

Easement in gross: An easement laid upon a servient tenement, the easement being personal to its owner, and independent of any dominant tenement.

Easement by implication: There are two types. A way of necessity and those growing out of quasi-easements. Both types are created either by implied grant, or implied reservation.

Economic life: The remaining economic life of a building is the number of years remaining during which the building will produce a reasonable return on the investment and at a reasonable recapture rate to recapture that investment.

Economic obsolescence: A deterioration in the economic character of a neighborhood.

Economic rent: A theoretical figure. What an appraiser would say space in the area should rent for in the open market.

Efficient cause: As used in the text, the cause which necessarily sets in motion all causes leading to the consummation of the transaction between the purchaser and the broker's principal.

Equitable redress: Remedy in a court of equity.

Equitable servitude: A servitude or *use* enforced in equity which permits restrictive covenants not running with the land to be enforced as though they did run with the land; usually for the mutual benefit of persons purchasing lots in a subdivision.

Equity of redemption: The true meaning of the term is *the right to redeem* the land from the mortgage, that is, to recover the land which, under the early common law, had been transferred to the mortgagee. However, today this right to redeem, or equity of redemption, is thought of as being an equitable interest in the property itself which may be recovered.

Escrow: A written instrument delivered conditionally "in escrow" to a third party to be delivered unconditionally and as an effective instrument "out of escrow" upon the happening of a specified event.

Escrow holder: One who holds an escrow.

Estate at sufferance: An estate held against the right of the owner to take possession of the premises, and usually against his will and consent.

Estate at will: A tenancy for an indefinite period of time at the pleasure of both lessor and lessee.

Estate for years: An estate of less than freehold. It may be for any fixed period of time.

Estate for life: Two kinds. Estate limited upon the life of the grantee, or devisee; or limited upon the life of a third person. This latter life estate is known as an estate *pur autre vie.* Neither is an estate of inheritance. But see *Descendible freehold.*

Estates of inheritance: Those capable of passing to the heirs of the owners.

Exchange agreement: In practice, a firm offer to exchange property made by one party to another, which must be accepted by the latter to become binding.

Exclusive agency contract: A listing agreement appointing the broker an exclusive agent to sell the property. Would not exclude the owner from selling without liability for commission to broker, the owner not being an "agent."

Exclusvie authorization and right to sell employment contract: A listing agreement giving broker exclusive right to sell property, which excludes the right of the owner to sell his own land without liability to the broker for commission.

Executed contract: A contract the object of which has been fully accomplished and there remains nothing left to be done on the part of either party.

Executory contract: A contract all of the terms of which have not been performed. Any contract which is not an executed contract.

Executory limitation: A future interest in land created usually by a devise in a will.

Express contract: One the terms of which are stated in words, either oral or written.

Fee simple: An estate of inheritance.

Fee simple absolute: The greatest interest which may be held in real estate.

Feudal tenancy: Land held under the feudal system as it existed in England. As opposed to allodially held land. See *Allodial.*

Fixture: That which is affixed to the land. Fixtures divide into two general classes—fixtures proper and trade fixtures.

Formal contract: A contract or promise which is enforceable by reason of its being under seal; or because it contains certain formal characteristics by which the law recognizes it as a formal contract. Such contracts are promises under seal, recognizances and negotiable instruments.

Fraud: Briefly stated, any act fitted to deceive and intended to deceive another or induce him to enter into a contract by reason of such deception.

Functional obsolescence: Loss in value due to poor design, lack of modern facilities, out-of-date equipment and poor capacity in relation to site.

General deposit: In banking law; in effect, a loan to a bank of the depositor's funds.

Grant, bargain and sale deed: A deed commonly used to convey real estate, containing certain implied warranties.

Grant deed: A form of deed used to convey real property, containing certain implied warranties.

Grantee: One to whom a grant is made.

Grantor: One who makes a grant.

Gross multipliers: A quick, rule-of-thumb approach to value taking gross income as the measure; net income to be inferred from like properties in the neighborhood.

Ground rent: Price paid for use of bare land.

Guaranty of title: A contract of indemnity guaranteeing record title in a certain person, subject to named exceptions. Not title insurance.

Hard money: Money which is not used to pay on the purchase price of property securing its repayment. Brokerage in hard money loans are strictly regulated in some states.

Highest and best use: That use capable of producing the greatest net return on an investment.

Holder in due course: A holder in due course is a holder who takes the instrument for value, in good faith and without notice that it is overdue, or has been dishonored, and without knowledge of any defense against it or claim to it on the part of any person.

Homestead exemption: A statutory provision protecting home owners against demands of creditors.

Immovables: Real property.

Implied contract: One the existence and terms of which are manifested by conduct.

Improvement: In a subdivision sometimes refers only to street work and utilities to be installed by subdivider on land to be used for public or private streets, highways, and easements, as well as local neighborhood traffic and drainage needs.

Incorporeal hereditament: A right or use issuing out of a corporeal hereditament and collateral thereto, such as an easement, or right of way.

Indenture: A deed executed by both grantor and grantee.

Independent covenant: One the performance of which is not dependent upon the performance of another covenant by the same or other party.

Inducing cause: See *Efficient cause.*

Infants: Infants in law are minors, generally persons under 21 years of age.

Informal contract: See *Simple contract.*

Integrated contract: Generally speaking, a contract in which all the terms and conditions have been expressed in a whole, complete instrument.

Interpleader: An equitable remedy to settle the rights of contesting parties to a thing in which the party interpleading the contestants has no title or interest himself, but stands in the position of having custody of the thing, or some obligation for its proper disposition, or some other duty towards one or the other of the contestants with respect to the thing. Interpleader asks the court to determine the matter.

Intestate: Dying without leaving a will.

Joint tenancy: A form of co-tenancy in which the right of survivorship is the distinguishing characteristic. The interests of the co-tenants are equal.

Judicial decision: See *Court decision.*

Jurisdiction: In law the right, authority or power of a court to adjudicate a particular matter. It also refers to the territory in which such power may be exercised.

Land contract: An executory contract for the sale and purchase of real estate.

Lateral and subjacent support: Support the soil gives an adjacent owner's land; the support of the surface by the underlying soil, the surface including what rests upon it.

Lease: A conveyance of an estate, usually of less than freehold, coupled with a contractual obligation written therein fixing the terms and conditions upon which the leasehold estate is to be held, and limiting the term thereof.

Legal estates: A term sometimes used to denote estates created by operation of law, as distinguished from conventional estates, or those created by the parties.

Legal redress: Remedy in a court of law as distinguished from a court of equity.

Lien theory of mortgages: Under this theory title to the mortgaged real property remains in the mortgagor, the mortgage being merely a lien on the property.

Limited ownership: See *Perpetual ownership.*

Lineal heirs: Heirs in the direct line from a common ancestor, as distinguished from collateral heirs.

Listing agreement: A contract of employment between a principal and a real estate broker for the services of the broker in selling or offering to sell the principal's real property.

Mechanic's lien: A statutory lien which has for its purpose to secure payment of labor performed on and materials going into a work of improvement on real property.

Meeting of the minds of the parties: In contract law, the term generally means that which the reasonable interpretation of their acts and the language of their contract intends and the mutual assent of the parties in that respect.

Menace: For all practical purposes, menace is a form of *Duress,* which see.

Minor: A person under the age of, usually, twenty-one years; the law recognizing the general capacity to contract at 21 years.

Mistake: Mistake is of two kinds, mistake of fact, and mistake of law; in the former the parties are mistaken as to what each intended and expected of the other by the terms of the contract; in the latter, the parties misunderstood the law applicable to the facts involved.

Mortgage: A security instrument. Ordinarily a lien on property to secure the payment of a debt. It can likewise secure performance of an act.

Mortgagee in possession: A mortgagee in possession may not be ejected until the debt is paid, even though both the note and the mortgage is outlawed by a statute of limitations.

Movables: Personal property.

Multiple listing agency contract: Usually, a devise employed by groups of real estate brokers to obtain a wider market for the sale of property.

Mutuality of obligation: This means that the mutual promises of the parties to a contract must effect binding obligations between themselves; i.e., each promise must be sufficient consideration to support the other.

Naked power: A mere collateral authority.

Negative easement: The right to prevent the owner of the servient tenement from doing an act on the servient tenement he would otherwise have a right to do. See *Affirmative easement.*

Negotiable instrument: An instrument which establishes certain rights, not found in ordinary paper, in the indorser or holder. The instrument may be transferred or negotiated freely in an exchange of credit discharged of undisclosed equities and unrestricted defenses; the holder is capable of maintaining an action thereon in his own name.

Negotiable promissory note: A formal contract to pay a sum certain at a specified time, and otherwise meeting the requirements of negotiable plaper.

Non-continuing covenant: One that binds the covenantor to perform but a single act.

Note: See *Negotiable promissory note.* A note need not, however, be negotiable.

Notice of dishonor: A notice given to an indorser or drawer of a negotiable instrument that the maker or acceptor has failed to meet his obligation and that such indorser or drawer will be held responsible for payment.

Notice of non-responsibility: A notice available to the owner of real property to prevent mechanics' liens from attaching to it for labor and materials not authorized by him, or of which he had no knowledge.

Notice to quit: A notice to a tenant to pay rent due or quit the premises. It is preliminary to an action in ejectment.

Objective test: This is a rule of construction. What the language of the contract says is made the criterion, not the secret intentions of the parties. To make the latter the criterion would be a *Subjective test.*

Object of the contract: It is what the parties intend by their agreement. It is, actually, the "consideration" by which the promise or the act of a contract is supported. It must be lawful.

Obligation of contract: The sanctions of the law validating and binding the terms and conditions of a contract.

Offer: A proposal, which if accepted, is capable of creating a binding legal relationship between the parties.

Offeree: One to whom an offer is made.

Offeror: One who makes an offer.

Open listing agency contract: May be revoked at any time before broker has performed.

Operating statement: A statement supplied a prospective purchaser of income property showing net income before depreciation.

Operation of law, by: By the force and effect of the law without any act by a party. Rights may be so acquired or lost.

Option: An option is a continuing offer [usually limited in time] to do or perform a certain thing upon certain terms and conditions and which may be accepted, within the time allowed, by the party to whom it is given. To prevent its withdrawal before the expiration of its limitation it should be supported by a sufficient consideration.

Optionee: One to whom an option is given.

Optionor: One who gives an option.

Ownership: The right to possess and use a thing to the exclusion of others; the right to share such use and possession.

Parol contract: Any contract, whether written or oral, other than one recognized by law as a formal contract. A simple contract.

Particular Estate: "Particular," from the Latin *particula,* meaning a small part of the inheritance. The commencement in possession of reversions and remainders are preceded by particular estates.

Patent: A government conveyance of public land.

Payment guaranteed: The indorser by so indorsing engages that if the instrument is not paid he will pay it.

Peaceable entry, foreclosure by: Some title theory states permit foreclosure by peaceable entry of the mortgagee into possession of the land and retention of it for a statutory period of time.

Periodic tenancy: A tenancy which continues from period to period, as for example, from week to week, month to month, the term not being fixed, and determined, usually, by the rental period stipulated.

Perpetual ownership: Duration of ownership equal to the property itself, as compared with limited ownership when duration is less than that of the property.

Police power: The power inherent in the sovereign state to regulate its internal affairs and insure the welfare and best interests of the greatest number of its citizens.

Power of sale: Contained in a mortgage or a deed of trust. It is an authority to sell the property to satisfy the mortgage debt upon default of the mortgagor.

Practice of the law: A term which means not only doing or performing services in a court of law, but the giving of legal counsel or advice.

Precedent authorization: The ordinary agency contract is created in this manner. Authorization given before the happening of an event contemplated by the authorization.

Prescriptive right: A user for a period of time the law requires for the perfection of such a right, usually equal to the period of time fixed by the prevailing statute of limitations barring an action for the recovery of land. An incorporeal hereditament is involved.

Primary liability: A person primarily liable on a negotiable instrument is one who by the terms of the instrument is absolutely bound to pay it, such as the maker of a note or the accepter of a draft. All other parties are secondarily liable.

Principle of substitution: In property appraisal, a property is no more valuable than what people will pay for a substituted like property of equal quality and utility in the area.

Privity of contract: The legal status of parties necessary to a contractual relationship between themselves.

Privity of estate: While there is difference of opinion as to what constitutes privity of estate in relationships outside of that of landlord and tenant, the weight of authority seems to be that there is privity of estate when the fact of *succession* is found, such as takes place between grantor and grantee. In the landlord and tenant relationship it is generally conceded that simultaneous ownership of an interest in the land by both parties creates privity of estate, such as a reversion in the landlord and an estate for years in the tenant.

Procuring cause: See *Efficient cause.*

Profit a prendre: The right to take something from the land of another.

Progression: Of properties of like type, that of the lesser quality in the better neighborhood will be advantaged by its location and have more value. See *Regression,* this glossary.

Promise: A pledge or commitment given by one party to another to do or not to do some specified thing, or act, which if supported by a sufficient consideration becomes binding upon the party making it.

Promisee: One to whom a promise is given.

Promise under seal: A formal contract in those states which recognize a seal to the same extent as did the early English common law.

Promisor: One who makes a promise.

Promissory note: See *Negotiable promissory note.*

Property: That thing of which there may be ownership. The right to dominate and use a thing.

Proximate cause: See *Efficient cause.*

Punitive damages: Exemplary or vindictive damages, awarded because of the malicious acts complained of.

Purchase: Property is acquired in one of two ways, by *purchase* and by *descent.* Property acquired by purchase is acquired by contract, gift, devise or bequest.

Purchase money: Money which is used to pay on the purchase price of property securing its payment, hence the purchase-money mortgage, or purchase-money deed of trust.

Purchasing power: In real estate appraisal, the financial ability to pay for a thing in the open market.

Qualified ownership: See *Absolute ownership.*

Quantum: The quantum of an estate is measured by its duration. The word means amount, quantity.

Quasi-easements: Certain practices or uses established by the owner on his own land for a more convenient use of a part of it.

Quitclaim deed: A deed without warranties used to convey interests in real property. A mere quitclaim does not pass after-acquired title.

Real defenses: Defenses which may be made against a holder in due course of a negotiable instrument.

Reality of consent: Implies the freedom with which the consent was given. Contract law.

Real Property: The land and that which is affixed to it.

Recapture rate: The rate determined upon to recapture the investment in an improvement within the economic life of the improvement.

Recognizance: Sometimes referred to as a "judicial covenant."An obligation entered into before a court and made a record therein, conditioned upon the doing of some specified act, usually to appear and answer to a criminal charge. The entry in the court records is actually substituted for the signatures of the obligors, and dispenses with the need for a seal. It is considered a formal contract.

Regression: Of properties of like type, that of the better quality in the cheaper neighborhood will suffer loss of value. See *Progression.*

Remainder: That portion of the whole estate disposed of passing to the remainderman upon termination of a particular estate. A remainder is vested or contingent.

Rescission: The termination of a contract for lawful cause, and compliance with the law relating thereto.

Restrictive covenants: Covenants which restrict the use of land. Usually inserted in deeds by grantors retaining a portion of the land sold, for the benefit of themselves or the land retained. See *Equitable servitude.*

Reversion: The residue of an estate left by operation of law in the grantor after the grant of a particular estate of freehold or less than freehold. It commences in possession upon the determination of the particular estate granted.

Right of re-entry: The right to take possession of premises formerly parted with, in the event of a breach of condition.

Right to redeem: See *Equity of redemption.*

Sanction: It has two meanings in law. The *penalty* of the law. The *approval* or *authoritative force* of the law.

Scarcity: A thing in short supply is scarce in the market. Scarcity represents that condition.

Seal: In modern practice usually the word "seal" enclosed in a scroll or circle and intended as a seal and so indicated in the body of the instrument to which it is affixed. The need for an instrument to be "sealed" is done away with in most of the states, except for government purposes, or particular organizations.

Secondary liability: See *Primary liability.*

Seized: In possession. Having ownership, as *seized* in fee.

Servient tenement: The tenement upon which an easement is laid, which easement may be appurtenant to a dominant tenement, or in gross.

Several ownership: Property held by a single person. See *Sole ownership.*

Simple contract: A contract which complies with those essentials, other than form, which are demanded by the law for all contracts other than formal contracts.

Social obsolescence: A deterioration of the social character of a neighborhood.

Sole ownership: Property held by a single person, as distinguished from a co-owner.

Sound: In law the term means to be of the nature of, or have the characteristics of a legal concept, such as, for example: to *sound* in contract; to *sound* in tort.

Special deposit: A deposit with a bank to be held for a particular purpose or use, or to be held in trust. Funds so deposited are not the property of the bank.

Spouse: A married woman, or a married man, or the survivor.

Stipulation: In its broadest sense an agreement between two or more parties which they agree to recognize and give effect to.

Stop-payment order: An order on a bank to stop payment of a check drawn on the account of one giving the order.

Strict foreclosure: A procedure used in very few states. Title to the mortgaged property being in the mortgagee, and the mortgagor having an equity of redemption, i.e., a right to redeem the land, an action is brought to *foreclose,* that is to say, to close out, this equity of redemption. The decree in such a procedure gives the mortgagor a definite period of time after the decree is rendered in which to pay the debt, or lose the land forever to the mortgagee, whose title, if there is no redemption, becomes indefeasible.

Subject to the mortgage: A term used to indicate the position a purchaser of mortgaged land is in with respect to personal liability for the mortgage debt. One who takes land *subject to the mortgage* is not personally liable for the mortgage debt.

Sublease: The lease created by a subletting.

Sublet: To underlet; It occurs when the lessee gives a lease on the property to a third person for a period of time short of the expiration of the lease held by such sublessor.

Subsequent bona fide purchaser: One who acquires an interest in property, or who has purchased the fee or other interest for a valuable consideration, in good faith, and without knowledge, actual or constructive, of the prior rights of third parties.

Subsequent ratification: An agency contract is often created by subsequent ratification; that is to say, where the act of the agent performed without authority from the principal is approved or ratified by the principal and adopted as his own act, an agency by subsequent ratification is said to have been created.

Sufficient consideration: A consideration which the law recognizes as capable of supporting a promise or an act.

Tenancy by the entireties: Essentially a joint tenancy. Held by man and wife by a single conveyance or devise. Cannot be defeated by one party transferring to a stranger, as in the case of joint tenancy.

Tenancy in common: In this tenancy the interests held by the several co-tenants are undivided interests in the whole estate. The several interests may vary in fractional amounts. They need not be equal as in joint tenancy.

Title theory of mortgages: Under this theory title of the mortgaged real property passes to the mortgagee.

Trade fixtures: Chattels affixed to land and used for carrying on a trade or business.

Transferable in law: A thing is transferable in law when it may pass from the ownership and possession of one person to the ownership and possession of another.

Undue influence: Undue influence is said to be present when one party is dominated by another, and the former, by reason of the relation between them, might reasonably assume that the latter will not act in a manner harmful to him.

Unilateral contract: A contract in which a promise is given for an act.

Unilateral offer: An offer made by one party for the act of the other party. This is sometimes not accurately referred to as a unilateral contract.

User: See *Usufruct.*

Usufruct: The right to a limited use of the property of another.

Utility: The power to satisfy human wants. Appraising.

Value judgment: An operation of the mind with relation to the facts and reality, which fixes value.

Vested: A present fixed right to present or future possession and enjoyment; as distinguished from contingent, when the right to such enjoyment or the person who may enjoy the thing is uncertain.

Vest: In real property law title "vests" when there is given an immediate fixed right of a present or future estate or interest in the land.

Void: A void act in law is a nullity, of no effect whatsoever, and incapable of being ratified.

Warranty deed: A deed in some states used to convey real estate, carrying certain warranties.

Without recourse: An indorsement without recourse changes the ordinary warranty contained in a negotiable instrument, by operation of law, to the effect that no defense of any party is good against the indorser, to the lesser warranty that he (the indorser without recourse) has no knowledge of such a defense. The other warranties of an indorser are not affected.

Writ of entry, foreclosure by: Employed to put the mortgagee in lawful possession of the mortgaged land if payment is not made as directed by the court. Once thus in possession, the mortgagee is in the position of one entering peaceably, and after a statutory period of time, if there is no redemption, the mortgagee has an indefeasible title.

Writ of scire facias, foreclosure by: A writ commanding the mortgagor to show cause why the land should not be taken in execution for the mortgage. Upon judgment for the mortgagee a writ of *levari facias* issues, under which the land is sold.

Suggested Publications

Law

American Jurisprudence (Rochester, N.Y.: The Lawyers Cooperative Pub. Co.: San Francisco, Calif.: Bancroft-Whitney Co., 1964) See appropriate titles.

Arthur G. Bowman, *Real Estate Law in California* [2nd ed.] (Englewood Cliffs, N.J.: Prentice-Hall, Inc., 1965)

William Everett Britton, *Cases on the Law of Bills and Notes* [5th ed.] (Chicago: Callaghan & Company, 1961)

California Land Security and Development, *Continuing Education of the Bar* (California, Practice Handbook 14: The Filmer Brothers Press)

Corpus Juris Secundum (Brooklyn, N.Y.: The American Law Book Co., 1963) See appropriate titles.

Everett Fraser, *Cases and Readings on Property*, 3rd ed. (Brooklyn: The Foundation Press, Inc., 1954)

Edith J. Friedman, *Handbook of Real Estate Forms* (Englewood Cliffs, N.J.: Prentice-Hall, Inc., 1957)

Edith J. Friedman, *Real Estate Encyclopedia* (Englewood Cliffs, N.J.: Prentice-Hall, Inc., 1960)

Harry W. Jones, E. Allan Farnsworth and William F. Young Jr., *Cases and Materials on Contracts* (Brooklyn: The Foundation Press, Inc., 1965)

Robert Kratovil, *Real Estate Law*, 4th ed. (Englewood Cliffs, N.J.: Prentice-Hall, Inc., 1964)

Melvin B. Ogden, *California Real Property Law* (Los Angeles: Parker & Son, 1956)

George E. Osborne, *Cases and Materials on Property Security*, 2d ed. (St. Paul, Minn.: West Publishing Co., 1954)

Real Estate Guide (a periodical newsletter), (Englewood Cliffs, N.J.: Prentice-Hall, Inc.)

Robert W. Semenow, *Selected Cases in Real Estate* (Englewood Cliffs, N.J.: Prentice-Hall, Inc., 1964)

Robert W. Semenow, *Questions and Answers on Real Estate*, 6th ed. (Englewood Cliffs, N.J.: Prentice-Hall, Inc., 1969)

Appraisal

American Institute of Real Estate Appraisers, *Appraisal Terminology and Handbook*, 4th ed. (Chicago, 1962)

American Institute of Real Estate Appraisers, *Problems in Urban Real Estate Appraisal with Suggested Solutions*, 3rd ed. (Chicago, 1963)

American Institute of Real Estate Appraisers, *The Appraisal of Real Estate*, 4th ed. (Chicago, 1964)

Ray H. Arnold, *How to Estimate Market Value in Selling Real Estate* (Englewood Cliffs, N.J.: Prentice-Hall, Inc., 1962)

Edith J. Friedman, *Encyclopedia of Real Estate Appraising, Revised and Enlarged*, (Englewood Cliffs, N.J.: Prentice-Hall, Inc., 1968)

Clifford L. James, *Principles of Economics*, 9th ed. (New York: Barnes & Noble, Inc., 1962)

Stanley L. McMichael, *McMichael's Appraising Manual*, 4th ed. (Englewood Cliffs, N.J.: Prentice-Hall, Inc., 1951)

Alfred A. Ring, *The Valuation of Real Estate* (Englewood Cliffs, N.J.: Prentice-Hall, Inc., 1963)

George L. Schmutz, *Condemnation Appraisal Handbook*, revised and enlarged by Edwin M. Rams (Englewood Cliffs, N.J.: Prentice-Hall, Inc., 1963)

Harold S. Sloan and Arnold J. Zurcher, *A Dictionary of Economics*, 4th ed. (New York: Barnes & Noble, Inc., 1965)

Robert W. Winstead, *Real Estate Appraisal Desk Book* (Englewood Cliffs, N.J.: Prentice-Hall, Inc., 1968)

INDEX